French Gay Modernism

French Gay Modernism

Lawrence R. Schehr

UNIVERSITY OF ILLINOIS PRESS

URBANA AND CHICAGO

Manufactured in the United States of America
C 5 4 3 2 1

∞ This book is printed on acid-free paper.

Library of Congress Cataloging-in-Publication Data

Schehr, Lawrence R.
French gay modernism / Lawrence R. Schehr.
p. cm.
Includes bibliographical references and index.
ISBN 0-252-02945-3 (cloth : alk. paper)
1. French fiction—20th century—History and criticism.
2. Homosexuality in literature.
I. Title.
PQ637.H65S44 2004
843'.9109353—dc22 2004003480

FOR ALLEN WEISS AND ROBERT HARVEY

CONTENTS

ACKNOWLEDGMENTS

My thanks first to my colleagues at the University of Illinois in the Department of French and in the College of Liberal Arts and Sciences. I have found a cohort of talented researchers and teachers in the humanities who have been most inspiring to me as I thought and wrote. Special thanks go to Jean-Philippe Mathy, head of the Department of French, and Jesse Delia, dean of the College of Liberal Arts and Sciences, for their generosity and support of my work. I extend gratitude as well to Michael Bérubé (now at Penn State), Suvir Kaul (now at the University of Pennsylvania), and Matti Bunzl, all of whom were or are associated with the Illinois Program for Research in the Humanities. I owe a special debt of thanks to Chris Catanzarite, also of the Illinois Program for Research in the Humanities, who kindly and generously read a late version of this manuscript and provided helpful and much needed suggestions on making it more readable.

I am grateful as well to Willis G. Regier, director of the University of Illinois Press, for his support of this book and other projects over the years. My extreme gratitude to Bruce Bethell, associate editor at the press, who took my rough prose, cleaned it up, removed many infelicities, and generally improved it.

Some of the material in chapter 1 appeared in *Proust in Perspective,* ed. Armine Kotin Mortimer and Katherine Kolb (Urbana: University of Illinois Press, 2002). I thank the press for permission to use this material. All translations are my own, except where noted.

I have received valuable advice and guidance from Kal Alston, David F. Bell, C. L. Cole, Jed Esty, Andrea Goulet, Robert Harvey, Alex Hughes, Masumi Iriye, Katherine Kolb, Elisabeth Ladenson, James Mandrell, Armine Mortimer, David O'Brien, Denis Provencher, Dina Scherzer, the late Naomi Schor, Franc Schuerewegen, Naomi Segal, Siobhan Somerville, Adam Sutcliffe, and Alexandra Wettlaufer.

French Gay Modernism

INTRODUCTION: Gay French Modernism

MALE HOMOSEXUALITY enjoys a noticeable presence in French narrative from the twentieth century's first four decades, especially from the end of World War I through the early 1930s. Works by writers such as André Gide, Marcel Proust, Jean Cocteau, René Crevel, Francis Carco, and Willy, as well as those by a host of less well-known writers, portray overtly gay male characters having social and often sexual relations with one another. Of course, earlier works of canonic French narrative had depicted homosexual characters: Balzac's Vautrin is the most obvious and important example, and many of Sade's male characters perform sex acts with one another. It is only with the early twentieth-century rise of modernism, however, that an entire discursive field comes into play. In a certain sense Gide's narrative *L'Immoraliste* began the process of gay French modernism, although not in a programmatic way and with only scattered, encrypted references to same-sex desire between men. In that work, which precedes the main period of gay modernist production by about fifteen years, Gide develops a strategy whereby he inscribes the homoerotic rather than the homosexual, but it is still a convenient starting point for examining the tropes through which male same-sex desire is articulated in modernism.

Modernism and the articulation of male same-sex desire are not necessarily or naturally related to one another, but the conditions under which both phenomena developed are interrelated and share a number of factors. Moreover, although literary history (whether of an individual work or of a literary movement or form) does not merely reflect the world—if only because literature and literary forms have a semiautonomous status as organizing or modeling systems—it is useful to start with the conditions of producing the "modern" at the end of the nineteenth century. In addition, even though the articulation of same-sex desire has its own long history, the means by which that desire was articulated found their own distinctly modern forms during that same period.

Paris emerged as the "capital of the nineteenth century," to use Walter Benjamin's well-known phrase (*Arcades* 3–26), with physical and visual changes and a concomitant demographic shift making the city a singular urban landscape during the Second Empire and the early years of the Third Republic. The modern look associated with Paris arose from two projects that remade the urban space. First, the "Haussmannization" of public spaces involved destroying older neighborhoods with their small streets and creating the wide boulevards for which Paris is now famous (11–13 and passim).[1] Haussmannization was meant to prevent the construction of barricades on the streets of Paris, as had occurred during the Revolution of 1848, but it also created a distinctive public space in which a new architecture would shortly make itself visible in the famous Belle Époque apartment houses. Many of these structures were built according to a recognizable model: seven stories above the ground floor, with apartments on all stories between the ground floor and the top story, maids' rooms above, the concierge's booth on the ground floor, and distinctive railings marking the second and fifth floors.

The original reason for Haussmannization may have been military, but this massive construction related primarily to a great demographic shift from country to city as industry and business developed. The peasants came to Paris by methods of transportation newly available, and this urban migration quickly found its way into literature, echoed by writers such Zola, who chronicles the Second Empire as he shows the development of Paris from the neighborhood of the "Goutte d'or" in *L'Assommoir* to the invention of the department store in *Au bonheur des dames.* Baudelaire's solitary *flâneur,* the premier figure of decadence before the fact, became, in Naomi Schor's phrase, "Zola's crowds."

As often as not, these new urban residents were separated from their extended families in the countryside. Frequently alone in the city, these individuals had a relative freedom from the conservative moral constraints prevalent in the village, where everyone knew everyone else and any adult and the church could act as a parental force. Far from the curé, and especially after the creation of the Third Republic as a secular state, urbanized individuals were far less subject to a totalizing moral fabric than were their peers in the country, where the normalizing code continued strongly to reinforce the familial model. In the city it was easier to find solutions to matters of inheritance, primogeniture, and personal freedom. One did not have to become a priest or a soldier; one could be a worker. One could live outside the family model.

The city also allowed freedom of movement and relative anonymity: a walk through the streets of Paris need not imply a particular destination. Certainly there were the police and surveillance, but the sheer size of the city, the accessibility of public transportation, the number of people, and the general heterogeneity of the population allowed for a kind of freedom or openness to life (*disponibilité,* to use a word central to Gide), at least to the male individual, not present in the country. People living in a village or even a small town could deduce where someone else was going simply by observing the path he or she took. No such prediction could be made in Paris. And if the individual *flâneur* is multiplied into an anonymous face in the crowd, he can become a loiterer, idling here or there, pretending to look in a shop window or a courtyard without too great a fear of discovery. Certainly there would have been arrests of men loitering in parks or in the famous public urinals that have now disappeared from the urban landscape. But who would be arrested for chatting casually with a stranger and then disappearing into a private space? Who could not have an assignation in a bachelor flat? Indeed, although the city continues to demarcate classes—in many ways doing so even more decisively than before—it still permits members of different classes to mingle. There will be borders to cross as one scales the hill of Montmartre after having left the fashionable neighborhoods of western Paris, but these are not insuperable obstacles.

I have not yet separated the real factors determining where modernism and the modern articulation of male same-sex desire would land. As I shall show, both were articulated against that initial background of urban heterogeneity. A retrospective reading of modernism shows that it developed from what could be considered an impasse of realism or its final incarnation in naturalism: the increased inability of a third-person omniscient narrator to define and interpret a world full of unknowns. The nineteenth-century narrative developed parallel to a relation between omniscient narratives and a positivist, scientific approach to knowledge and determinism. Whereas Balzac's interpretation of the world is based on structuring narrative relative to ideological absolutes, Zola's is based on the accuracy and limitless power of scientific observation. Nevertheless, even if science continues to control ever greater areas, and even if there are two master narratives, those of Marx (before modernism) and Freud (concomitant with modernism), the literary master narrative appears to be in a precarious position, for it seems no longer to cover the world it once purported to describe.

What could realism do in this situation? As I have shown in *Figures of Alterity,* realism can—and did—assimilate its alternative others, normalizing them in the process. Realism thus extended its reach by including voices and subjects other than those that had been determined by Balzac and others. As writers who in some ways continued the realist tradition, both André Gide and Marcel Proust extended the possibilities of what would be described "normally" by a reasonably dispassionate, albeit subjective narrator. Yet decadent fin-de-siècle narrative can be seen in part as a reaction to the limits of realism: faced with the acceleration of urban life and its host of matters that cannot be known, decadence slowed things down, froze them, and offered set pieces or tableaux. Instead of presenting the frenzy of the white sale in *Au bonheur des dames,* Huysmans freezes time and space in *A rebours,* and Mirbeau does the same in his work.

Perhaps the most important literary event is not the introduction of a single technique but rather the reintroduction of a fragmented, multilayered subjectivity at the locus of narration, where realism had insisted on a unitary voice. This subjectivity and this fragmentation did not arise in literature alone, and as Everdell shows, there is a correspondence among various features of modernism, including Picasso's painting, the concept of entropy, blank verse, pointillism, and relativity, among others, not to mention the first experiments in "modern" writing, such as the early works of Gide, Proust, and Joyce. Joyce retrospectively made stream-of-consciousness writing the mark of modernism, attributing the technique to a rather forgotten work by Edouard Dujardin, *Les Lauriers sont coupés* (1887). Yet this technique does not mark the writing of Gide or Proust, and they are every bit as modernist as he is, albeit less visibly experimental. Their works remain more classical in form and voice than are Joyce's, but Proust and Gide still fit the pattern of the modern writer, for their narratives are multidimensional rather than linear, with numerous subjectivities, patterns, and discourses.

Proust and Gide wrote the last great French master narratives in a style, both a fulfillment and a deconstruction of the Balzacian realist model, that was marked by verisimilitude as well as irony. In the *Recherche* and, to a lesser extent, *Les Faux-Monnayeurs,* the authors construct a world that they proceed to mine from within to undercut any sense of totality, fulfillment, or completion. Their actions were not revolutionary, for they followed other practices that separate language from the world it purports to describe; they merely finished breaking down the possibility of master narratives. Between

Balzac and the modernists, Flaubert began to unseat the objective, using psychologically based legerdemain to replace an individual analytical subject with an intervening and incontrovertible discursive system, a system of objects, and a collective object of desire. It would require the two modernists, however, to pull off the trick. Proust's multiple revisions of the subject position and the role of analysis endlessly challenge the possibility of the objective as well as the stability of the subjective. Gide voids the position of the agent of reason, and following Flaubert, he replaces an implicit or explicit psychological argument with the noncausal, unmotivated act (*l'acte gratuit*) and availability to act (*disponibilité*). In a kind of dialectical sublation of the form, Proust and Gide fulfilled the master narrative and simultaneously produced the modernist novel.

Modernism thus found its voice and place with this urban landscape as a backdrop, and the articulation of male same-sex desire is generally set against that special space. Although Paris is not the only locus in which these texts inscribe male homosexuality, the city and its relative anonymity became that against which it was set. Gide seems at first to have eschewed the centrality of this particular cityscape, for *L'Immoraliste* and *Si le grain ne meurt,* to name just two works, focus on other settings. The former is based to some extent on Gide's own life (the second is purely autobiographical) and retrospectively looks at a period—the 1890s—considerably before the main period to which this book is devoted, when new modernity was not yet possible, so that the author had to resort to sexual tourism. And even then, the issue in *L'Immoraliste* is not homosexuality but homoerotic desire. Nevertheless, in his novel of high modernism, *Les Faux-Monnayeurs,* Gide maintains Paris as central to the setting. For his part, Proust situates his work predominantly in three places: Paris, Combray, and Balbec. Whereas Combray forecloses on the unknown, except as a displacement or an accident—as when Marcel masturbates in "the little room smelling of orrisroot [l'iris]" or when he wakes up to see ritualized foreplay between Mlle Vinteuil and her friend—Balbec at times allows for anonymity and availability. So Marcel can see Charlus on the street, and Charlus can go to Marcel's room. Cocteau's work relative to homosexuality follows much the same pattern: scenes in Paris, accidental events in the country, and anonymous encounters in a brothel. Much of the popular literature, too, follows the same pattern: *Jésus-la-Caille* and *Metallo, mon ami* are set in Montmartre; *L'Ersatz d'amour* and *Le Naufragé,* in various cityscapes and all-male societies.

Thus, as this generalized discursive field developed over the quarter-century between the world wars, male-male desire and male-male culture were repeatedly encoded in French literature. But how should one talk about that desire, given that all the language is fraught with secondary meanings? If *queer* is eschewed as a postmodern and post-gay-liberation coinage, it still is not easy to choose between *gay* and *homosexual* or *homosexuality.* The words *homosexual* and *homosexuality* may once have seemed to be neutral words, but post-Foucauldian queer theory has increasingly read them as overly determined by medical and juridical discourses. Moreover, although *gay* has precedents in the time period I am discussing—indeed, Gilles Barbedette and Michel Carassou entitled a study of the period *Paris Gay 1925*—the word was much more prevalent during and after gay liberation, starting in the late 1960s. And turning to the language of the period, with its discourses about pederasts and inverts, would serve no purpose.

Rather, I take the clue not from the language of the era but from the effect of that language. That so much of this literature quickly became considered canonic demonstrates that male homosexuality itself, at least so encoded, had become perhaps not "normal" but at least something representable relative to the dominant discourses, and not merely as an abject other rejected by them. To the extent that the canon includes, supports, and reinforces those dominant social values, it begins to encode male homosexuality as part of those social values in modernity. So I have used both *gay* and *homosexual* precisely because many of these works caused the articulation of same-sex male desire to be encoded in twentieth-century Western culture at a time when multiple discourses existed: a celebratory discourse was often coupled with a moral, legal, juridical, or medical one. Gide and Proust did not create gayness or a gay sensibility; rather, the way in which they inscribed male homosexuality contributed greatly to the century's understanding of the matter, as did Freud and others along with them. And what would eventually become queer theory at the end of the twentieth century owed as much to the figures of male homosexuality in those authors' works as it did to Freud or Foucault (Schehr, "Filiations").

Let us examine the corpus a bit more closely. Some of these works place homosexuality at center stage; other narratives treat it as one subject among others. At the beginning of the century, with the publication of *L'Immoraliste,* André Gide began to explore discourses related to homoeroticism and latent homosexuality. Although this work perhaps gives less than free range and complete visibility to matters he would more fully explore in *Corydon, Les Faux-Monnayeurs,* and *Si le grain ne meurt,* Gide opens a space for desire and begins to articulate that desire in a tentative manner. Between that first publication and the key moment a quarter of a century later came *Corydon,* his apologia for masculine homosexuality, as well as the first volumes of Proust's *Recherche*, in which the subject is evoked and explored. The critical moment comes in the mid-1920s, which saw not only the last, telling volumes of Proust's *Recherche*, starting with fairly explicit material in the first pages of *Sodome et Gomorrhe*, but also André Gide's *Les Faux-Monnayeurs*, which is both less explicit and more matter-of-fact. These two novels quickly entered the literary firmament, permanently changing the literary map in the process.

The rapid consecration of these two authors' works created a change of epic proportions in the literary landscape. They somehow "normalized" male homosexuality as a valid subject for serious literary narrative. Proust and Gide permanently altered both narrative itself and the way in which male homosexuality is presented through literary language. To be brutally direct: narrative could no longer pretend that it is heterosexual and that homosexuality does not exist. This change was due not to Proust and Gide alone, however, but also to a general discursivity, to changes in cultural practice, and to a whole host of writers who also were involved in that change.

In their extraordinary book *Paris Gay 1925*, Barbedette and Carassou provide a wonderful overview of the social and cultural aspects of gay life in the 1920s. As did Willy before them in *Le Troisième Sexe*, they focus on Paris's many institutions that were venues for this developing gay culture. Barbedette and Carassou effectively show how the literary vanguards were not alone, how there was a whole gamut of more popular institutions, including bars and saunas; well-known cruising spots; and even a short-lived magazine, *Incidents*, which they call "this 'gay' magazine, the first of its kind" (it began publication at the end of 1924 and lasted only four issues). Indeed, Barbedette and Carassou (151–303) present long excerpts from the magazine, which published work by Suzanne de Callias, among others, and was extremely gay friendly and gay supportive. A year later another magazine, *Les Marges*, published an "inquiry" on homosexuality in literature that, over the course of two issues, included some of Willy's preliminary material for *Le Troisième Sexe* as well as a supplement on lesbianism and poetry. Gay culture was visible in a more general sense, too, and although literary writing constitutes the primary medium for expressing culture's high end, the evidence of a gay popular culture is more plentiful.

Gide and Proust became the cartographers of a new inscription of gay culture, discourses, and existence. They were not alone among the major writers, for Colette certainly remapped articulations of gender in her writing. Colette remained a "woman writer" for a long time, however, and she was perhaps taken less seriously during her lifetime than in the last twenty years. Proust and Gide were canonized early on; Crevel was part of the surrealist movement despite its raging heteronormativity and homophobia (words to which I will return in this book); Cocteau had high visibility in several arts; and Jean Genet, as the first of a new generation, would be consecrated by Sartre.

I previously referred to Gide and Proust as cartographers, and although it is always dangerous to pin a thesis on a metaphor, this one is apt. Writers such as Gide, Proust, Cocteau, Crevel, and Genet remapped gayness in their writing. To a lesser extent and in a different way, more popular writers such as Willy, Francis Carco, Francis de Miomandre, Abel Hermant, and Suzanne de Callias, just to name a few, did likewise. The popular writers tended more generally to reflect the world they saw. In their works they describe, often in a kind of stereotypical way—even if they are in the process of inventing the stereotype—the world around them. Their writing is a kind of direct reflection of that reality, often subtended by a mode of prose that does not alternate between realism's mutually exclusive poles of formless verisimilitude and the exigencies of novelistic form. Rather, these works often vacillate between murky melodrama and light romance. While blazing new trails in subject matter, they were not in and of themselves literarily innovative. Aside from appealing to prurient interest, authors make their subject matter accessible not by using modernist or even realist techniques but by employing safer and more melodramatic ones. These authors provide a comfort level for readers who can safely watch the marginalized or the quasi criminal from a secure voyeuristic or sensationalist perspective. The authors create a theatrical play for the readers—superior to the subjects of the text—who remain protected (and invisible) behind the invisible fourth wall that is the stage.

Stronger writers, whose texts are thicker or more opaque, sometimes do that as well, faithfully mapping into their work the dispositions of the world they see beyond their writing tables. The world as mapped by Proust or Gide becomes a hermeneutic figure and a problematic within writing, so that these writers effectively produce a new world instead of just faithfully reproducing the one at hand. It is as if they change perspectives, use a different kind of projection, or discover that the world is not flat. Such "strong" writers redefine sexuality, put the givens into question, and reinscribe the world for their readers, who then can—and this is the "effect" of literature—use that remapping as a means of envisioning what a new world might be. Proust and Gide are among the first to have provided a hermeneutic, a rhetoric, and a general discourse in which a modern version of male homosexuality is articulated. They held a mirror to the gay men of their worlds; in so doing, they told the world how to look at that mirror (so different from Stendhal's), what they were seeing in the mirror, and what language to use to react to what was depicted.[2]

The distinction between the two worlds is approximate at best and perhaps even specious, for the very fact of choosing to look at something new, such as that on which the gaze of the popular writers lingers, is itself a redistribution of material. A knowledgeable reader must make some sort of distinction between writers who have been guaranteed a spot in the literary firmament and those who, although not always hacks, did a more journeyman kind of work. The difference becomes palpable in this thickness of text, especially evident in the work of Proust and its upheaval in Genet. The thickness is present in Gide's work, especially *Corydon, Les Faux-Monnayeurs,* and the various journals, where the writing of homosexuality interrelates to a personal aesthetic and to a sense of explanation and confession, an apology for Gide's life.

Proust offers us literature's most complicated depiction of male homosexuality, a distinct and dynamic multiple representation and hermeneutic that has never been equaled before or since. In the two chapters on Proust I focus on the way Charlus encounters sexuality and homosexualizes, or "queers," the space in which he figures. I examine Charlus's initial encounter with the narrator; his intermittent relationship with Morel, that episodically appearing character so important in the explication of Charlus and his homosexuality; and a strange wartime free-for-all in a blacked-out metro station set during a German raid on Paris. In the section set in Balbec, Proust shows how Marcel initially perceives cruising as inexplicable behavior and then, as he comes to understand Charlus, begins to view the behavior as a bit less odd. With the thickness of his narration and the distance between his narrator and Marcel understood as the future narrator, Proust also develops a system of differentiated knowledge about homosexuality: the narrator knows what Marcel will only come to learn. At the same time, the narrator—or even the unconscious structures of the novel—constructs impossible positions in which his own sexuality is questioned. Thus does Proust queer the novel by destabilizing the binary opposition between heterosexuality and homosexuality and the former's presumed precedence to and dominance over the latter.

Proust develops two things in the material dealing with Charlus and Morel. First, he develops the notion of a gay relationship—not just a single act of sex between two characters, as with the initial encounter between

Charlus and Jupien, but also something with an emotional dynamic and the jealousy that characterizes the important straight relationships discussed in the book: Swann and Odette and Marcel and Albertine. Second, he uses the character of Morel to insist on the fluidity of sexuality; in certain situations a given character can be straight, gay, or bisexual. In one sense this takes the sexual fluidity ascribed to women and inscribes it in male domains; in another, it constitutes a materialization of the destabilizing rhetoric at the beginning of *Sodome et Gomorrhe,* in which the sheer excess of figurality contributes to the impossibility of defining the "men-women" of whom Proust will write. Both the figure of the couple and the fluidity of sexuality are reflected in many of the more popular works as well.

In chapter 3 I look at two other strong writers, André Gide and Jean Cocteau. For Gide, I turn to matters of homoeroticism and latent homosexuality that Proust never addressed and that Gide himself largely omitted from his more overtly "homosexual" writing. A study of *L'Immoraliste* not only illuminates these areas of desire and separates them from sex but also shows how Gide introduces male appreciation for the beauty or the sexuality of another male. Gide's concept of the homoerotic provides a means of forestalling both the explicit description of homosexuality in *Corydon* and *Les Faux-Monnayeurs* and the complete transparency of Gide as practicing homosexual. By this I do not mean anything as trendy as Gide's coming out of the closet or outing himself in some confessional scheme (although, symptomatically, *L'Immoraliste* is presented as a confession and *Corydon* is presented as an apologia). Rather, Gide had to find the language and rhetoric appropriate to describing his own homosexual "bent," to use Michael Lucey's felicitous word.

As for Cocteau, he wrote the most about homosexuality in his unsigned volume *Le Livre blanc.* Cocteau develops a series of figures and constellations for male-male desire in that work and in others such as *Les Enfants terribles.* Deftly jumping from genre to genre, expressing his talent and depicting male homosexuality (and homoeroticism) in a variety of ways, Cocteau seems always to be gamboling through life, and even at his most serious he never quite plumbs the depths of his subject. His feverish productivity from 1925 to 1932 (squarely within the period under consideration), however, and the entire personal mythology and constellation of figures of male homosexuality he creates in his interrelated works, including his first film, make it suitable to explore this set of figures as a focal moment in the inscription of male homosexuality in the realm of the modern.

The picture of the inscription of modern gayness would not be complete without a reading of more popular texts in which modern gayness figures. Through an examination of Francis Carco's *Jésus-la-caille* and Willy and Ménalkas's *L'Ersatz d'amour,* I try to gauge the extent to which more popular culture reflected changes in the mapping of homosexuality and how that more normalized map was seen through the eyes of the writers and their characters. Carco's work deals with the depiction of a male gigolo; Willy and Ménalkas's, with a fairly cosmopolitan situation involving a French artist and a German nobleman. These writers also demonstrate the extent to which male homosexuality had become representable, even without the protective literary thickness offered by Proust or Gide.

These chapters follow the mapping of male homosexuality in the interwar years as each author or group of authors looked at the way it was troped, be it in high literary language or popular fiction, in master narratives or in singular objects shaded in a unique fashion. These mappings will give readers a set of interrelated readings of that map, one that will emerge after World War II as the map of a brave new world, far different from the one in which those maps were originally produced.

1 Proust: Forgetting Homosexuality

HAD BORGES not already used the titles for two magnificent short stories about narrative, meaning, and death, one might rename Proust's novel "The Garden of Forking Paths" or "Marcel El Memorioso." Like the image described in the first tale, this is a novel of a seemingly infinite number of pages in which various possibilities are explored and time changes meaning in a revision of a moment or a locus. Unlike Borges's tale, however, it is a space in which some of the paths, having forked, meet again. This is the sense of the initial separation of and subsequent magical reencounter between the two "ways" of the novel, Méséglise and Guermantes, once thought separate but eventually seen to meet and merge in a variety of ways. For Marcel as a youth, there is no literal or symbolic connection between the two paths of the novel: the Méséglise way is the more familiar path and is "Swann's way," whereas the longer, less familiar "Guermantes's way" is associated with the noble and seemingly unreachable family of the same name. Moreover, evoking the total recall of the second tale by Borges, the narrator seems to remember or want to remember in detail every important event in his life or in those of others. The narrator duly inscribes each important moment in his coming to be an author and even includes a novel within the novel, "Un Amour de Swann," written about events prior to his birth that will nevertheless help form his understanding of the world.

It is strange, then, to find a moment in which the narrator forgets, seemingly willfully, for his project is to create the narrative in which every sign is deciphered (Deleuze 36–50) and everything is remembered. This is not to say that the narrator remembers everything or that he does not change opinions about matters as he goes through his process of deciphering; in so doing, he sometimes forgets his earlier opinion. But most of the time he reminds the readers of his earlier opinion as he tells them how and why it needs to be modified. The novel is not about forgetting; it is about having forgotten, trying to remember, and eventually remembering. In his search for the truth, the narrator will stop at nothing.

Consider a pointed example. In Balbec Marcel is speaking with Robert de Saint-Loup, his new friend. Marcel is ostensibly still trying to pinpoint the truth of Combray, a truth that will come from the Guermantes perspective. At this point Marcel is attempting to discover the truth behind a rumor of a relationship between Odette, now Madame Swann, and the Baron de Charlus, and he feels he has briefly espied them (hundreds of pages back) in one of the novel's early scenes. To find out the truth, Marcel indirectly elicits information about Charlus's personal life from Robert, who is also Charlus's nephew. Saint-Loup explains his uncle's character, saying: "As handsome as he was, he must have had some—mistresses! Besides, I could not tell you exactly which ones, because he is very discreet" (Proust, *Recherche* 2:110). Saint-Loup's comment deserves our attention. First, he does not know who Charlus's mistresses were because his uncle is so discreet—a character trait that any reader of the whole novel would be unlikely to ascribe to Charlus, this often outrageously forward individual who, only a few pages later, will give the lie to this supposed discretion by apparently cruising Marcel quite openly. In addition, the oblivious Saint-Loup makes a logical supposition based on an idea rather than a fact: Charlus "must have had some mistresses [a dû en avoir]." It is an inescapable and logical conclusion based on incontrovertible suppositions: as are all men, Charlus is heterosexual; all men of his station and especially in his family have mistresses; therefore, he must have had mistresses. In an ironic turn the Saint-Loup who will eventually have homosexual relations is making a blanket assumption that everyone is straight. Could we ascribe this to his youth? Or is there another game going on here, one that the narrator/author is imposing on the novel, a game in which the assumption of heterosexuality is necessarily and falsely taken as a starting point? In this light, the correction that will eventually ensue fits into the novel's characteristic pattern of revised opinion.

For the moment, however, Marcel accepts the logic, even though the older and wiser narrator knows that this is not the whole truth. The narrator is setting the stage for what will be gradual revelations about the character: Charlus may have had mistresses in the past, just as he had a wife, yet the truth of Charlus is that he is gay and not a skirt chaser. Marcel solidifies the assumption by turning the hypothesis become foregone conclusion into a recognizable, visible truth: "But among the numerous mistresses you said that your uncle, M. de Charlus, had had, was not Mme Swann among them?" (2:115). Yet Saint-Loup has said nothing of the sort; he has said that his uncle "must have had" mistresses. Furthermore, Saint-Loup does nothing to correct Marcel's reinterpretation of what he has just said, for were he do so, he would have to question his own knowledge about his uncle, and Proust does not want that to happen here and now. Although Saint-Loup cannot confirm exactly who Charlus's mistresses were, he can avoid the matter by indicating that Odette was not one of them, and were such a supposition to be voiced, he opines, it would cause a lot of "consternation" in their circles ("dans le monde"). It would be a preposterous situation and mismatch. Thus, while ostensibly learning about Charlus from Saint-Loup, Marcel learns instead that, the rumor in Combray notwithstanding, Odette has never been Charlus's mistress. It little matters at the moment that, although Saint-Loup can rule out Odette as one of Charlus's mistress, he does not really know whom the list includes. Marcel has forgotten Saint-Loup's previous remark about the mistresses, that he does not know who they are and thus cannot say with total assurance who they are not. Saint-Loup seems to have forgotten this as well. What allows them both to forget is the certainty of Charlus's infidelity and heterosexuality.

The narrator is reenforcing the role already ascribed to Odette, that of a character with an ambiguous relation to the intersection of class and sexuality. Throughout "Un Amour de Swann" Odette's ambiguous class status, supported by the role of mistress she has ostensibly played with Uncle Adolphe in her figuration as "la dame en rose" (the woman in pink), makes her the prime figure of the woman who crosses class lines in the social kaleidoscope. As such, her sexuality evokes the social climbing that in a different register will mark the behavior of Mme Verdurin, who herself will eventually make an even greater leap to become Princess de Guermantes. In addition, the construction of Odette as sexual shifter will also pave the way for her daughter Gilberte gradually to shed the marks of Jewishness, thus allowing her to become first Mlle de Forcheville and then Madame de Saint-Loup. In that, Odette is distinct from someone like Rachel, who while eventually changing station from prostitute to mistress—of the same Robert de Saint-Loup—never makes a quantum leap.

Simultaneously, Odette's function as sexual shifter retrospectively remarks the initial view of Charlus in Combray. We now know that she has not been his mistress; we will come to learn that the situation of heterosexual adultery falsely perceived in Combray is itself a shift. The truth is is that of a friendship between two beings, Odette and Charlus, who desire men. In addition, just as Odette will act to move up in the class structure, Charlus continually acts not really to lower himself but at least to slum from time to time and to raise up others, at least temporarily, in a class structure that he has refigured according to his desire. That revision of class structure is temporary, at least for acceding to the highest classes, for it is there that Charlus will draw the line; participation in that revision lasts only until Charlus's favor or desire is played out, although he often rewards those he loves by finding them a modest position, thereby raising them on a more permanent basis.

The moment is odd, because once we separate the narrator from the protagonist, we realize that the narrator is forgetting to tell us something, to tell us the truth, or to indicate that we will later learn something that will change his and our reading of the scene.[1] To wit, he forgets to tell us that Charlus is homosexual. How could the narrator forget such an important matter? It is not as if he has not encountered homosexuality before; there has already been an explicit scene between Mlle Vinteuil and her friend, although it is not a foregone conclusion that a familiarity with female homosexuality would necessarily make Marcel aware of male homosexuality or that he would recognize it when he sees it (Ladenson, *Lesbianism* 28–57). As elsewhere, we do not see the sex act itself. This rule will be bent as Marcel overhears the sounds of sex between Charlus and Jupien at the beginning of *Sodome et Gomorrhe* and will be bent again by the scene in Jupien's bordello—although this is not genital, anal, or oral penetration but rather a scene of performed sadomasochism.[2] Even ritualized foreplay gives us more information about the nature of the relations between Mlle Vinteuil and her friend than Saint-Loup provides, in his hasty and abortive conclusion, about his uncle's private life.

In terms of the narrative and rhetorical constructions of the scenes to come, the narrator does not want to tip his hand, and perhaps simply stating that we will find out more about this matter later would be enough to make even the dimmest readers understand what is at stake. Moreover, the narrator desires to have readers focus on the subjective position of the adolescent character, who is unaware of exactly what is happening and who is still confused by contradictory information and signs. To identify with the learning process and apprenticeship of Marcel as he becomes the narrator and to follow the bildungsroman as such, readers cannot occupy a position totally superior in knowledge to Marcel; rather, they should sympathetically identify with Marcel's incomprehension.[3] The self's coming of age is a measure of relative freedom compared to the structures imposed on the child in

Combray. Here Marcel has the possibility of exploring his own life and making his own personal contacts in this world in which he has some independence of movement, some freedom to separate from members of his family, and some possibility of meeting people on his own. The protagonist is also beginning to explore a world that he has only glimpsed before: the world of the aristocracy. It is not just any aristocracy, moreover, but the crème de la crème, the Guermantes clan; it is a world whose members he has long known by name but with whom only now does he begin to have his first real contacts. Like Julien Sorel in the salon de la Môle, hearing a language "that he understood but could not speak" yet eventually learning it well enough to fill a secretarial position in it, Marcel is beginning to speak the language that will allow him access to the world of the Guermantes, "dans le monde," as Saint-Loup has said. Understanding that world and speaking its language will entail a process of apprenticeship that will not be complete for quite a long time. Exploration of this world involves a total revision of received knowledge, including, for example, reassessing the fact that Marcel's grandmother, through having renewed her schoolgirl friendship with Mme de Villeparisis, has had a relation all along with the mythic Guermantes family, albeit one circumscribed by a whole set of behaviors and possibilities. The Guermantes were always more strangely familiar than the narrator ever suspected—as is homosexuality.

By drawing a line at the question of Charlus's sexual interests, the narrator differentiates what the character knows from what he is about to discover. Despite his knowledge of lesbianism in Montjouvain, this separation leaves the protagonist in the position of nonknowledge; he is puzzled at some of Charlus's behavior and remarks. At the same time, Marcel/the narrator offers details that will eventually become meaningful, even if they are not yet now. These details, such as Charlus's wandering eye or his penchant for helping young men of the lower classes, will make sense when the truth—for the moment, I mean the reductive truth—of Charlus's behavior and his character is revealed. Once Charlus's homosexuality is out in the open, all these other "accidental" details will make sense: we will understand, for example, that his aid to some young men of the lower classes probably relates to the bestowal of sexual favors.

In the sense of narratology, this difference of homosexuality is cause—here more than anywhere else in the novel—for a clear distinction between what the narrator knows and what his younger self knew. That is, even if the protagonist as a child, an adolescent, or a young man making his way in the world always knows less than the narrator, the narrator clearly indicates that this is a voyage of discovery. Here, however, he is content to leave his former self befuddled. The narrator seeks to distinguish between the knowledge given the reader and the knowledge given the character. The reader knows more than the character; the narrator keeps Marcel at a distance while reading the semiotics of Charlus's behavior. Because this is a gift from the narrator, not a permanently inscribed position of superiority, we can follow along, reading the multiple layers of discovery without abandoning our position of sympathy to the characters' development and experiences.

The role of the family in the *Recherche*—specifically, the role by which the family of the other makes that other familiar—constitutes the means by which homosexuality is introduced and made part of the narrative. We discover that filiation and affiliation—or siblingship and bonding—are related. The irony surrounding the lesbian couple of Mlle Vinteuil and her nameless friend lies in the initial presentation of this model, but it is depicted in a way that will eventually be inverted, as homosexuality is subsumed by the aesthetic. Made familiar by the Combray relations of the Vinteuil family, Mlle Vinteuil is involved with her friend in a taboo-shattering relationship visible to Marcel's wandering, wakeful eye. Much later the various images of Vinteuil will coalesce, as it becomes clear that the provincial piano teacher is also great composer, and, in the final irony, it is the nameless friend who translates the unreadable hieroglyphics of Vinteuil's hand into the magisterial septet (Schehr, *Flaubert,* 235–55).

Here the pattern is repeated and reinforced as it is solidified. Mme de Villeparisis, the grandmother's friend from schooldays, is revealed to be not some mere minor noble from the provinces but one of the matriarchs of the Guermantes clan, a near relation of the book's two most important male characters other than Swann and Marcel: the aunt of Charlus and grandaunt of Robert de Saint-Loup. As Marcel's grandmother has long maintained, Mme de Villeparisis is a member of that august family. More to the point, the two characters whom she introduces will both turn out to be homosexual, or at least to have homosexual interests, a trait more pronounced and sustained in Charlus yet ultimately revealed as an aspect of Saint-Loup's personality (and the personalities of a number of other characters). The noble path—the path of the noble family—is thus the means by which male homosexuality is introduced to the narrator, made familiar to him, and given a fundamental part in the world he is to describe.

The point is not so much that homosexuality is intrinsically related to the nobility but that revealing the homosexuality of one of his noble characters pleases the narrator far more than doing so for a member of the lower classes. It becomes a sign of a complex personality in a noble, an additional aspect of a character whose cumulative interest and aggregate personality are always the sum of the layers of noble family preceding him or her. Thus Charlus's homosexuality is as essential as his name, his heritage, and his family's alliances. The revelation of a noble character's homosexuality is always related to the most essential part of the character's being, the accreted essence of a thousand years of structuring of an individual. The homosexuality of a character from the lower classes is always more situational, accidental, or incidental than it is essential: be it Jupien or Morel, not to mention the large number of lower-class individuals on whom favor is bestowed, the homosexuality of the character relates to the situation in which he is found, a means by which a movement, in the economic if not the social sense, can be effected. I will come back to this later.

The sense of filiation in this specific instance thus relates to role of Mme de Villeparisis, who, if not exactly a go-between, is the instrument through whom male homosexuality is made familiar to Marcel. Guaranteed by his grandmother, she is marked as a woman outside social norms by her longstanding relationship with M. de Norpois and her inability to keep it permanently enshrouded in secrecy: she knows, for example, what Marcel's father is doing on a mission, thanks to secret communications from her paramour. So Mme de Villeparisis is marked as one who facilitates sexualities other than those marked as appropriately bourgeois or noble.[4] In introducing her nephew and grandnephew into the same circles as Marcel, she enables the exploration of other sexualities that challenge Marcel's bourgeois propriety. Mme de Villeparisis is nothing short of a fairy godmother who makes the miracle of male homosexuality happen for the adolescent Marcel.

There is thus an immediate tension perceptible between behaviors, even at the level of the nobility: sexual identity may be essential, as seems to be the case for Charlus, going back uncountably through layer on layer and year on year, but it is not always what the society officially sanctions, even within the class structure. Mme de Villeparisis's liberal and vaguely libertine sexuality should remain private, just as Charlus's should. In that respect Mme de Villeparisis contrasts dramatically with her old friend, Marcel's grandmother, whose philosophy—although never touching the sexual—combines artlessness with a conservative recuperation of essence. Through Mme de Villeparisis this broadening and re-marking of the private does two things to modify what our modern conceptions of sexuality—especially those inherited from a rapid application of the insights of gender studies—have wrongly wrought on the system. First, it clearly forecloses on homophobia, or what is gathered under that rubric, as the operative concept; rather, there is a distinction made between public position on the one hand and private rhetoric, discourse, and behavior on the other. It is a lesson that Marcel will receive repeatedly from Charlus, as well as from others, such as the Duchesse de Guermantes and Robert de Saint-Loup, during the odyssey to authorship. Second, it shows that the behavior of the upper classes bears no necessary relation to what those not "to the manner born" believe to be their essence, for for to think otherwise would be to impose a middle-class morality that seems to view all qualities as fungible. Throughout the novel, Charlus's message will be that this is not the case: that certain qualities are essential but that the untrained bourgeois, epitomized by the narrator, will misread which signs indicate which essences, so concerned are they to maintain all possibilities for transformation.[5]

Class difference plays a fundamental role in the apprenticeship of the signs of homosexuality. Beyond the intrinsic difference *of* class—the absolute difference that the narrator seems to suggest makes the nobles' situation essential, not situational—is a difference *between* classes. This class difference is marked as an example of noblesse oblige, at least from the narrator's point of view: it is behavior shared by many, if not all, members of the Guermantes clan, be it learned or inherited, along with name, title, and sexuality. Completely at ease with the bourgeoisie, at least with her childhood friend, Mme de Villeparisis still occasionally shows that her behavior is not natural (2:83) and that the relation between the classes is marked by an excess of this learned behavior: "And the only absence of true politeness there was in her was in the excess of her politeness, for one recognized in it the professional move [le pli professionnel] of a lady of the Faubourg Saint-Germain." Apparently Mme de Villeparisis's previously established role as a facilitator of difference is in fact her profession; Proust's description of Mme de Villeparisis not only reflects her paramour's diplomacy (likewise the facilitation of difference) but also makes her the spiritual descendant of Balzac's Mme de Beauséant, who explains life's mysteries to Eugène Rastignac in *Le Père Goriot* and thus foreshadows de Villeparisis's ability, both native and professional, to "ex-pli-cate," to unfold the layers of the social and, especially, to clarify the purported heterosexuality of her nephews.

Mme de Villeparisis learns her behavior or comes by it naturally, for she has seen such behavior in her youth, as when the Duc de Nemours, having received a *commission* from the concierge, brings the mail to her father. This recounted anecdote is remarkable, for the act entails crossing not one class line, between the nobility and the acceptable bourgeoisie, but two, between the concièrge and the duke, skipping over the middle class. It is a proleptic reminder of the leapfrogging of class structures that will mark Robert de Saint-Loup, madly in love with Rachel: "His aunt let my grandmother understand that he had unfortunately fallen into the claws of a bad woman about whom he was mad" (2:87–88).[6] Moreover, Saint-Loup will reinforce his climbing over class lines by seizing the reins not of power but of a waiting coach: "The nephew of Mme de Villeparisis, taking the reins the coachman handed him, sat next to him and, while opening a letter that the hotel manager gave him, made the animals take off" (2:89). Most notably, however, it proleptically hints at the behavior of Charlus, who, despite his incredible snobbishness and closure to numerous social situations in which he would have to associate with those whom he perceives as beneath him, is always ready to lend a helping hand to certain members of the working classes or the peasantry.

Sight, vision, perspective, and reading seem already to be related to or invoke the possibility of homosexuality. In the scene in Montjouvain the concern is that the lesbian couple may "be seen reading." Could it be that homosexuality is, within the constructions allowed by the development of the novel and of Marcel's "apprenticeship" in specific, initially and textually a matter of vision, sight, and perspective? The change in focus and the arrival of the two nephews is predicated on the turning of a blind eye both to the bourgeois friends and to the foibles of the two nephews: "Mme de Villeparisis warned us that she would soon not be able to see us so often" (2:87). She cannot see Marcel and his grandmother because of the exigencies of her heavily coded family obligations. But the unread and unsaid word *homosexual* could apply to her nephews as well. She is no longer able to separate herself from her family or from her class, and the indulgent (grand)aunt is unwilling or unable to see Saint-Loup and, especially here, Charlus for who and for what they are. Since her code has no word for "homosexual" (for this world is presumed always to be heterosexual), it is always a question of sight and vision in this introduction of the male homosexual, for all involved will refocus vision, sharpen perspectives, and change sights and sites. Vision is introduced by a moment of blindness that evokes the second sight that comes through hearing; it will be the means of discovering homosexual lovemaking hundreds of pages later. Nevertheless, unsighted, unseen, and unseeing, Marcel can already fantasize about a romantic friendship between himself and Saint-Loup: "thinking of the short time that was reserved for our friendship, already so great in my heart without my ever having seen him" (2:88). That is quite a leap into the unknown. Smitten with Saint-Loup, in a post-

Swann-like moment and a recollection of the maternal kiss, Marcel counts the days until the end of the affair that will be this summer love. Sightless, he can speak this friendship or love, even if it is only to himself; with sight, however, things will change. He will see, as will the other; the relation, once organized by a line of sight, takes on different forms.

Heretofore everything in this section has taken place in an unsigned world. Then comes the first vision of the beloved: the one who is loved before having been seen and the one who is adored for his family, although Marcel does not yet know that it is *the* family. But Saint-Loup, focusing his vision, sees at least as well as Marcel does, and perhaps better than that:

> One afternoon when it was very warm, I was in the hotel dining room which had been left in half-darkness to protect it from the sun by drawing the curtains—for it yellows them—and which, through their interstices, let the blue of the sea blink through, when in the central path [travée] that went from the beach to the road, I saw, tall, thin, his neck free, his head high and proudly set, pass a young man with penetrating eyes and whose skin was as gold and hair as golden as if they had absorbed all the sun's rays. Dressed in a supple, whitish cloth, the likes of which I would never have thought a man dare to wear, and whose thinness evoked nothing less than the freshness of the dining room, the heat, and the fine weather outside, he was walking quickly. His eyes, from one of which a monocle repeatedly fell, were the color of the sea. (2:88)

Saint-Loup—for it is he—is already intimately tied to the dining room, which is the space of exchange, for he is yellowed/golden as are its curtains; he is tied to the sea as well by the color of his eyes. He marks this space by his association with it and by the similarity of words with which they are described. It is his jaunty freedom—the same freedom that will allow Marcel to wander and that will mark the advent and event of the uncle—that is invoked here, as well as the repeated leitmotif of correct or incorrect vision. The passage is noteworthy for its other related details. The blue sea winking through the curtains, matching the blue eyes of Saint-Loup, already predicts the scene between Marcel and Charlus. And there is nothing as blatant a challenge to the received knowledge of sex roles and gender performance as the comment about the clothes Saint-Loup wears, or rather the thinness of the material, as if somehow that thinness reveals something that should have stayed swathed, hidden, or shrouded in the folds or thickness of a more masculine and less revealing fabric.

The intermittences of vision—as if there were a pattern of light and darkness—and the penetrating eyes of the sea/seen interrupt, as does the blue of the ocean that precedes them. Whereas the blue of the ocean is forced into a pattern by a play of light and dark, Saint-Loup's eyes penetrate, either seen or unseen, present or not, and reach Marcel's eyes. Resembling the Guermantes we have seen and those we have not, especially his cousin become his aunt, the Duchesse de Guermantes, Saint-Loup looks like who he is supposed to be but sees even more than he is seen. He is caught in his vision of self and other, constantly seeing and actively looking as his monocle rises and falls, albeit moved by no hands. More precisely, Saint-Loup is always in a position of having seen and having been seen: the monocle falls constantly from his eye as he has seen what he wants; having been seen, he becomes the lion or scion of a society looking for models and finding the chic elegance of the young marquis.

But who sees whom? If Marcel is in love with Saint-Loup before seeing the young marquis, what does he think when at last he finally sees him? At the same time, has Marcel already been seen? Does the monocle fall from Saint-Loup's eye even before Marcel can get in a word, a sight, or an eyeful of elegance? Does Saint-Loup already know something about himself, about Marcel, and about his or their fate? An abyss lies between vision and knowledge or language, the same gulf that separates any two who observe each other. For we may surmise that Marcel is seen by Saint-Loup, with his penetrating eyes and his fluttering monocle, as the latter man seems "to pursue his monocle, which fluttered in front of him like a butterfly" (2:89). Long before the insect imagery at the beginning of *Sodome et Gomorrhe,* Saint-Loup's gaze, if not his whole being, flutters like a fritillary, taking in and alighting on everything and everyone on which it focuses. That flitting gaze is even described using a word related more often to sexuality than to the field of vision: "His monocle started its jaunts [ébats] on the sunny road" (2:89); the word *ébats* is often used to describe the movements of lovemaking. What lies in this gap of knowledge and language is a word, an allusion, something hinted at but immediately abandoned because of common knowledge: "Because of his 'chic,' his impertinence as a young 'lion,' especially because of his extraordinary beauty, certain people thought he had an effeminate air, but without reproaching him for it, for one knew how virile he was and that he passionately loved women" (2:88–89). Yet what one knows is not always the truth, for all Combray "knows" that Odette is the mistress of Charlus, yet this is not true. So the "they say" is as fleeting as the presence of a butterfly flitting from one object to another; indeed, the whole *Recherche* will be devoted to dismantling what "one knows." Both this effeminate air, whatever the cause, and Proust's reasons seem as specious as the arguments against this effeminacy, for the argument against inferring anything from this effeminacy is nothing more than what one knows, and that knowledge is potentially wrong. Simultaneously, whatever effeminacy may be in the novel, it is not intrinsically linked to either heterosexuality or homosexuality but is rather a free-floating category unto itself.

In his displacement of vision, the narrator perhaps gives us a truth that will be developed subsequently in the strange encounters between Marcel and Charlus. This displacement of an argument as a perception is easily stated: consider a young, sickly adolescent, moonstruck at the sight of an extraordinarily handsome man he has not yet met and ready perhaps to bring the beloved back from the edge of madness and mental illness caused by an evil woman—"this kind of love finished fatally by mental illness [l'aliénation mentale]" (2:88). Although he has reached the age of reason, the adolescent depends on his grandmother for comfort, solace, friendship, company, and acquaintance, and he has no male friends or acquaintances aside from Bloch, a Jewish parvenu and thus a social outcast. What might one say of such a youth? Might not some people think him more than a tad effeminate? And there are neither stories of virility nor romantic adventures to give the lie to the assumption.

Silence and recognition come at the same moment, although there is no word, contact, or sign. Saint-Loup focuses his attention and ours while focalizing the process of encounter, meeting, and exchange—or rather, there is no exchange, even if all the other possibilities are there. This lack is registered as a defeat of both love and writing. The expected contact does not take place, and perhaps most disappointing is the substitution that occurs; expecting letters, Marcel receives nothing but icy tones, signs that say there are no signs, far more extreme than the mother's answer in Combray that "there is no answer." After all, the statement that "there is no answer" is still an answer, albeit a disappointing one to the young hero of Combray. Here, however, there is no registering of a yes or no, and despite repeated proximity and repeated focusing of monocles and attention, there is no indication that anything is there: "These icy manners were far from the charming letters I imagined only a few days before, written to me to express his sympathy" (2:90). Marcel searches for signs and contact through writing, but he receives nothing: he has written a letter to his mother in Combray, Saint-Loup has received a letter, and Charlus will fake writing, but there is no letter for Marcel, who in the absence of same cannot read signs of love for him from anyone.

What does Saint-Loup understand to be happening? We have no sense of his consciousness beyond knowing that his mien, his manners, and his behavior are automatic and inflexible. Nothing will change them; even before we meet his uncle, we find someone who seems to have stringent requirements for meeting someone else—literally and etymologically stringent, for they create a narrowing, a bottleneck. Saint-Loup will not even acknowledge Marcel's existence until the road is so narrow that they are inescapably put together in the same space. Then the rules of proxemics can be violated and physical and social distances can be obliterated, yet Saint-Loup still seems to refuse any contact or emotion. The dancing eyes that had been perceived in their multiple focusing are devoid of interest: "His eyes where not the faintest light of human sympathy shone, showed simply, in the senselessness [l'insensibilité] and inanity of his look, an exaggeration without which nothing would have distinguished them from lifeless mirrors. Then, focusing those hard eyes on me as if he wanted to get information [se renseigner] on me" (2:91).

And still there is a difference, for even in that senselessness Saint-Loup's look is exaggerated and not merely transparently or reflectively blank. That same look is a search for information, literally a "reteaching" (*renseigner*) and a search for signs. Saint-Loup's search for signs does not mark his character to a great extent, for he tends to be a bad reader compared to astute and subtle readers such as Swann, Charlus, and the narrator, but this search for information prepares the reader for the penetrating, information-seeking looks of Charlus, the master reader.[7] Saint-Loup seems to be seeking information about Marcel, but this is a classic displacement, for Marcel projects his own search for signs and recognition onto Saint-Loup. Marcel wants information, he has a thirst for signs and what they simultaneously hide and reveal (never the same thing in Proust), and he wants to know what is behind those seemingly lifeless eyes—specifically, whether that senselessness and inanity mask a sympathy, a love, or a devotion.

Again, how might Saint-Loup understand the situation? Forced to acknowledge the presence of the other, he stops his eyes from doing what they seem to do naturally, stops their radiation of ultramarine blue, and stops anything from being emitted by them. Suddenly, after a stringent encounter in which his grandaunt is now in the position of arranging meetings, things change. Previously uninvolved with Marcel or having refused to "see" him, Saint-Loup does Marcel's bidding, writing him or at least offering the semblance of writing with a calling card sent not to do battle, and certainly not to have sex, but to talk about literature: "I thought that it was at least a question of a duel, when he had his calling card brought to me the next day. But he spoke to me only of literature, declared after a long chat that he had a great desire to see me several hours every day" (2:91).

The previously mentioned projection is reciprocal rather than being something more complex: the narrator states that Saint-Loup wants to know about Marcel, which also means that Marcel wants to know about Saint-Loup. Here the motif of the calling card presents the possibility of reciprocal and ritual exchanges of information, for a calling card is a fixed sign, a kind of semiotically controlled writing in which the card itself—the enunciative structure—states what the message states. This moment recalls the novel's original writing scene, in which, the child Marcel writes his mother seeking an answer and her presence, but the answer is that there is no answer. With Saint-Loup's calling card the answer—which is in a sense "no answer," for there is no real message other than what is always already written on the card—has finally come, and Saint-Loup answers where the mother would not. Saint-Loup will provide the kiss of conversation about literature, and this for several hours a day. Saint-Loup's card also predicts Charlus's announcement of himself: Charlus announces himself without a card but with the repetition of his name, as if he were his own calling card. The scene repeats itself later: a nocturnal kiss, yet this time desired by the other—Charlus—and unrecognized by the somewhat naive adolescent. Again, the scene is accompanied by a book, this time one that Charlus brings along to lend to Marcel: Bergotte replaces Saint-Loup's general conversation about literature, but more important, the volume of Bergotte replaces the one by George Sand that the younger Marcel received.

The letter to the mother, the calling card, and the announcement of self as if Charlus were his own calling card are all accompanied by literature, as if the writing of the individual one knows—the self, the mother, Saint-Loup, and Charlus—were the prologue to the immortal writing for all time: Sand, literature in general, and Bergotte. This association is seconded by an erotic intimacy that is either the overvaluation of a relation—between mother and son—or the difference from acceptable norms: homophilia, as is the situation of Marcel for Saint-Loup, and ephebophilic homosexuality, as is the case with Charlus for Marcel.

Perhaps Marcel is not Saint-Loup's type. Perhaps Saint-Loup, having recognized a kindred spirit, also sees a spirit who is willing to deflect his secret sexuality into another realm: one into heterosexuality, the other into letters. The common language between the two will be the love of literature instead of the literature and language of love. Love is safely transferred into heterosexuality or made socially acceptable in the realm of friendship with someone whom Marcel describes as "the most likable and caring [prévenant] young man I had ever met" (2:91). Decidedly, the contact will have been made.

How should we explain the sudden change in Saint-Loup's attitude? A sudden thaw might be understandable, as would a civility brought on by the stringent encounter. But how should we explain a move from the impassive to the emotional and from the indifferent to the "friendliest"? It is hard to justify the "love at first sight," for it is not as if Saint-Loup has read Marcel's narrative. No, the answer lies elsewhere, in other relations, in family plots, and in family traits as Mme de Villeparisis's other nephew—Saint-Loup's uncle, the Baron de Charlus—finally comes on stage. And he enacts what Saint-Loup hides from himself and from Marcel. Charlus turns silence into signs.

Charlus's arrival introduces the concept of machismo, which will be a fairly transparent mask for what Charlus will eventually reveal. The signs emitted, radiated, and manipulated by Charlus are there for all to read. He is far and away the most macho character in the whole *Recherche,* which means that he is also the gayest. Charlus makes an athletic entry into Balbec, his lungs filled with fresh air, for he has been nourished by the sun and the earth: "very devoted to physical exercises, especially long walks, it was for the most part on foot, sleeping at night on farms" (2:107–8). A figure like Baden-Powell or Coubertin, Charlus, "in his travel on foot, after hours of running, threw himself, burning up, into icy rivers" (2:121).[8] Accompanying the mastery of self in the realm of the physical, which is a kind of poise and physical equilibrium, goes a mastery of station, tantamount to social poise. With that social poise goes a critical sense of station, for Charlus is also the character most focused on his own station and his relation to others. Moreover, he is acutely focused: he realizes what Saint-Loup flirts with and does so without a monocle. Contrasting with the veritable bonhomie of his brother, the Duc de Guermantes, who endlessly evinces a familiarity in his conversations and who has none of the wit of his wife, Charlus is the most distant and unapproachable of men; he is characterized as "difficult to get access to, disdainful, infatuated with his nobility" (2:108). Although he belongs to the Jockey Club, which also includes Swann, he will not allow himself to be presented to some two hundred of its other members.

Distant, this "prince" (2:109), this member of the circle of Phoenixes (2:108), and this member, in his youth, of the "Three Graces" (2:109) seems to fulfill the destiny and the description of the most unreachable of men.[9] He chooses his company, belonging to select groups of those reborn (the phoenixes) or those who bless human endeavor (the Graces); one simply wonders whether Charlus was cast as Aglaia (Splendor), Euphrosyne (Festivity), or Thalia (Rejoicing). Above all, he is a man's man and appropriately focused on the signs of masculinity and the rejection of effeminacy: "He would not allow a man to wear even one ring [bague]" (2:121; I will return to this phrase later). Perhaps most distinctively, the rejection of effeminacy goes so far as to be a moralizing homophobia, or at least it was so in the past when he was one of the Three Graces.

The information comes from Saint-Loup, who, totally enchanted by his uncle's mythology of self, repeats a story that happened when Charlus was a bachelor and shared an apartment with the two other Graces. One of their circle who "showed bizarre tastes" (2:109) wanted access to the bachelor pad. Once there, however, he failed to turn his attention appropriately to women, instead declaring his intentions to Charlus. To correct this unacceptable behavior, the Three Graces seize the guilty man, strip him, beat him until he bleeds, and throw him out in the subzero temperatures.[10] Charlus's honor is saved, the man has been taught a lesson, and heterosexuality remains the way of the world. Or does it?

Already in Marcel's confidence and complicitous with him—as well as having been *made* complicitous with him by textual maneuvers—Saint-Loup has no need to seduce Marcel directly. Proust tries to seduce Marcel and the reader into reading the homosexual content of the story. Reversing the role of the naked man, the novel's real homosexual (Charlus) stays dressed, while the one for whom it is a passing fancy—or who is of only passing interest to the reader—is victimized. Safety is in the body: the three homophobic Graces, although compared to women through that sobriquet, maintain their manhood by a homophilic bonding that will victimize the one who declares his homosexuality. All is safe. And yet Proust wants to tell us that things are not as safe as they appear.

No tale told by Saint-Loup is just for the adolescent Marcel; the narrator further intends it for our eyes and ears, which are not the same as those of the more naive teenager. Even within the story Saint-Loup tells there is information important for us—its deeper meaning unknown to him—soon to be revealed to those who can read. This information remains impenetrable to Marcel as protagonist but is transparent to the narrator, who once again forgets to tell us what it means. Although the infinitely disdainful Charlus remains unapproachable to most members of society, even many members of his club and the upper classes, he is open to crossing class lines when certain occasions present themselves: "Nowadays, my uncle would not permit himself such a cruel execution and you cannot imagine the number of men of the people [hommes du peuple]—he who is so haughty with the worldly set [les gens du monde]—that he has developed affection for, that he protects, ready to be paid with ingratitude. One time it will be a servant who served him in a hotel and whom he will find a position for in Paris or a peasant whom he will have learn a trade" (2:109). The first use of the conjunction *and* here is telling, for Saint-Loup, although not the greatest stylist in the *Recherche,* associates Charlus's previously described act of delivering a lesson to someone who had been sexually forward with a seemingly unrelated anecdote about his attitude of noblesse oblige with men of the lower classes: "hommes du peuple." The two apparently disjoint stories are made harmonious only when we read the content of both as homosexual.

This passage is remarkable for several reasons. The first relates to what remains unsaid in the first clause: "my uncle would not permit himself [taken word for word, "no longer deliver himself to"] such a cruel execution." What would he do, then? Would he let an attempted homosexual seduction pass, would he find a less cruel response, or would he himself be in the position of having "delivered himself to" cruelty for having tried to seduce another? Charlus, self-fulfilling victim and prophecy, will deliver his own gay body to a beating, albeit a ritualized one, in Jupien's brothel. Just as he did with the question of Charlus's supposed mistresses, Saint-Loup utters what he supposes to be the truth given the world in which he lives. Yet what is not said and what he misunderstands is as fascinating. Beyond the question of what Charlus would do today lingers other questions: why would he not do what he did, and why would he do something else? Has he become more moderate, tolerant, and understanding? No, not really: he remains the haughty, opinionated snob that he always was. Or is there a secret history that we may soon begin to suspect and that we will definitely learn a bit later? Would he not do what he has done precisely because he is a homosexual? Might he not find a different solution, a complicity with the other or an assignation?

The second important matter is an error that seems to have escaped the editors of both Pléiade editions of the *Recherche:* Saint-Loup addresses Marcel with the familiar pronoun *tu* instead of the more formal *vous.* In the next part of the novel, *Le Côté de Guermantes,* Marcel makes much of a hoped-for use of the less distant forms, for he would take the intimacy of language to reflect the intimacy between the two characters (2:401). It would not be an easily won linguistic intimacy, given Saint-Loup's aristocratic airs, which are almost as severe as those of his uncle. Here, however, during their first encounters, the *tu* is clearly a textual error. At the same time, this error seems to serve as an index of the confidence that is being made about Charlus's tastes, even if neither of the participants recognizes that confidence. Although I suppose it to be nothing more than an oversight by the author and the editors, it perhaps reflects Proust's unconscious desire to create intimacy in the relationship between Saint-Loup and Marcel long before it can happen, precisely to tell the truth about Charlus where it cannot yet be told.

The crux of the passage lies in the attention Charlus pays to some of the "little people" who cross his path. A retrospective reading shows that the young men placed in such service are those granted favored status for services rendered or expected. This fact raises the possibility of the "ingratitude" Saint-Loup mentions, for the men may not come through or put out, or they may cease doing so. The choice is not a choice, for it could be either or both. Were Charlus's favors bestowed on young women instead of young men, there would be no ambiguity whatsoever about the baron's actions. Whether in the past or in a desired future, a young woman so placed would be "compromised," or at least placed there for a reason. Accepting such a placement would, according to the rules of hospitality and etiquette, be a tacit acceptance of the situation and an assent that one's silence or one's favors have been purchased.

The narrator reminds us that, like Saint-Loup but even more so, Charlus is a model for society. The world invariably follows Charlus's lead except in the one area the world about which it is unaware. This reminder of mimetic behavior on the part of the world's followers also serves to remind us, once again retrospectively, that this is one of the points at which textuality separates from reality and verisimilitude. Verisimilitude cedes to textual coherency, even when the narrative remains seemingly within the bounds of the apparently true. Although it is unlikely that so many people in a social group would turn out to be homosexual or to have homosexual interests or proclivities, it is strictly consonant with the textual dynamic.

With all this information in our hands, we are ready to meet the singular character who will dominate much of the remainder of the novel, even when he is absent. Prepared as we are for a manly man who is a paragon of society and a model of masculinity, we finally meet him. Again, the narrator seems to give distance, for he leaves open the path for the adolescent Marcel to do a reading. Assured narration itself seems to have taken a temporary backseat, given the narrative about Charlus that Saint-Loup relates to Marcel and the narrative of a narrator who does not inform his earlier self or his readers of the knowledge he has. So we are given what amounts to a naive or faux-naive reading of Charlus, for it is less a direct presentation of the character than an incomplete description from which certain analyses have been eliminated. By filtering the narrative through the perceptions of the adolescent Marcel, Proust can leave his protagonist in a position in which he has no special knowledge, no special insights, and no benefits from the later self that he will become. Without his future power to narrate, Marcel can thus become fair game for the eyes of another. Not only does he observes; he is observed as well:

> I walked alone in front of the casino when returning to the hotel; I had the feeling of being looked at by someone who was not far from me. I turned my head and saw a man of about forty, very tall and rather heavy, with a very black mustache, and who, while nervously hitting his pants with a walking stick, focused his eyes, dilated with attention, on me. At times they were shot through in every way with an aspect of extreme activity, such as occurs only in men in whom, for whatever reason, an unknown stranger standing before them inspires thoughts that would never occur to anyone else—as is the case, for example, with madmen and spies. He gave me such a meaningful glance that was daring, wise, quick, and deep, like the last blow given before one flees, and, having looked all around him, suddenly took on a distracted and haughty air, through a brusque bending of his entire body, he turned toward an advertisement, the reading of which he became absorbed, while humming an air and arranging the moss rose in his lapel.[11] (2:110–11)

Charlus scarcely resembles the portrait that Saint-Loup has painted of his uncle, for he hardly seems to be the fine specimen of manhood that was once one of the lionized Three Graces. The point lies not there, however, but in the vision or multiple vision: what Marcel sees and what we presume Charlus sees are two very different images.

While keeping the critical information directly from us and from Marcel, the narrator cannot tell exactly what he sees. The network or constellation of textual linkages foregrounds the nature of the unknown individual who will turn out to be Charlus. The walking stick—*une badine,* related to the words *badinerie* and *badinage,* or "banter"—already hints at playful bantering, often with erotic overtones.[12] As I have already indicated, the central focus is focus itself: the narrowing of vision, the scoping out of the other, and the features of the eyes. Charlus seems to be looking with his whole body; whereas Saint-Loup focuses on his monocle dancing like a butterfly before him, his gaze impassively flitting from object to object in his path, Charlus stares with his whole being. He looks, he is intent on looking, and he focuses his every muscle on that attentive gaze. Reprised as well is the important leitmotif of repeated hitting or striking: here self-inflicted; previously inflicted on the homosexual other—the episode from his youth; and finally, in the whipping scene in Jupien's brothel, inflicted on himself by another. Also repeated is the hummed tune with no words, a tune that draws attention to itself and its absence. As readers may remember, when Marcel brought home a Jewish friend, his grandfather would wordlessly hum the tune of an aria with "Jewish content," such as "'O God of our fathers' from *La Juive,* or 'Israel, break thy chain'" (1:90; see Schehr, *Figures* 178–96). We will never know what tune Charlus might whistle, although it is safe to say that it is neither the wordless melody from the Vinteuil violin sonata, which figures prominently in Swann's courting of Odette, nor an aria from *La Juive.* The analogies and the comparisons reinforce the images and move even the simplest reading off the mark to indicate that there is an outlaw or abnormal status to this behavior: the last blow rendered before flight, the behavior of spies, madmen, or a hotel thief (Deleuze 205–19).

What Marcel sees, therefore, is a man who differs from any other he has ever seen: a homosexual. The mark of that homosexual is that he too sees, remarks the other, and gazes as intently at his vis-à-vis—in this case Marcel—as the observing writer-to-be gazes at his prey. The homosexual writes. Not content merely to hand over a calling card, as his nephew did, the homosexual figures an absorption in reading (Saint-Loup is content to talk about literature) and a subsequent writing that is equally intent: "From his pocket, he took out a notebook in which he seemed to note the title of the performance in question" (2:111). Certainly Charlus fakes writing or feigns interest in what he is writing. The difference between the homosexual and the writer is that, whereas the latter believes in the truth of his act of writing, the former fakes it, just as he fakes wanting to know the time—Charlus "took his watch out two or three times" (2:111). Charlus cannot even breathe without signing the fictional nature of his act, for he exhales theatrically: "He exhaled that noisy breath made by people who are not too warm but who want to show that they are too warm" (2:111). Proust repeats the word *air* in these pages, as if everything were merely phenomenal, an act of surface appearances that need not have anything to do with the underlying essence or reality. This repetition of the word *air* is finally translated into the referent of the breath itself, but that breath is theatrical: the breath of those who want to have an air of being warm.

Despite all these comparisons, Charlus believes he sees a reflection of himself: another homosexual in the form of an adolescent observing intently, writing things in a real or imaginary notebook, and spying on others. Think of Montjouvain, where Marcel had espied Mlle Vinteuil and her friend: Charlus seems to have a writer's second sight for knowing Marcel's previous activities. He sees a second self, an earlier self, or a self recognized by "gaydar," a sign system that Marcel remarks and that the narrator possesses without knowing what it is: "I had the feeling of being looked at" (2:110). If the word *gaydar* seems out of place, one should remember that the narrator speaks of Charlus's looks as a "coup de sonde" (2:113), or "test of a plumb line." The dynamic here between two characters unknown to each other reverses the general dynamic of the novel as a whole, for the spying, the observing, and the sleuthing ordinarily performed by Marcel and inscribed by the narrator are now one-upped by the one individual who can read Marcel's mind, or so he thinks. But that is the novel's one taboo, the one impossible point: the narrator cannot be gay, cannot be perceived as gay, and must remain steadfast in his heterosexuality, even if it does not yet exist.[13] Charlus perceives a gay man in the making, and no one can do anything about it. That perception will set the scene for the events to come.

Charlus's gaydar is often a hit-or-miss phenomenon, even if he seems to be on target here, at least in terms of the gayness of the future textuality, and he will be on target later in his assault on Morel. It is Morel, however, who will give fullest expression to this gay sixth sense, showing that the talent can be applied to lucrative as well as platonically desirable situations. During a dinner with Charlus, Morel has zeroed in on two possible members of the gay brotherhood: "'But how do you know all that?' asked M. de Charlus astonished at Morel's prescience. 'Oh! I can guess in a second. If the two of use were to take a walk, you would see that I would not be wrong twice.' And whoever would have looked at Morel at that moment, with his air of a girl in the middle of all his male beauty, would have understood the obscure divination that indicated him no less to certain women than did they to him. He felt like supplanting Jupien, vaguely desiring to add to his 'usual take' the monies that he believed the haberdasher got from the baron" (3:396). In the Balbec passages Proust deploys a system of recognition that lacks any material component, for it seems to be based entirely on a recognition of desire. In the relations between Charlus and Morel and in the male brothel, which also plays on a semiotics of recognition, Proust somewhat cynically yet pragmatically shows the labile nature of desire, which can be motivated by other means. Gaydar can be coin operated as well as free flowing.

The initial contact between Charlus and Marcel involves hard looks and penetrating glances. Attention wavers: the forced attention that is the focusing of desire hides behind a host of activities meant to seem as if there were no focus, no direction of desire, and no evocation of the other as potential object of sexual desire.[14] For what is gaydar here? It is double, with two sensations that I have not distinguished. First, there is the recognition of the other as as "*semblable*," as "*frère*": as another homosexual. It is a recognition of sexuality without necessarily a conscious consideration of sexuality as an object. Second, there is the recognition of the other as potential—real or fantasized—sex object, regardless of whether he is gay or not. The two are not necessarily the same. The first always involves a moment of phantasmic sexuality, even if it is not conscious or directly libidinal, simply because the act of identification that occurs at a subconscious level is, at least in the modern West, based on a categorization of humans into groups based on their presumed sexual behaviors, desires, or "identities." If gaydar is considered to be a complex preconscious or subconscious recognition of a series of internalized signs and behaviors, often remaining invisible to members of dominant sexual groups, this subtle semiotics relates to a sexual disposition. The blip on an internal gaydar screen is fundamentally a sexual one, even if, at the conscious or performative level of self, there is nothing more than the recognition of a peer. Recognizing the other as gay is tantamount to recognizing that the other has sex with other men, either in reality or in fantasy.

The second movement involves the recognition of the other as sexual object, whether gay or straight. This is a fleeting or enduring phantasm, focused on something in the other, which is not necessarily the same focus as the sounding system of gaydar. Certainly recognizing the phantasm is a more wholly conscious act than simply recognizing the other as a peer or believing the other to be gay as well. The phantasm surfaces as a daydream that interrupts the flow of the ordinary with a sexual event, a momentary division of consciousness and presence into two zones, one of which is private. In this second case, even if the initial process that signs recognition and the one that signs desire are the same, there is a difference and a danger. The gaydar recognition is immediate, just as the phantasm can be—or more appropriately, as focusing on the real presence of the other can be. Beyond that, extended focusing might have consequences other than those envisioned in the daydream, for example, if the other, recognizing the focusing of the desire stripped by the mind's eye, fails to appreciate such attention for reasons at the most basic level, that of not being a member of the same sexual group. The other might go so far as to call his friends together and collectively administer a beating to the unfortunate one who declared his intentions with his mind's eye.

What is the case with Charlus? To what extent could we impute one of these interrelated desires and recognitions to the behavior and signs that Proust painstakingly ascribes to the character? The conclusions necessitated by both those recognitions are taboo within the realm of the novel: we cannot conclude that Marcel is homosexual, nor can we conclude that, straight or gay, he is a suitable object of homosexual desire. Nevertheless, although both conclusions are taboo, the first is decidedly more problematic than the second. In the second the narrator can claim unwonted attention, but it is nothing that challenges his manhood. Rather, there would be an implicit praise of his attraction and his desirability. He would have, as is said in French, *le beau rôle* (i.e., he "comes off smelling like a rose"). As the object of desire, Marcel is placed in that position of desirability by the other's observant eye. For the narrator, this repeats what he has always done and will continue to do with the other protagonists: envision them as desirable and seek to fulfill that desire, albeit not necessarily a sexual one, by getting to know them. As was the case with Gilberte, Odette, and Saint-Loup and as will be the case with the Duchesse de Guermantes, not to mention Albertine, so it is here with the projection of desire on the safe interpretation of Charlus's desire for Marcel. Made desirable, Marcel thus fits symmetrically and reciprocally into the system of desire Proust has created for his other characters.

Most specifically in the realm of the immediately mimetic, Marcel is therefore like both the male characters just described: Saint-Loup, the lion of Paris, and Charlus as described by Saint-Loup. Each of them becomes a paragon of behavior that sets the pattern for those who follow. Signs taken as memes become law: "If for eating a piece of cake he used, instead of his spoon, a fork or a utensil of his own invention that he had had made by a goldsmith, or his fingers, it was no longer permitted to do anything else" (2:110). Desirability makes Marcel as respectable a he-man as the figures Saint-Loup and Charlus project of themselves. Thus does his desire for the unattainable other perversely make him more heterosexual. Then he too is a ladies' man, and no matter if he may have an effeminate air; his heterosexuality, like that of Saint-Loup and Charlus, is not in question.

The alternative explanation is more dangerous, for it would project the narrator as homosexual, or at least as someone producing signs or behavior that others might conclude are those of a homosexual. Parading about and emitting a trail of semiotic pheromones, Charlus has already clearly done so. Whereas the lionizing attitude of general desirability would guarantee his masculinity (i.e., his heterosexuality), considering Marcel to be gay can threaten the sense of self established for the protagonist at the textual level. It may ultimately have an impact on the writing project as a whole: can one imagine the consequences of having a gay narrator? Readers may conclude that this is a homosexual text, a different, more radical, and more far-reaching conclusion than that this work, although grounded in heterosexuality, has homosexual themes. The preening, parading behavior ascribed to Charlus, a foreshadowing of the dance with Jupien in the courtyard, can leave no other impression on the reader. Would Charlus risk such an audacious display were he not sure—had his gaydar not told him unequivocally—that Jupien is also gay? Would Charlus behave as he does in this scene were he not sure that the delicate adolescent he perceives walking alone is not like himself, a fellow traveler in Sodom by the sea?

What does Charlus see? What does Charlus do? What signs does he emit? Sensing someone in his field of vision whom he believes to be a young homosexual and having had his gaydar emit a lavender ping, Charlus goes into attack mode and removes his cruise control. First, he draws attention to his person—indeed, to his lower body—its physicality, materiality, touchability, and capacity to receive force and violence, for he is "nervously hitting his pants with a walking stick" (2:110). His reaction occurs at both conscious and unconscious levels, with the word *nerveusement* linking the two systems. Charlus's will perceives the other as prey, but his unconscious does the same, and libidinal juices start to flow as he opens his eyes wide (2:110) to show interest and attention. While piercing with their stare, his eyes—the windows to his soul or mind—are pierced as well in a strange reversal of penetration that evokes sexual versatility whereby one is top or bottom. His mind fills with curious thoughts and strange ideas "that would occur to no one else" (2:111). But they do occur to someone else: Marcel. Is he a spy, a madman, or another homosexual?

Charlus goes for broke and makes his move with his eyes: "He gave me such a meaningful glance that was daring, wise, quick, and deep" (2:111). This last-ditch effort reinforces Charlus's belief that he has found a like-minded traveler. Charlus seems more convinced that he has found another homosexual than that he has found an object after whom to lust. Still, there is no response from Marcel, so perhaps Charlus has been wrong to make the assumption he has made. Tactically retreating from the direct plan, therefore, Charlus follows up with a series of false activities, all of which seem to be calculated to show their artificiality to anyone who may be in the know. And the narrator knows, even if Marcel does not. The narrator knows what those signs mean, while his earlier self can recognize merely an aberration, a strangeness, or the outlaw status of a madman, a spy, an assaulter, or a hotel thief. For the narrator has gaydar, even if his character is blissfully unaware of the implications of those roving glances shot in his direction by penetrating, wandering eyes.[15]

Shall we say, then, that the position of narration is doubly homosexualized? It is homosexualized because the narrator manifests that same gaydar as does Charlus: the narrative vision focuses on specific aspects of Charlus's behavior just as Charlus's eyes linger on Marcel. The narrative flirts with Charlus, makes him a sexual object, and brings the reader together with this other who is neither madman nor spy; the narrator thus repeats, in another triangulation of narrative desire, the intermittent actions of Mme de Villeparisis. Yet the position is also homosexual, for, as Kristeva has argued, novelistic narrative is the locus of nondisjunction of values in which the opposite category is always implied even as it is elided. Once Marcel is marked as potentially homosexual, therefore, he is always marked as such. It is not that an accusation of homosexuality makes someone a homosexual (the juridical tone here seems acceptable, for medical and juridical categories of abnormality intersect). Rather, within a set of potentials associated with any textual position lies the accumulation of values and semioses associated with that position.

Making an advance is no guarantee that the other will accept, and rejection occurs as often as not. With the suit or pursuit rejected, the body is convinced and convincing in its manifestations and thereby becomes a negative version of itself. The body plays out a game of an alienated suitor who still radiates that same aberration—madness, skullduggery, criminality, or homosexuality—through the torsion and distortion of the physical: "His goal seemed [. . .] to be to give me the idea, not that he had not seen me, but rather that I was an object of too little importance to attract his attention. He bent his waist with an air of bravado, pinched his lips, rearranged his mustache, and in his look, adjusted something indifferent, hard, almost insulting. So much so that the unique nature of his expression made me think of him as a thief or an insane person [aliéné]" (2:111). This rejection perceived as an insult augurs the one to come, which takes those physical moves and redoubles them with an explosive reverse discourse that rejects instead of allowing the wounded pride that comes with having been rejected. Yet the reversal is also repetition. Charlus first bends one way and then another: he is taken for a spy or a madman and then for a thief or an insane person. His glance was penetrating, and now it is hard. To rework a famous title of Gilles Deleuze, in this case difference *is* repetition.

If the reversal means playing it straight for Marcel, the narrator is informing us that the retrograde movements repeat the original ones; there is no closet to return to, for there never was one to begin with. For Proust, the bond between two homosexual positions is exclusive. It is singular by nature, and though it can be espied by a third—such as Marcel at Montjouvain; in the hôtel de Guermantes, where he overhears rather than sees; or in Jupien's brothel—it can neither lean or be leaned on by another kind of social intercourse, at least at this level. If there is a significant difference in social rank, there may be an economic interest that parallels the homosexual bond. But the homosexual bond cannot coexist with the bonds of social amiability described by etiquette. Thus Charlus dehomosexualizes himself for Marcel, if not for the narrator and the readers, and Marcel is once again clueless as he sees Charlus suddenly go straight: "With the speed of lightning, his look went through me [me traversa] as it had at the moment that I first saw him, and returned, as if he had not seen me, to organize itself, a little lower, in front of his eyes, dulled [émoussé], like the neutral look that feigns seeing nothing without and is capable of reading nothing within, the look that expresses only the satisfaction of feeling around oneself the eyelashes it brushes away from its inane roundness, the devoted and confected look that certain hypocrites have, the stupid look that certain fools have" (2:112). Molière's Tartuffe and certain characters from La Bruyère may come to mind, but we should also recognize the recurrent language: the relation of reading to these penetrating glances and the repetition of the penetration in a feigned turn toward the self-satisfied, the autoerotic, and even the asexual.

Mme de Villeparisis makes an error, one that seems superfluous, presenting her nephew as the "Baron de Guermantes"(2:112), a nonexistent character who is the mythical straight version of Charlus, the incognito prince who maintains his anonymity. The Baron de Guermantes is Charlus, who does not look, for the narrator insists on the absence of eye contact: "without looking at me" (2:112), "without having raised his eyes" (2:112), "Saint-Loup's uncle honored me neither with a single word nor even a look" (2:113). No fear, Charlus has been stricken with neither modesty nor blindness. His eyes still work: "and during this short walk, two or three times, he cast his terrible and deep look like a sounding [coup de sonde] on insignificant people walking by who were of the most modest extraction" (2:113; see also Deleuze; Doubrovsky; Genette; Infantino; Shattuck). These soundings are the same gaydar pings that we have already seen. If, in the presence of his family, he cannot act on his recognition of another gay person—or a person perhaps or potentially available for gay sex—this does not prevent a quick glance and confirmation of recognition.

Charlus is no longer a bad guy, for like Vautrin transformed into the head of the secret police—and thus, in Balzac's eyes, albeit quite ironically, having found the straight and narrow—Charlus has also metamorphosed from hotel thief into a "policeman on a secret mission but who keeps his friends outside his professional surveillance" (2:113). Thus does Proust underline that the separation of fields of vision remains in place, at least for social intercourse: the homosexual mission remains unknown to anyone within the regular social group. The star-struck Marcel is rapt in his own thoughts and in his ecstatic meditation on the golden name that he has just heard dropped from the lips of Mme de Villeparisis. Engrossed as he is, he probably does not have the necessary focus to play spy/counterspy.

Where is Marcel before he breaks rank, when he sees Charlus look at "insignificant people"? How can he follow that withering glance so quickly and clearly? Is Marcel next to Charlus and able immodestly to look at him watching and focusing his vision precisely when he turns to use his penetrating eyes elsewhere? Or is Marcel, too, attracted by the same insignificant people? Presumably he is not walking backward in front of Charlus, so he must be doing what Charlus does, stealing looks, with Marcel focusing on the vision and on vision itself at the very moment when the same phantasmic gaydar look occurs. For a brief moment Marcel has possibly become Charlus, raising his head and eyes in unison with those of the cynegetic older man; Marcel, becoming the narrator, is a scribe, an amanuensis, or a pantograph of that other position—Charlus's homosexual one—that is perhaps made safe by narration itself, which, while homosexualized, prevents or protects Marcel from becoming a full-fledged homosexual.

The look is like the taste of a madeleine dipped in an infusion of linden flowers, for it is a retrospective glance and a recognition: "I now recognized [reconnaissais] in the hard look that had made me turn around [retourner] a little while ago near the casino the look that I had seen focus on me at Tansonville at the moment that Mme Swann had called Gilberte" (2:115). So Charlus will have taken Marcel—as a child—for a homosexual even earlier, and the iterativity of *reconnaissais* and *retourner* emphasizes that repetition. The look now is perhaps the recognition of a familiar face or the belief that Charlus recognizes someone he has already seen but cannot place. This may be part of the reaction, but it does not correspond to the flirtatious and theatrical behavior that characterizes the encounter between Charlus and the adolescent Marcel. We may thus assume that the first look also gave him that information. Significantly, this is what the narrator says at the time of the first visual encounter; speaking of the still unidentified Charlus, he mentions a gentleman who "focused eyes on me that were popping out of his head."

The narrator needs to maintain heterosexuality to protect his earlier self from sexual ambiguity; all the characters must do the same, whether for self-protection or for social and ideological reasons. There is a general concern about maintaining the perfect veneer and ubiquity of heterosexuality, and Marcel jumps to a conclusion when he assumes that Saint-Loup has specific knowledge about the identity of Charlus's mistresses. What Saint-Loup knows is known by negation: he knows that Odette has not been Charlus's mistress. The brief perception of the two in Tansonville, which Marcel took as a confirmation of the local gossip that they were having an affair, is set aside, although without any further question as to the reason behind it. This still does not explain what Marcel thinks he sees. Let us assume that his initial view of Odette and Charlus at Tansonville was perceived as importunate by Charlus, perhaps an unfortunate overhearing or a case of involuntary espionage (Marcel's future stock-in-trade) that Charlus does not appreciate and receives with a glacial stare. There is nothing similar in the second encounter to warrant the same stare. The two situations could not be further apart. What ties them together is the stare of one individual at another, the "sounding" that characterizes all Charlus's penetrating glances.

Tea time arrives, but this is not the tea of Combray later recalled when Marcel eats a bit of a madeleine while drinking a cup of infusion; rather, it is a much more formal tea with the Guermantes. Having invited Marcel and his grandmother to Mme de Villeparisis's rooms for tea, Charlus seems to have forgotten that he did so and intimates that it was the grandmother's idea, something totally inconsistent with her modest, retiring character, as Mme de Villeparisis would be the first to know. Charlus's flickering memory reminds us of his wavering attention to others and of his alternation between penetrating glances and their denial: Charlus inscribes the game of absence and presence, intimating the Freudian *fort-da,* but in this case it indicates not attachment to the mother but rather his perception of the homosexuality or interest of the other.

While Marcel remains perplexed and commits a faux-pas by reminding Charlus of the invitation's correct origin, Charlus continues to mix his penetrating glances with a willful ignoring of Marcel to probe the situation even further. Departing from the normal train of narratological events in these pages, the narrator makes a remark that indicates that his views of people and their intentions and innermost thoughts will eventually change: "with a scrupulousness for precision that I kept until I was of an age at which I understood that it is not by asking a man about it that one learns the truth about an intention that he has had" (2:119). Although cast in the *passé sim-*

ple and thus adequately distant from the moment of narration, the realization is still some time in the future for the adolescent that Marcel is or the adult that the narrator was. Moreover, although Marcel seems to remain clueless about Charlus's intentions, wondering why the baron invited them only to ignore him or feign not remembering the invitation, the narration tells a different story: "He was merely content, turning (away) from time to time the investigative look of his penetrating eyes, to attach to my face, with the same seriousness, the same air of preoccupation, as if it had been a manuscript that was difficult to decipher" (2:119). All the previous signifieds are there, with the reader reminded of the nexus of signs that the narrator is connecting not so much to the construction of homosexuality but to the inscription of homosexual seduction: having an air, penetration, reading, and the like. In moving from a simple inscription of writing and reading to the act of deciphering, the narrator is giving us a taste of things to come, as "the friend of Mlle Vinteuil will turn her own penetrating regard on the hieroglyphic scrawl that marks the posthumous masterpiece of a composer so that she can produce a readable and playable manuscript for Vinteuil's posthumous septet. I might even suggest that the penetrating glance that characterizes active reading is associated not just with voluptuousness in general, as Paul de Man (57–78) suggests, but with sexuality: in *Du côté de chez Swann*, with masturbation in the room that smells of orrisroot, and here, with (male) homosexuality. After all, it is once again in the natural progression of things to move from autoerotic to homoerotic pleasure.

From having been described as a big, heavy man, Charlus has regained the graceful beauty of his youth: "Undoubtedly, had those eyes not been there, the face of M. de Charlus was like that of many handsome men [Sans doute s'il n'y avait pas eu ces yeux, le visage de M. de Charlus était semblable à celui de beaucoup de beaux hommes]" (2:119–20). This strange sentence demands a bit of attention. The editors (2:1391) comment that although the Nouvelle Revue Française proofs from 1914 lack the *y*, it is undoubtedly a printer's error, so that they are restoring it. They remain silent, however, regarding the awkward sequence of tenses between the pluperfect of the protasis and the imperfect of the apodosis, where one would expect the past conditional in one form or another. That is, one would have expected *il aurait été* or *il eût été*. Such constructions do occur, so perhaps this is nothing more than a singular agrammaticality, rather than a grammatical error, or even merely a more casual, oral French. At the same time, the imperfect implies another grammatical structure present as a ghost: "Si il n'y avait pas ces yeux, le visage serait semblable . . . ," that is, "if those eyes were not there, his face would be like . . ." Whereas the structure using the pluperfect describes a completely unchangeable state of affairs, having occurred in finished past, the structure of the imperfect-conditional "if-then" sentence implies a possibility of hope for the future. In this case we would be witness to a wish fulfillment that is yet another sign—like the error in room numbers so well discussed by Lavagetto—that places the narrator *in* the scene of homosexuality.

Previously there was no reason to think Charlus handsome. Here the narrator offers nothing more than Charlus's aristocratic airs, which suddenly make him attractive. Despite the long appreciation of masculinity and effeminacy that soon follows and in direct contradiction to those ideas, we learn that Charlus wears makeup: "A light layer of powder gave [his face] a bit of the appearance of a face made up for the theater" (2:120). The comparison emphasizes Charlus's artifice and shows that some of the previous comparisons were justified, at least on a hermeneutic level. Charlus does have a state secret to hide; at the same time, the artificiality created by the makeup already undercuts the disquisitions on masculinity associated with Charlus's macho posturing.[16] Yet his eyes are telltale, and they are literally and figuratively a loophole in his face: "like a crack, like a loophole [meurtrière] that alone he had not been able to plug and through which, according to the point at which one was placed relative to him, one felt brusquely crossed by the reflection of some internal mechanism that seemed to have nothing reassuring about it" (2:120).

Charlus's look is put into question because it is the sign of a secret. The narrator has indicated the effect of the look and the behavior associated with it and has underlined the discomfort Marcel feels when being penetrated by Charlus's X-ray vision. Having connected the look to a host of secretive or furtive activities and behaviors, the narrator now moves closer to focusing on what he knew from the beginning, the look's relation to secret knowledge: "I would have wanted to guess what the secret was that other men did not carry within themselves. . . . But with what I knew now about his family background [parenté], I could no longer believe that it was that of a thief, nor after what I heard of his conversation, could I believe it was that of a madman" (2:120). Antisocial behaviors have been eliminated because of Charlus's pedigree; aberrant behaviors such as madness have been eliminated because of Charlus's logic of discourse. Whatever the unknown secret is, it is vouchsafed by family, personal logic, and order. Thus the secret presents only limited danger because there is a safety net guaranteed by pedigree, which for Proust and many of his characters, including Saint-Loup and

Charlus, means authenticity and cratylism. It is guaranteed as well by language. Whatever this secret is, it cannot go beyond the limits of the orders established by time and by language.

Marcel still recognizes that he is the object of the look, both earlier, when perceived near the casino, and later, while taking tea in the rooms of Mme de Villeparisis. Because there is nothing singular—idiotic, idiomatic, or idiopathic—about Marcel, there must therefore be something that he typifies or illustrates. Marcel recognizes Charlus's benevolence when it comes to Marcel's grandmother, and indeed, Charlus is generally good-natured toward women. For him, women remain an indivisible group: "he had good will toward women" (2:112) whether they are liked or unliked, for Charlus's behavior toward a certain group of men is like that of misogynists for women in general (2:112). Distinctions are made only among men, and that is where gender plays a distinct and ultimately disquieting role:

> As far as men were concerned, and particularly young men, he had a hatred, with a violence recalling that of certain misogynists for women. Of two or three "gigolos" who were related to or in the intimate circle of Saint-Loup and of whom the latter mentioned the names by chance, M. de Charlus said with almost a ferocious expression that cut through his habitual coldness: "They are little rascals [canailles]." I understood that he reproached today's young men for being too effeminate. "They are really women," he would say with disdain. (2:120–21)

Does the narrator understand this effeminacy before Charlus says it? Why does he say this repeatedly while saying only once that they are "little rascals"? Shall we assume once again that the narrator reads the character's mind? Generally speaking, neither family connections nor the reputation of being gigolos guarantees anything. If the reputation of being a ladies' man or a gigolo does not guarantee masculinity in Charlus's eyes when it comes to other people, however, what can it possibly guarantee for Saint-Loup and Charlus, two characters just described as being masculine? Charlus's dislike of effeminacy, related to a public position and performance of masculinity, will eventually return to and turn on both of them.

The implication is clear, logical, and disquieting because the conclusion is inevitable but unannounceable. Charlus has perceived Marcel earlier in the day and then again at the tea. Charlus must have concluded Marcel to be a rascal or a womanly man. Marcel, then, must be effeminate in Charlus's eyes. The narrator excuses Marcel's behavior by asking a rhetorical question: "But what life would not have seemed effeminate compared to that which he wished a man to lead and which he never found energetic and virile enough?" (2:121). The focus has shifted slightly from a scene of attempted direct seduction to a discussion of affective, ancillary, and accidental behavior. Beyond that, no source is given for the narrator's knowledge of what Charlus wants or desires, although what Charlus arguably wants or desires is repeatedly and clumsily hidden behind a flimsy set of readings. That the explanation does not hold water is clear, because nothing explains Charlus's flirting, dancing, and preening behavior earlier in the day when there were no observers. Charlus's truth comes out only when there is no one to observe it. As soon as there are witnesses, he moves to a behavior that is the antithesis of his individual psychology, a position that validates traditional masculinity and excoriates effeminacy in all its forms.

If Charlus likes women, moreover, or seems to like women, or likes them when in public, and if the young men are "really women," he should logically like them as well. But they are not "true women"; they are women in men's bodies, to use the late nineteenth-century expression that defined the "invert." For Charlus, then, this effeminacy is to be excluded because it is a negative value. It is to be excluded also because the difference between container and contained or between signifier and signified is a false one that leads to problematic logics and inappropriate conclusions.

What precisely would the signifier and signified be in this case? These gigolos show all the signs of masculinity, but Charlus alone—along with his double, the narrator—is capable of seeing the secret effeminacy hiding behind that cloak of masculinity. According to the narrator, there are telltale signs of effeminacy; at least one has already been mentioned: "He would not allow a man to wear even one ring" (2:121). It goes no further than that. Certainly no suspicion attaches to the sensitivity that one might otherwise associate with effeminacy, a sensitivity of which Charlus is the first and best example. Charlus is capable of speaking of the *Letters* of Mme de Sévigné, the grandmother's favorite author, exactly as she herself would speak of them: "She was amazed that a man could understand them so well. She thought M. de Charlus had feminine delicacies and sensitivity" (2:121). If Charlus could see himself through her eyes, would he revise his opinion and move from the banishment of rings to the banishment of sensitivity? Or would such an action be impossible, as we have been led to believe by the narrator's assessment of Charlus's loophole? At this point, one must think the latter.

Thus we are treated to a new and different point of view, the grandmother's essentialist view on sexuality and gender. Marcel's grandmother considers Charlus to think as does a man yet possess feminine qualities. Since the unthinkable *is* the unthinkable, however, the position of essential masculinity has undergone a transfer of qualities, much like the metempsychosis discussed in the novel's first pages. For all his denials and rationalizations, Marcel and his grandmother agree that there has been a transfer of feminine qualities to Charlus from some woman: a woman, his mother, or his daughter, for example. No other explanation is possible for the grandmother, and the various heterosexual explanations help Marcel distance the truth that has more than once entered his textual preconscious. The only difference between his position and his grandmother's is that he believes that the woman in question must have been one of Charlus's mistresses. He thus continues to admit that the event lies outside legitimate lines; like his nephew Saint-Loup, Charlus must have had a mistress who tamed him.

Significantly, the little exchange between Marcel and his grandmother—which happens both after the tea and after the final event of this sequence, the encounter between Charlus and Marcel in the latter's hotel room—is the means by which the freedom to examine Charlus's feminine side appears. It is as if the grandmother serves as a safety net for the discussion, a guarantee that the discussion will not go further than a certain acceptable point. This is important precisely because of the placement and timing of the events. The conversation between Marcel and his grandmother about Charlus's feminine—as opposed to effeminate—sensibility, occurring as it does after the conversation between Charlus and Marcel, should psychologically lead to conclusions other than those at which they arrive. But Proust strategically places it here as the narrative means by which a reflection on Charlus's "side" can occur. Thus the later event permits a reflection on femininity that could not have taken place if psychology and sequential order had been observed. Opposed to the narrator's subsequent summary and analysis, it also allows for a strikingly revolutionary point of view: Charlus's opinion of love.

An admirer of Racine, despite his own nephew's disdain for the classic author, Charlus offers a radical revision of love that takes on tragic overtones: "But the important thing is not what one loves, it is to love" (2:122). Racine's tragic love knows no boundaries: extramarital, adulterous, and necrophiliac in *Andromaque;* incestuous in *Phèdre;* and always criss-crossed, as Roland Barthes shows in *Sur Racine* (35)—A loves B, who does not love A. The important element, then, is neither the nature of the relation nor the validity or worthiness of the love object but the fact of loving itself. In that Charlus seems to reflect a position not unlike Augustine's before his conversion: "amabo amare," I loved to love"; the object of that love matters little. According to Charlus's pronouncement, there would be nothing wrong in his loving a tailor, a music student, or a peasant perceived from afar. The fact of loving is the important one. In loving, therefore, Charlus is anything but aristocratic, and he evinces the most democratic of positions imaginable.

This double invocation—on the one hand, Charlus's reflection on love; on the other, Marcel's and his grandmother's reflection on Charlus's sensitivity—allows for a direct perception of Charlus's intrinsic effeminacy. For there is no flirting and no social contact outside his self-absorption, which is what blinds him from seeing himself as others see him and more specifically from seeing in himself what he execrates in others:

> His voice itself, like certain contralto voices in which the medium has not been adequately trained and whose singing seems to be the alternating duet between a young man and a woman, lay, at the moment during which he was expressing such delicate thoughts, on high notes, took on an unforeseen sweetness and seemed to contain choruses of fiancées, sisters who spread their tenderness. But the brood of young ladies whom M. de Charlus, with his horror of all effeminacy, would have been so devastated to shelter thus in his voice, was not limited to the interpretation and modulation of bits of feeling. Often, while M. de Charlus was chatting, one heard the sharp, fresh laugh of boarding-house residents or coquettes settling matters with their neighbor with smart quips and fine remarks.[17] (2:122–23)

Regardless of the signs it emits and the words it produces, the voice itself is the true sign of gender and sexuality. No matter how masculine the statements Charlus makes and no matter how much he despises effeminacy in others, his voice tells the narrator and the readers the truth. Marcel does not yet recognize the import of the contrast, but his associations let us read the sexuality of the baron. In a prescient foreshadowing of the events that take place at the beginning of *Sodome et Gomorrhe,* the baron's voice is doubled in a pairing of the voices of a young man and a woman. Proust goes even further here in deconstructing the voice, however, for the voice is anything but the presence of sound unto itself in this situation. Like many another motif in the *Recherche,* the baron's voice echoes all those voices past and thus absent; all those who are not present; and, one might surmise, all those who, at one moment or another, will no longer be present.

Usually understood as a vehicle for or way to communicate his comments, a role to which it will shortly return in the bedroom scene, the baron's voice here is the channel and summary for the entirety of the feminine, as Proust recalls all those women who exude and spread tenderness. While this is not a quality one would normally associate with Charlus unless one were the grandmother, here he represents that summation of the feminine other. And this feminine other is situated not in effeminacy, which would be associated more with a surface of signs, peremptory or superficial figures or affectations, but in a deep-seated essence. Charlus's voice is the sign of his soul, and that soul is feminine, if not effeminate.

This perceived tenderness is the emotive truth of his voice and is associated with the strange preening dance and a diffidence that borders on the impolite. How to regroup the various threads becomes clear by the end of the paragraph. Whereas the feminine and tenderness are associated with all women, and especially with those in whom one respects inviolate virginity—fiancées and sisters—all those women are potentially capable of entering into sexuality, which would be Marcel's wish, for they, with their dose of narcissism, come into bloom as "boarding-house residents" or "coquettes." Alternatively, as the narrator notes later on the same page, Charlus's behavior resembles that of "a modest [pudibonde], though not innocent, woman" (2:123). So the step here is not a big one: like the young ladies who constitute the cluster of femininity that marks the novel's beach scenes and like Albertine, who along with many others will eventually take center stage, Charlus, too, is a young lady in bloom. Charlus's essential voice contains the feminine, and if only for a moment, Charlus displaces women with his version of the feminine, which is a singular combination of wild masculinity and delicacy that the adolescent Marcel has yet to understand.

For Marcel can still not piece together the various parts of this behavior: the peacock-like displays of bravado, bravura, and feathers; the dissimulation and distance; and the feminine behavior to which Charlus himself seems oblivious. Everyone else seems oblivious to the meaning of this femininity as well, even though the grandmother notices a delicacy in Charlus's behavior. Given the strict code of masculinity by which he was supposed to live, it is hard to imagine that Charlus's truth is not visible to all those who see him, especially Saint-Loup or the usually perceptive Duchesse de Guermantes, who rarely misses much, although she may see this matter simply as a question of discretion: turning a blind eye or keeping family secrets is essential to the Guermantes "way." Still, readers might suppose that the number of those who understand Charlus (none at this point, with the possible exception of Mme de Villeparisis) would be larger than it in fact seems to be.

As any reader of the *Recherche* knows, its dramas often happen at bedtime, whether it is the narrator's insomnia on the first page or young Marcel's wait for his mother's bedtime kiss. Here the day has passed, and we join

Marcel in his bedtime ritual. Charlus has seen Marcel in his morning attire, with his dark-colored jacket; in day clothes; and ostensibly in some sort of evening wear. Now, after a long day of intermittent flirting and diffidence, Charlus perhaps hopes to see Marcel in his last set of clothes for the day, his sleepwear—or perhaps he hopes to see Marcel change into his sleepwear, for, knowing that Marcel has gone to prepare for bed, Charlus follows rather quickly on his heels. Contrary to the announced severity of Charlus and his specific intolerance for anything effeminate, he shows a docility, a delicacy, and a concern that hitherto have not been seen and that have been heard only in the tenderness of his voice. It is that voice, returned to a public performance, from which the tenderness is suddenly gone once again; it is marked now by a dryness, both in public and in private: "I heard the voice of M. de Charlus who was saying in a dry tone: 'It is Charlus. May I enter, sir? Sir,' he repeated in the same tone as soon as he had closed the door again" (2:124). As soon as Marcel shows his own vulnerability, perhaps flattered by Charlus's presence and touched by Charlus's concern and caring—for the latter has offered to lend Marcel a book by Bergotte—the tone of voice changes and Charlus becomes both sweeter and more flirtatious.

Without invoking sex itself, Charlus straightforwardly tells Marcel what the latter should have realized all day: his adolescence and his youthful appearance have seduced Charlus, who uses the word *seduction* to describe, at least in the abstract, his position (2:124). Additionally, he espouses a position of catholicity, indicating that all tastes and all choices of pleasure are for him equally valid, and he certainly would refrain from condemnation. At the same time, he is uncovering his position, at least for those who wish to read it. He remarks the extent to which Marcel has tender feelings for his grandmother, feelings that are obviously reciprocated, in contrast to the many unilateral Racinian relations. The choice of language is significant: "But at least you have well placed your affection in your grandmother. You see her a lot. And it is a tenderness that is permitted, I mean a tenderness that is paid back. There are so many of them of which that cannot be said!" (2:125). The contrast is with the unconsciously feminine tenderness that effuses from Charlus. Though focused on an object, that tenderness is given without any thought of return, reciprocity, or permission, to use Charlus's strange word. This tenderness contrasts with the kind that is given in expectation of or hope for reciprocation but receives none. Is Charlus contemplating such tenderness now, be there be reciprocity or not? This slip in language, the redefinition of tenderness from what is permitted to what is reciprocated, is a slip of the tongue; Charlus quickly moves to recover a presence of mind—that is, a position of falsity—whereas he had first indicated what he was really thinking: a forbidden tenderness with an adolescent with whom he has already flirted.

But nothing happens. Charlus paces the floor yet finds no language in which to communicate his thoughts: "I had the impression he had something to tell me and did not find the words in which to do it" (2:125). Charlus has been doing nothing else but announcing what he had to say the whole day long. Marcel wants specific words, however, and those words are not forthcoming, nor can they be. They are not permitted: they would be the emission of signs where none is proper. The language here is among the most banal in the book, including even that between Charlus and Jupien in the courtyard, and it is the signs—the same signs of availability, or Gidean *disponibilité,* that Charlus has been emitting all day at Balbec—that tell all.[18]

Here, however, words are necessary, if only because Marcel needs things explained to him the first time. No supplementary signs work: the presence of Charlus in his bedroom can be associated only with other innocent bedroom matters, that of his mother comforting him in Combray and that of his attentive grandmother listening in the next room to see if he has any problems or if he needs her. It would not cross Marcel's mind that there is something importunate in Charlus's very presence. Charlus leaves, but not without having regained the masterful voice of control, order, and dominance associated with his station and his unapproachability.

The next morning arrives. Figuring that he has been rebuffed, Charlus has no more use for the adolescent with whom he flirted only twenty-four hours before. In an ironic twist Marcel can finally read Charlus's mind and knows what Charlus is supposed to say: "M. de Charlus had approached me to let me know that my grandmother was waiting for me" (2:125). I invoke mind-reading because Charlus says nothing of the sort: "I was quite astonished to hear him tell me, while pinching my neck, with a vulgar familiarity and laugh: 'So, you don't give a fig about your old grandmother, huh? Little scoundrel!' [je fus bien étonné de l'entendre me dire, en me pinçant le cou, avec une familiarité et un rire vulgaires: "Mais on s'en fiche bien de sa vieille grand-mère, hein? Petite fripouille!"]" (2:125–26).

Will Marcel then be a scoundrel because he refused advances, because he is too thick, because he prefers family love to the adoration of an older man, and because he remains steadfastly heterosexual? All of these and none of these. The scoundrel—the outlaw character who is at the same time the protagonist at the center of his experiential development—will thus be the apostle of other outlaw characters, including Charlus, who is about to assume his full role in the rest of the novel.

2 Un Amour de Charlus

Revelation

As with so many other matters in the *Recherche,* the main scenes in which both Charlus and sexuality come to the fore are offered under a sign of revelation. What was not known will be read and perhaps misconstrued, yet eventually it will be revealed for what it is, either when the events occur or, more likely, at some later moment. In revelation one sees what one has not seen before: a vision is presented to the eyes, and that vision manifests the truth. One sees that to which one has been blind. At the same time, this revelation has the sense of a repetition; we are reminded of the extensive use of the iterative prefix *re-* in describing Charlus's activities. As Harold Bloom tells us, revelation relates to the anxiety of influence and therefore is a kind of repetition. In a more general sense, however, revelation is often an undoing or deconstruction of the uncanny, that strangely familiar unfamiliar realm. For the *Recherche,* this means that homosexuality is always present. Thus, we should turn once again to the scene at Montjouvain.

Mlle Vinteuil and her friend are seen, as if in a vision, after Marcel has fallen asleep and reawakened. The very rhetoric of the scene underlines the visual aspect of what is going on, for the lesbian couple might be seen "reading." There is an insistence on vision, as well as an early instance of the novel's tendency to associate sexuality with reading and writing; vision is the most revelatory and most important of the senses at this point in the novel. What Marcel sees at Montjouvain is something that, even as young as he is, he realizes he has not seen before. Montjouvain becomes a kind of primal vision of alterity, in this case lesbianism but in a general sense homosexuality—or perhaps simply that which is not heterosexuality.[1]

This scene is queered by the theatricalization of the event. The window frames Mlle Vinteuil and her friend as if it were a picture frame or, better yet, a proscenium. The two are like actresses on a stage, performing for some invisible man, be he a voyeur or a client at a peep show, and their sexuality quickly metamorphoses into an amalgamation of sexualities: sapphism overflows into a theater of sadomasochism, role playing, and (implicitly and explicitly) voyeurism.[2] Their performance for the lusty about-to-be heterosexual child is a foretaste of the performance of homosexuality that stands at the heart of the first section of *Sodome et Gomorrhe;* in its use of the window, this scene also recalls a scene of sexual window dressing that is the masturbatory experience already mentioned. Many thousands of pages later it will be the retrovision, the base, and the function that motivate the observation of Charlus in the brothel. Marcel will remain a voyeur, but this time Charlus will be the lesbian being beaten. This final scene will be a return to the first volume of the novel, a return that buckles the buckle, when vision and knowledge have come together, are combined, and work synchronously.

Certainly, then, there is a privileging of vision in one of the last great narratives, after which both the modern novel and modern Continental philosophy will turn away from vision "with downcast eyes" (Jay). Yet the classic novel, of which Proust has provided arguably the last great French example, continues to use the phenomenon of sight to get to the truth of knowledge. This is not to say that vision is the only mechanism, but it is certainly the classic one. In the classic novel those who refuse to see and those who give precedence to other means of knowledge are doomed, expelled, or condemned to a bad plot: Tristram Shandy and his talking cure, Eliot's Casaubon and his books, and the hapless antiheroes of Balzac's *Études philosophiques.* Even Emma Bovary sees, through reading, what she would become.

Proust, however, is both classic and modern, and vision is not the only mechanism available; lack of vision is not equated with a lack of knowledge. In the anatomy of cruising already described, sight is complemented by voices and hearing that tell the truth about Charlus, even when the eyes do not seize it. In the encounter between Charlus and Jupien, Proust creates an anatomy of seduction with a great metaphoric web that undoes all received knowledge about homosexuality. The language of the section and the construction of a network of metaphors give the lie to homophobia, unless one is reduced to a "poor," simplistic reading of the event or reads so poorly as to think that a novel is just about characters meeting: narrative as the poor subject of a weak narratology. In so doing one falls into the vision trap: the only knowledge allowed is that of visible surfaces. The section in question sets up an entire metaphorics for the novel, linking it to many passages before and after, to a semiotics of revelation.[3] The revelation occurs when Marcel is blind, when he has crawled to a spot in which he cannot see, and when hearing—and specifically hearing something that is not language as such—provides the revelation he needs. If, as Martin Jay cogently suggests, vision has been devalued, Proust moves here from a classic narrative to a modern one and abandons the possibility of a totalizing narrative in the process.

Let us think, then, about the major scenes with Charlus. The anatomy of cruising depends on a kind of knowledge and a semioticity Marcel belatedly discovers in himself; there is a set of mistranslated, misconstrued, and misinterpreted signals. Marcel attributes various antisocial behaviors—those of a madman, a spy, or a thief—to Charlus when all the latter wants to do is reaffirm his perception of signs, namely, signs that the character he is perceiving is a member of the set of society that "recognizes its members everywhere." What is misconstrued in Balbec is read correctly in Paris by the new vis-à-vis, Jupien, and it takes an inability to see at the hôtel de Guermantes for Marcel finally to understand what is going on. The situations are parallel, for in each case there are two players who have knowledge and one who does not. At Montjouvain and in the courtyard in the hôtel de Guermantes, the two actors on stage know what is going on, but the audience—Marcel—remains clueless. Only when shut away in the dark, in a position miming that of his own nonknowledge, does Marcel finally figure things out. When he can no longer see the theatrical representation of homosexuality and when the signs are not visibly displayed for anyone to see, he understands. The meaning of the sign is in its final, silent echoes. The scene in Balbec is parallel as well, for there is one in the dark and two with knowledge: in this case, however, it is Charlus and the narrator who know and Marcel who remains in the dark. On the one hand, then, Marcel is always the one in the position of nonknowledge; on the other, it is not always the two actors who are the knowledgeable ones.

Scales fell from his eyes: having occupied a position of nonknowledge and one of knowledge, Marcel now knows that visible signs are not the only ones that inform and that he now has knowledge of their meaning. Without that knowledge the signs are like words in a strange language—like a Chinese opera for a Westerner who recognizes the production as an opera or something similar but does not know what the signs mean. Certainly the analogy finds its parallel and support in Marcel's first visit to the theater, which proves to be a disappointment to him, because what he imagined would be the delivery of Racine's noble verse is not at all the reality of the theater. With the beginning of *Sodome et Gomorrhe* the paradigm changes completely. No longer can Marcel be in a position of nonknowledge. No longer can he feign not knowing what homosexuality is about. The visibility of the paradigm—produced through the "blindness and insight" of invisibility—changes the game.

The Nexus That Is Morel

Hundreds of pages before he is needed as a participatory character in what will prove to be the heartache of Charlus's life, Morel is presented in Marcel's retrospective glance at the reception of Madame de Villeparisis. As is often the case in the *Recherche,* the framework into which this memory is presented sets the stage—again, the matter of the theatricalized moment is never far in such parts of the narrative—and provides the semiotic framework for this character. Marcel is making his way in the world, moving into the outer realms of aristocratic society. He has already befriended Saint-Loup and been befriended by Charlus. He has recognized the truth of his grandmother's assertion that her former classmate, now Mme de Villeparisis, is indeed a Guermantes, although he does not yet know the ins and outs of this society and will only belatedly discover that Charlus is the brother of the Duc de Guermantes (2:574).[4] So it is not merely that he is beginning to make his way along the Guermantes way but also, and perhaps more important, that he is beginning to recognize the connections among the various parts of that path.

This initial foray into the world of aristocracy does not take place in full-blown sunlight, for in the "social kaleidoscope" of Paris the salon of Mme de Villeparisis is not particularly in favor. It is nevertheless still a venue where various individuals can meet and where the bonds of kinship allow the author to have the various members of the Guermantes clan parade by with the feeble but plausible narrative excuse of having them visit an old aunt. The unfavorable marker of the salon is a means by which unsavory encounters can be discussed; there can be near misses, avoided contacts, and unfortunate collisions. The presentation of the memory comes under the sign of a double nonencounter in which the Duchesse de Guermantes implicitly and Saint-Loup explicitly do not wish to meet Odette. The duchess gets up and takes French leave, for she has seen Odette, who, she says, "seemed rather annoyed to see me" (2:560). Saint-Loup is explicit in his refusal, even though the information is superfluous: "'I don't want my mother to introduce me to Mme Swann,' Saint-Loup said to me. 'She is an ex-hooker [une ancienne grue]. Her husband is Jewish, and she shoves nationalism down our throats. Look, there is my Uncle Palamède'" (2:560). Whereas Charlus will show signs of anti-Semitism at various points, Saint-Loup is not particularly known for being associated with such remarks, and his position on the Dreyfus affair relates more to his fealty to the army than to any inherent prejudice on his part. In fact, his longtime mistress Rachel, who could also be accused—and more accurately—of having been a streetwalker, is purportedly of Jewish origins, and his wife to be, Gilberte, is a bit less than half-Jewish. Beyond that, his own mother, Mme de Marsantes, is accused of philo-Semitism and even of being Jewish.

These crossed encounters lead to a consideration of which paths are crossing, which are not, and which may someday do so: Jew and non-Jew, aristocracy and bourgeoisie, Swann and Guermantes, and heterosexual and homosexual. In this moment of crossed paths, the re-presentation of Charlus echoes several pages later in Madame de Villeparisis's consternation at Marcel's expressed desire to leave with Charlus, as if Charlus's homosexuality now risks spreading to Marcel (2:580).

The introduction of Morel is framed by a set of events where both chance and determination play roles and in which the narrator-novelist's desire to put characters under the same roof allows for a plot turn that brings the question of homosexuality to the forefront. Morel's introduction retrospectively imitates the situation I have just described. Morel is the son of Uncle Adolphe's butler, and as readers may remember, the last encounter between Marcel and his uncle was on the fateful day on which he was being visited by the "lady in pink," who was Elstir's "Miss Sacripant" and who is Odette, described here in Morel's words as a "demimondaine" (2:563). Marcel finally makes the link and draws a metanarrative conclusion about connections, encounters, and identifications: "As for me, in shaking his hand, I was thinking of Mme Swann, and I told myself with astonishment, so separated and different they were in my memory, that I would henceforth have to identify her with the 'lady in pink'" (2:563). The meeting with Morel provokes a revisionist aesthetic that associates elements so widely different that it is hard to believe they refer to the same being. Even though the narrator has already told the story of "Un Amour de Swann," in which the reader has learned that Odette is anything but noble in origins, only now does she come to incarnate the nondisjunction of values and the association of two previously separated realms, bourgeois society and the demimonde.[5]

Whereas the uncle's rooms had been at the threshold of these two worlds, and whereas it was precisely the unfortunate encounter of these worlds that provoked Marcel's having been prohibited from future visits, the re-representation of the event as a forced memory makes its future repression impossible. Just as the ways of Guermantes and Swann are now inextricably crossed and intertwined, so are the worlds of licit and illicit sexuality, without a negative or condemnatory value having been assigned to "illicit" sexuality. Perhaps a better term would relate to the viewing of that sexuality or of the relationship that frames that sexuality: licit relationships—not sexual relations—are those viewable by Marcel's mother. This means appropriate marriage to someone of one's own station, neither too high nor too low, which is also the position of Marcel's grandmother, who in Balbec chooses not to see Mme de Villeparisis for as long as is humanly possible. Illicit or improper entanglements would include Uncle Adolphe's consorting with women from the demimonde, Swann's marriage to Odette, the relations between Mme de Villeparisis and M. de Norpois, Charlus's various assignations, the relations between Mlle Vinteuil and her friend, and those between Marcel and Albertine. Some of these remain delicately hidden; some can be avoided; some can be banished.

What changes here is the forced remembrance of that world, which is prompted not only by its incarnation in Morel, worthy son of his father, but also by material memories of it, especially photographic representations. Just as Marcel's grandmother has always felt that, in a Swann-inspired aesthetics, accreted layers of good artistic representation add to the value of an object, Morel bears the inscription of the event in aesthetic form. Instead of giving photographs of famous sites, the grandmother prefers giving paintings of them by great painters (1:40); Morel will do the same. In the one case the form of representation and the represented object seem to coincide in a harmony of aesthetics and value. In this, the other case, the situation seems to be the opposite, for art represents the improper: "The goal of his visit was the following: his father had, among the keepsakes of my Uncle Adolphe, put aside some that he had thought inappropriate to send to my parents, but which, he thought, were of a sort to interest a young man of my age. They were photographs of well-known actresses, great cocottes whom my uncle had known, the last images of that life of an old high-liver [vieux viveur] that he separated with a watertight barrier from his family life" (2:561). This barrier, which hitherto has been an impermeable, opaque membrane, is now put into question and seen through, if not quite yet torn down. The encounter of motifs (representation of the aesthetic object), the encounter of paths (Odette), the encounter of sexualities licit and illicit (Adolphe and Charlus): all combine to weaken the wall that separates the parts of Marcel's existence into logical categories, making it a semipermeable membrane. Aesthetics breaks down division and produces the nondisjunction that is the mark of the novelistic.

Here already, long before Gilberte is adopted by Monsieur de Forcheville during Odette's marriage to the latter, the novel addresses the question of adoption, with the author planting the seed for a nonfilial relation to develop. The first, avuncular version is the one that strays the least from the path of marriage and legitimacy: "Morel considered me an adopted son, a chosen child of my uncle" (2:562). This remark suggests more than just the whole pattern of "uncles and nephews" that will pave the way for the similarities between Charlus and Saint-Loup and that has already been prepared by the double encounter at Balbec. In Balbec Marcel is linked to the eventually homosexual other through one acceptable relationship—the developing friendship with Robert—and through another that is less than proper: the dance Charlus performs around Marcel through the strange encounters of that visit. Marcel and his uncle share blood, but from that there will be a short step to Charlus's adoption of Jupien's niece.[6] For it is precisely that niece whose image is invoked here: "[Morel] had noticed in the courtyard Jupien's niece making a vest and . . . I felt that the young lady had made a great impression on him" (2:562). The single degree of separation between uncle and nephew or niece is doubled by that of the baron's eventual liaison with Jupien: the niece will be adopted not by the uncle but by the uncle's lover.

Morel and Marcel are ambiguous objects in this system of floating desire that is no longer anchored by the proper lines of family structure and station and no longer constrained by the morality and ethics of Combray. Paris has a different set of rules; as I discussed in the introduction, Paris allows the improper to occur. The partial anagram of Morel and Marcel may remind the reader that both are objects of desire for Charlus, one replacing the other, just as Morel's first name, Charlie, recalls both Charlus and Charles Swann and just as Mémé (de Charlus) recalls both a French diminutive for "grandmother" (*mamie*) and the other figure of care and concern in Balbec, M. Aimé, whose name reads somewhat like "mémé" as well. The crossing and bending of paths in this salon encounter is the first step toward opening the novel to a vast homosexual semiosis. If there are signs—and there are many in *Le Côté de Guermantes* that set the stage for the beginning of *Sodome et*

Gomorrhe—this is the full-blown encounter of worlds in which there is no longer an impenetrable wall of separation.

The novel continually presents walls of separation broken down by a penetrating glance or a sexual act: the first is the little room smelling of orrisroot in Combray, with its window to a world of sensuality. The character's and narrator's consciousness of sexuality begins to replace the primacy given to the visual, which becomes a part of the enunciation. Here the section of retrospective presentation of Morel closes significantly as Marcel realizes that Odette is "the lady in pink." The new paragraph starts with a juxtaposition of all these worlds, all these sexualities, now unavoidable: "M. de Charlus was soon seated next to Mme Swann" (2:563). Charlus has replaced the Uncle Adolphe of memory as the one seated by Mme Swann and has replaced Charles Swann in "Un Amour de Swann," just as Odette has replaced Marcel in the hotel room and bedroom in Balbec. Anyone can sit next to anyone; indeed, Marcel's observation about Morel's linguistic etiquette has just alluded to the breakdown of social structure: "He made a point of speaking to me as an equal. He had, in saying 'you' [vous] and and avoiding 'sir' [monsieur], the pleasure of someone whose father had, when speaking to my parents, used only the 'third person'" (2:561).

This encounter between Charlus and Morel takes its place as the third in this series, following Balbec and the courtyard of the hôtel de Guermantes. In the first the narrator questions the viability of visual signs; more exactly, through the schism necessary to the narrative consciousness, he creates a divide between the way the narrator reads and the way the adolescent Marcel understands. In the position of the one who is supposed to know things, the narrator triangulates the positions of his earlier self and Charlus, as he doubles that of Charlus—whose knowledge is tacit—and that of Marcel, who sees yet refuses to understand what he sees. In the courtyard, at the beginning of *Sodome et Gomorrhe,* the positions of knowledge and ignorance are shifted. Both Jupien and Charlus are adept at the mating, courtship, or pickup ritual that, while not a codification as such, is nonetheless a regularized set of signs (Bech). Although there is no gay primer, the behavior of both characters is an expansion of the initial gaydar ping mutually sent and felt; it is the silent sign that knows no codification. In the ensuing two-step dance, each character gradually expands that rather tautological perception of perceiving the other as oneself, as a kindred spirit, or as a member of the "club" and creates a semiotic web that, while always allowing for a retreat because of misprision, gradually lets the two sets of echoes from that ping conflate one with the other. Here the triangulated position, which is one not of desire but of knowledge, is fulfilled only when the prescience of the blind takes precedence over the testimony of the visible. During the courtship the betrayal by the visible is the ambiguity associated with the bivalence of the sign: what Marcel perceives—distinct from what the narrator knows—is the ambiguity of the dance, which at every moment allows a step back to a position of safety.

Where the narrator has changed his own position from the schisms of Balbec is in his creation of a metaphoric web, one that goes back semiotically and linguistically as far as the entire previous volume (*Le Côté de Guermantes*) and theatrically as far as Combray. The narrator's metaphors are a poetic rewriting of the dance of the characters; they are the linguistic fulfillment in the enunciation of the embroidered radar pings of the text. His metaphoric weavings in these pages are a means of direction that can be visualized in a very physical way. Charlus's and Jupien's signs are two-way streets. Should one of them be wrong in his assumption that the other is a homosexual, or should an innocent bystander be turned into a prurient observer, the bivalence of the semiotics allows for a reasonably innocent reading of the dance. There is thus a double failsafe mechanism, both internal and external. Where is the narrator in all this? Marcel may be the wide-eyed, voyeuristic, prurient observer, but the narrator uses his own language to point the reader along one lane of the two-way street: Charlus or Jupien might retreat to a position of safety, but the narrative pushes forward to make the reader reach one inescapable conclusion. This nuance or this overlay of a web of metaphors creates a poetic inscription of male homosexuality as the code is developed before our eyes. The web of metaphors subsumes even the prosaic statements about homosexuals, turning all the general statements not into some universal of self-loathing but rather into the banality that they are: the commonplace, with denotative remarks of the opinion becoming due fodder for the poetics of the text.

This third encounter—between Charlus and Morel—builds on the scenes in the novel and on the changing dynamic between knowledge and nonknowledge. Marcel knows what male homosexuality is—and here I am reductively confining that sexuality to the sex act—even if he has not *seen* it enacted. He knows its signs and those Charlus is emitting; no possibility exists for Charlus to be confused with a madman or a spy. The narrator ironically reminds us to think about Charlus on the prowl, not the Charlus of the salons: "In Paris, where I met him only in the evening, immobile, strapped into a black suit, maintained within the axis of the vertical by his proud bearing, his zeal to please, the spark of his conversation, I did not realize to what extent he had aged" (3:254). Now Charlus is on the move, and the signs emitted are readable by narrator and character alike. Most significant is the narrator's metanarrative remark directing the reader—who could not help but see—toward a position of anality: "a butt that was almost symbolic" (3:254). But Charlus's posterior is anything but symbolic. It is what it is: the locus of *jouissance,* the locus of passive anal intercourse, and the point of sodomy that is the material equivalent of the gaydar ping.[7]

The shift to visibility seems to imply that there is henceforth no need for a dance of recognition: gay semiotics is in the air. On the surface this seems to be the case for the meeting between Charlus and Morel, although a more perverse reading is possible. At the train station at Doncières, Charlus asks Marcel to hail one of the soldiers across the tracks who is supposedly one of Charlus's relatives, although it is a bit odd to think of a Guermantes as a musician in a military band. When Marcel arrives, he chances on Morel, who is also in the regiment. No sooner have they exchanged greetings than Charlus swoops in and makes a (financial) proposition to Morel: "All of a sudden, I saw M. de Charlus rush toward us. My lateness had obviously made him impatient. 'I should like to hear a bit of music this evening,' he said to Morel, with no introduction to the subject, 'I shall give 500 francs for the evening, which might have some interest for one of your friends, if you have any in music.' Although I was quite familiar with the insolence of M. de Charlus, I was stupefied that he did not even say hello to his young friend. The baron did not, moreover, leave me time to reflect. Extending his hand affectionately: 'Goodbye, old man [mon cher],' he said to me, to indicate that I had only to leave" (3:255). The idea of "making music" is an ambiguous one and is a well known metaphor/password for indicating male homosexuality.[8] The musical metaphor will come up much later when, the relation between Charlus and Morel being assumed by everyone, Mme Verdurin gives them two adjoining rooms and says complicitously: "If you want to make music, don't worry, the walls are like those of a fortress, there is no one on your floor, and my husband sleeps like a log" (3:431).

Here Charlus's gaydar seems to have gone off; he sallies forth to make a bold proposal to Morel, if not an indecent one. There are several puzzling points. From what is recounted, it hardly seems as if Marcel has been even slightly delayed in his errand by having run into Morel, even though Marcel allows that he forgot his mission. Charlus's mysterious, underachieving relative ("parent à lui") has been transformed a half-page later into a young friend ("son jeune ami"). Morel's concupiscence, of which the readers are already aware because of the seeds planted in the earlier scene, is not known to Charlus, and only the latter's boldness can explain some of the words exchanged, for Charlus does not directly proposition Morel and ask him to play music but instead seeks one of his friends ("un de vos amis").

There is much confusion between friends and relatives and between what is known in the enunciation and what the characters know. Indeed, one might think that Charlus has spent quite a bit of time reading the *Recherche,* for his knowledge mounts to the solidification of that reading: no longer does he need the other to participate in the dance; he completely recognizes the other. Moreover, in such encounters positions can change, and one person can substitute for another. If Morel is not available—Charlus does not even have to ask him whether he is, it so little matters at the moment—then perhaps a friend will be. Transforming relatives into friends and relations into complicities is essential to the structuring of this homosexual world in which everyone is potentially a lover or a procurer.

Marcel has brief recourse to a false rationalization as he explains to Albertine what has just transpired: "'You see,' I told her as I got back in the carriage, 'seaside and travel existences make me understand that the theater of the world has fewer settings than actors and fewer actors than 'situations.' . . . Because M. de Charlus just asked me to send him one of his friends, whom, just now, on the platform, I recognized as one of mine'" (3:255). Implicitly returning to the model of procurement (though totally innocently here), Marcel imagines that Charlus has already met Morel through Jupien: "It occurred to me first that it was through Jupien[,] whose daughter, as one will remember, seemed to be smitten with the violinist" (3:255). Marcel soon realizes that he cannot return to his former, naive ideas about relations based on a visible mechanism of contact, but he reaffirms what we have learned over these many pages, that Charlus and Morel did not know each other but that somehow Charlus and Morel both knew that the former could pick up the latter: "I grasped his resemblance with some of his relatives when they picked up a woman in the street. Only the object aimed at had changed sex" (3:256). What the narrator does not say, and what Marcel implies but does not seem yet to understand, is that Morel, who is compared to David ready to fight Goliath (3:257) and who is a suitable object of desire in a somewhat relaxed post-Gidean world, is not completely heterosexual.[9] Morel is ready to put out for some spending money. For the first time the text dissociates the possibility of homosexual behavior from effeminacy. Somewhat reminiscent of Saint-Loup, Morel combines grace and manly, authoritative behavior: "M. de Charlus was thrilled to see that manly, authoritative gesture made with his graceful hand for which it should have been too heavy, too massively brutal, with a precocious firmness and flexibility that gave that still beardless adolescent the air of a young David able to take on Goliath in a battle" (3:257).

Shifting relations between knowledge and signs are felt stylistically as Proust permits the narrator a moment of Balzacian omniscience, as if, at this point where walls no longer stand between levels of knowledge or capacities to read signs, everything could potentially be known: "'Now *there* is someone by whom I should like to be accompanied in my travels and helped in my affairs. How he would simplify my life!' said M. de Charlus to himself" (3:257).[10] It little matters that this role will eventually be assumed by Jupien and not Morel; the narrator, more knowledgeable about homosexuality than he can yet admit, can, at least in this one singular moment, read his character's mind.

Just as the salon Verdurin once served as a place for Odette and Swann to meet, it later does the same for Charlus and Morel. In the most socially elevated salons, entrance and appearance are themselves signs of social status; nowhere else is this clearer than in Balzac's *Le Père Goriot,* with the true aristocracy of Mme de Beauséant ironically doubled by the closed-door policy of Mme de Restaud. To the extent that the *Recherche* serves as a social bildungsroman for Marcel, the reader can chart the protagonist's gradual accession to ever more rarefied social strata, capped by his receipt of a "passkey" to all salons through his friendship with the Duchesse de Guermantes. Rank itself is not the only criterion, nor is attitude: despite the Baron de Charlus's aristocratic breeding and his sense of social class, being seen in his company does not guarantee social standing.

The bourgeois salon of Mme Verdurin functions in a different fashion in that it admits people who are amusing, tradespeople, artists, and people of dubious social background, such as Odette. Whereas Marcel's mother would never deign to receive Odette or even inquire directly about her, the salon Verdurin knows no such limitations. The Verdurins' wealth and recently acquired social position provide the means by which the stratified layers of high society are challenged; money breaks down certain barriers. Ostensibly the Verdurin salon could be considered a throwback to—or an ironic parody of—the intellectual salon of the Enlightenment, in which, for the sake of wit, class differences were less of a criterion than elsewhere for meetings among the middle and upper classes.

Into this salon, which is somewhat pretentious yet far more open than the Faubourg St. Honoré or Faubourg St. Germain, enters the new couple, Charlus and Morel. Once again the hearsay of the event is a mixture of friendship and relations. Morel said that he "would come that evening and would bring an old friend of his father" (3:286). The ambiguity is noteworthy. Although subterfuge has heretofore confused these two categories, in this case there is an additional "lie that tells the truth," for the only "old friend of his father" by any account, and that through a stretch, would be Marcel himself. This confusion of categories is repeated several pages later by M. Verdurin: "He is coming with an old friend of his family whom he rediscovered/met anew [*retrouvé*] and who bores him to tears, but with whom he would have been obliged, in order not to have complaints from his father, to remain in Doncières to keep him company: the Baron de Charlus" (3:294). Here the confusion is even more acute, given the invocation of Morel's father, for it is the latter whose view of Marcel, as the spiritual son of Uncle Adolphe, informs the initial meeting between Marcel and Morel. On several occasions Morel has sought to elevate his own standing by asking Marcel to retrospectively raise his father's status almost to that of a friend of the family rather than an employee. Morel has treated Marcel as if he were a peer, much to the latter's chagrin. Once again the novel has entered a dangerous zone by at least potentially making the character of Marcel a member of the "club" and implying some relational, if not real, confusion between Marcel and Charlus.

Far more important is the semipublic discourse about homosexuality that now becomes valid remarks in the Verdurin salon. The discourses of homosexuality have been particular up to now; every episode has been restricted to a limited group of participants: the two actors and a silent, notebook-wielding observer, whether Marcel or the narrator. In the expository pages in *Sodome et Gomorrhe* the enunciative framework changes, but rather than merely witness and comment on a scene, the narrator speaks directly to the reader. Nevertheless, until now homosexuality has never been the subject of conversation between characters. The long and complicated passage in which this occurs deserves commentary for the ways in which the text both mixes remarks and rumors relative to homosexuality and articulates homosexuality itself:

> The sculptor was very astonished to learn that the Verdurins accepted to receive M. de Charlus. While in the Faubourg Saint-Germain, where M. de Charlus was so well-known, one never spoke of his mores/morals [*mœurs*] (ignored by most, object of doubt for others who believed rather in exalted but platonic friendships, imprudent moments, and finally carefully hidden by the few in the know, who shrugged their shoulders when some ill-meaning Gallardon intimated an insinuation), these mores, known only to a few

> intimate friends, were, on the contrary, decried daily far from the milieu in which he lived, like certain cannon fire heard only after the interference of a zone of silence. Besides, in these artistic and bourgeois circles where he seemed to be the very incarnation of inversion, his important position in the world and his extremely aristocratic origin were completely unknown. (3:294–95)

There are two kinds of salons and two dynamics of knowledge and ignorance. In the aristocratic world such things are generally neither known nor mentioned, and those who know cover them up. We may infer that Mme de Villeparisis knows or at least suspects her nephew's predilections from her efforts to dissuade Marcel from coming under the influence of Charlus and, especially, from accompanying him after a salon: "That first emotional rush of Mme de Villeparisis, in different circumstances, would have resembled one of modesty. Her insistence and opposition could have, had one consulted only her face, seemed to been dictated by virtue" (2:580).[11] As it develops, the novel will eventually show that it is not merely Charlus whose morals are known to few; a slew of that social set's members, including the Prince de Guermantes and Robert de Saint-Loup, belong to the club as well. Aristocracy's public statements mark Charlus's behavior as idealized, Platonic friendship, homophilia, or homosociality, not homosexuality. Publicly, Charlus is unsexed and desexualized: what counts is not the action but the way it is represented. Charlus is unsexed by his society because it has no categories in which this behavior can fit, especially when it crosses class lines. The members of Charlus's circle cannot publicly rationalize his disdain for so many coupled with his particular friendship for a few, even though these aristocrats could hardly be accused of naïveté. Rather, there is nothing exchangeable about the relation, nothing mentionable or worth mentioning, nothing at all.

The Verdurin family and clan, especially Mme Verdurin, understand both the sense of relation (aristocracy) and the sense of production (bourgeoisie). Charlus's inversion therefore has no import for her, be it true or false: "'You are completely mistaken, besides, I never believe such things, and even if it were true, I would tell you that it would not be very compromising for me!' answered Mme Verdurin furiously, for Morel being the principal element of her Wednesdays, she wanted above all not to displease him" (3:296). Mme Verdurin illustrates a hybrid position combining a sense of relation with a sense of investment. It is not for naught that the narrator compares Charlus's initial reaction to that of a schoolboy on his first visit to a bordello (of which Mme Verdurin would logically be the madam): Charlus, "for whom dining at the Verdurins was not at all going into the world, but into a bad location [un mauvais lieu], was intimidated like a high school boy who goes into a public house for the first time and has a thousand respects for the owner" (3:298). Yet strangely—for her character is the most intellectually "Bovaresque" of the entire *Recherche*—Mme Verdurin both mimes Charlus's own position and provides a distinctly modern discourse of singularly in which each individual may choose his or her own subjectivity.

Mme Verdurin is the means by which a paradigmatic shift is effected in the perception of singular subjectivity. Despite her endless efforts to get her group to conform and be a collective, albeit with distinct members, she allows Morel's individual pleasure to remain distinct from her own. Her own belief or disbelief in the rumors about Charlus is part of the public discourse, as is her denial of any lowering of her social status were the rumors true; she is not interested in guilt by association. She does care about the production and productivity of her salon, however, and if that means feeding Morel's individual tastes, about which no remarks are made, so be it. Like a Balzacian character, she will succeed by any means possible. Marcel's trajectory parallels Madame Verdurin's: by the novel's end he has reached every social position that could have been attained by any princess, whether real or arriviste. He does so, in the hopes of becoming a writer, by dint of his charm, his wit, and his style: the social graces superior even to Morel's musical talent. In and of itself this parallel is not particularly enlightening, for this is a bildungsroman, and the success of the protagonist makes sense set against other successes and failures.

What does make it remarkable is that this translation of singularity in Mme Verdurin's salon—this acceptance both of Morel's desire, pleasure, and contentment and of Charlus's mores—is the means by which the narrator changes the modes he uses to describe the homosexual. On the most basic level he has recentered the character and brought Charlus back from the eccentricities of Balbec or the metaphorizations of the "First Appearance of Men-Women" (3:3–33). Charlus's inversion is no longer a sociopathic aberration or deceitful travesty; it is what and who the man is, without any implication of a lack of virtue. In fact, Charlus is compared almost immediately to one of the novel's few saints, his sister, Madame de Marsantes: "One would have thought it was Mme de Marsantes approaching, so much did the woman come out [ressortait] at that moment whom an error of nature had put into the body of M. de Charlus. Certainly the baron had toiled hard to hide that error and take on a masculine appearance" (3:300). Remarking the iterative often associated with the visibility or knowledge of Charlus's homosexuality, we may also notice that describing the homosexual as a woman in a man's body is itself a throwback to an old-fashioned model of homosexuality. At the same time, the narrator is saying even more forcefully that the situation is neither false nor condemnable. The only condemnable behavior is that which society foists on the individual who, through painful effort, seeks to make gender and sexuality coincide. This comment provides a strong antidote for all the critiques of Charlus's appearance leveled throughout the novel. It certainly shows the author, speaking through his narrator, voicing an ambiguity relative to assigning roles to male and female elements in the etiology or phenomenology of inversion. Whereas earlier metaphoric structure compensated for received knowledge and the prejudicial nature of some of the remarks, here there is something even more powerful: singularity.

Proust seems to have made a quantum leap beyond the position that Michel Foucault so eloquently describes for the social construction of homosexuality in the late nineteenth century. Foucault notes that the nineteenth century allowed for the creation of the homosexual as an individual with a distinct psychology; he (or she) is not just a teratological variant of everyone else whose categorization is determined by a set of behaviors—above all, sodomy—but a distinct person. This separation and this invention of psychology allows not only the notion of homosexuality as resulting from psychogenesis, or rather a mutually contradictory set of psychogeneses, but also of a set of bioethical proposals for dealing with "them" that range from extermination to normalization. In Foucault's model the individual derives from the category that makes him or her possible; if the individual subject is not, in the Althusserian sense, an effect of subjection to ideological state apparatuses, he or she is an effect of discursive grids and the structures of an episteme. Social constructivism becomes excessive, however, when the determinism of such categorization can never be changed by the actions or nonlogic of one individual. The current biological analogy makes the point: the genome is a roadmap, but in no way does it determine an individual. Although devout social constructivists in gender theory permit no such freeplay, I believe Foucault would have allowed for the singularity of the individual to rewrite otherwise determinative social texts.

Proust creates a specific situation for Charlus's absolute singularity, despite all family resemblance or predictability; beyond that, Proust never proposes a psychogenesis for Charlus's homosexuality. In this age of the bourgeois subject, the narrator valorizes the individual: "this habit of feeling to be a woman gave him a new feminine appearance, born, not of heredity, but of an individual life" (3:300). Thus in his singularity the baron is creating who he is or is having this self created. Charlus is no longer in mufti but is elevated to a noble and genteel position: "the baron would have merited the epithet 'lady-like'" (3:300).[12] It is only in a digression that the narrator speculates on some psychogenetic origin for Charlus, but really a rationalized one, for the underlying reason is never given: "Moreover, can one completely separate this aspect of M. de Charlus from the fact that, sons not always resembling their fathers, even without being inverts and looking for women, they consume in their faces the profanation of their mother?" (3:300). A retrospective, inverted allusion to the scene at Montjouvain, this comment and metacommentary are never really explored in what follows. Suffice it to say that the narrator immediately emphasizes that this behavior has its origin not in some general categorization but in the singularity of the individual: "the change here originated in the mind" (3:300).

Thus both the individual as homosexual and discourse about homosexuality find their way into society, a double entry whose significance cannot be overestimated. The creation or appearance of a social discourse attached to an individual changes the kinds and manners of statements floating through the system. It removes at least some of the stigma attached to homosexuality, because people who are well intentioned—or better yet, "bien-pensants" (perspicuous)—are at least begrudgingly acquiescing to the matter, not abstractly, but individually and subjectively. The impossibility of completely dissociating the individual from his behavior makes both abstract comments on homosexuality and any perpetuation of a medical-juridical discourse less than universal, because they have been given common currency.

The medico-juridical discourse does not completely disappear, however. Learning of Charlus's penchant, Cottard brings up the general idea of degeneration whose spiritual nature is matched by physical deformities—in nobles, pederasts, and madmen: "'Ah! But I did not know. Then this is a gentleman who knows how to turn himself over [se retourner] in life. What! He is in the club [de la confrérie]. But he does not have tired, red eyes [des yeux bordés de jambon]. [. . .] I see several nobles in the showers, in their birthday suits, they are more or less degenerates'" (3:324). The speaker packs a lot into a few words, starting with the pun about turning over, using a word marked by the iterative prefix already discussed. Charlus can turn over a new leaf and can metamorphose, but he can also turn over physically, to be prone or supine as needed. In addition to having Cottard mention the brotherhood of homosexuals, Proust has him, as a nineteenth-century physician, make a reference to the relation between biological and psychological structures.

Charlus does not fit the mold of those who have combined physical and moral degeneracy, as do some who, although clad only in the innocence provided by the Creator—"Adam's clothing"—have mores that have wreaked degeneracy on their bodies. One may wonder why Cottard is cruising the showers. Nor will the narrator abandon the medical discourse entirely, but he will mitigate it by sociotemporal structures: "The rapid, anxious, and charming style in which M. de Charlus played the Schumann-like piece of the Fauré Sonata: who could have discerned that this style had its correspondence—one dare not say its cause—in the completely physical parts and nervous defects of M. de Charlus? We will explain later this expression of 'nervous defects' and for what reasons a Greek from the time of Socrates, a Roman from the time of Augustus, could be what one knows while remaining absolutely normal men, and not men-women that one sees today" (3:344). Proust vacillates between discourses here, although it is difficult to say exactly what he means by "normal." Certainly he is developing a theory of homosexuality that in part relies on this older mechanism of a woman trapped in a man's body, and yet the developing characterization of Charlus undercuts that position with an idea of difference—a different normalcy. The discourses about Charlus tend to be less and less normative and normalizing, and those about the other male homosexual and bisexual characters in the remainder of the novel are barely tinged with this criticism. The idea of normalcy has no alternative here, but the means by which exchange is carried out, which amounts to a democratization and decentering of ideals and norms, is a means of replacing a specific discourse in the process of coming to the fore with a developing system.

The salon may be the locus of exchange in the most general sense, but it is also the locus of desire and emotion. Unlike all the novel's other male characters, Morel possesses a bisexual character untinged with subterfuge. Even though Charlus sometimes behaves in ways that show him to be a flaming queen, he generally maintains appearances and an aura of heterosexuality. Other characters, such as Robert de Saint-Loup and the Prince de Guermantes, cover up their homosexual infidelities with a perfectly unmarred surface of heteronormativity. Morel, however, is allowed the pleasure of both sexes and the readability thereof. He is the locus of the exchange of pleasure: "The way in which Morel was one of them [en était]—as far as I could learn—was that he liked women and men enough to please each sex with what he had experienced with the other" (3:302). Morel thus moves the contents of homosexual and bisexual behavior to a private but not hidden level; there is no opprobrium here, no unequal division between light and darkness or visible and hidden behavior. In this context Morel reflects the room—the salon—into which he is inserted.[13] Again, ironically, the negatively tinged arriviste world of Mme Verdurin gives freedom to both discourse and pleasure, whereas everything in her salon had previously been aimed at a conformity.

This makes eminent sense socially, even if the telos of *arrivisme* is basically a kind of retro behavior that seeks to replace heritage, history, and being to the manner born with arrival at a social station by bourgeois means. *Arrivisme* focuses on the assumption of authority, breeding, and power through a manipulation of signs, discourses, and fungible values. The social contradictions are palpable: by manipulating the class structure, one arrives in a class whose greatest goal is not to manipulate the class structure. This manipulation through signs rather than accreted essence is exactly what the introduction of a mutable, labile concept of desire requires. Desire is not fixed into its own heteronormative class structure simply because it has always been so. Desire finds its ground in an exchange of signs that can now be manipulated through knowledge without the benefit of an official blessing. Even Charlus's own discourse becomes ambiguous in this light. The mixture of light and darkness and the protective cover that was the noble position of a Maecenas or the lordly position of an aegis has been changed. In earlier encounters Charlus uses a vocabulary that suits his princely nature; with Morel the discourse may seem to remain the same, but there is an ambiguity at the level of the physical, as when Charlus echoes Saint-Loup's comments on his uncle's benevolence toward certain members of the lower classes: "The very fact that I am interested in him and extend my protection to him has something pre-eminent and abolishes the past" (3:306). Surprising is the fact that Charlus, as standard-bearer, would willingly abolish the past; equally surprising, but totally consonant both with Charlus's belief that the only real past is the noble past and with what I have been indicating, is the way in which the extension of protection incorporates a physical, tactile, and almost sexual set of connotations. The physicality will be realized in an adjustment of textual proxemics: "an admiration for Morel that extended through his manner of playing, to flatter him too, and finally, to explain the movement he made to lean on the shoulder of the violinist" (3:348).

The relatively liberal atmosphere of the salon leads to the characters' recognition that such discourses may be exchanged. This emerges not merely from the fact that people are talking; Proust also includes a moment of implied self-reflection about the linguistic and moral change in the environment. He chooses to do so in an amusing, almost slapstick fashion, for he has

Charlus do a double take at an innocently proffered remark. M. Verdurin is speaking to Charlus and trying to indicate the esteem in which he holds the baron: "'But from the first words we exchanged I understood that you were one of them [vous en étiez]!' M. de Charlus, who gave this expression quite a different meaning, snapped to attention. . . . 'Morel is one of them, my wife is, I feel you are' [Morel en est, ma femme en est, je sens que vous en êtes]—'What were you going to say to me?' interrupted M. de Charlus who began to be reassured about what M. Verdurin meant, but who preferred the latter yell those ambiguous words less loudly" (3:332). Whereas M. Verdurin is speaking of those who have artistic souls, Charlus believes at first that his interlocutor is speaking of homosexuality. It is only following the litany of the "in" crowd that the light dawns on Charlus, even as he recognizes that others might understand the expression "one of them" in this context as he himself has first understood it.[14]

What is remarkable is neither the joke nor the misunderstanding but the fact that it is now somewhat acceptable to speak of such matters, if only in private conversation, and to do so using the vernacular. An abstract or objective version of the language can be used, and even an individual can be said to have questionable or doubtful mores. Here, however, Proust goes one step further by introducing an informal way of talking about homosexuality: it has become a banality suitable for small change and small talk. And this comes from the mouth of a rather ignorant though very wealthy man to whom Charlus must, in the same paragraph, indicate the range of his titles (3:333). In this comedy of manners there are two kinds of misunderstanding: the ignorance of nobility and the misunderstanding of a statement. Yet equally important is the unimportance of that nobility, as Charlus himself indicates, albeit ironically (3:332 and 333), and the possibility of exchanging language and desire in a far more democratic manner than was possible before.

Misunderstanding the phrase "one of them/us" leads to a amusing confusion between minorities: "Mme Cottard made out only the words 'in the club [de la confrérie]' and 'tongue-flapper [tapette],'" and, as in the doctor's language the first meant the Jewish race and the second, the loquacious [les langues bien pendues], Mme Cottard concluded that M. de Charlus had to be a talkative Israelite" (3:425–26).[15] Having learned that Charlus is settling in the neighborhood, she nearly puts her foot in her mouth: "'I was very happy to learn that you had chosen this area to set up your tabern.' She was going to say 'tabernacles,' but the word seemed Hebraic to her and uncomfortable for a Jew who might seen an allusion in it" (3:426).[16] The effect is comic, but underlying it are two related ideological and indeed literary positions.

On the one hand, minority groups are interchangeable through linguistic confusion and a kind of language that separates and hierarchizes. Jews and homosexuals are the same relative to the dominant discourse. In this salon one respects them out of a republican sensibility that values individual liberty, and one tries not to embarrass them, but they must remain discreet, not too loud, neither too Jewish nor too homosexual. Unacceptable are the too queeny homosexuals or the Jews who invade the Normandy seaside resorts and turn them into the rue d'Aboukir. Thus the discourse of the other and the behavior of the other is limited by the discourse and behavior of the dominant groups, who determine what is acceptable. On the other hand, this very limitation attempts to preserve the sanctity of the status quo: assimilation is possible, but at a price.

This change in discourse becomes even more radical with one final remove from reference and denotation: "But in hearing M. de Charlus say in that acute voice and with that smile and gestures, 'No, I preferred its neighbor, the strawberry soda,' one could say, 'Look, he likes the stronger sex,' with the same certainty as that which allows to condemn, for a judge, a criminal who had not confessed, for a doctor, a general paralytic who perhaps does not himself know his illness but who makes such mistakes in pronunciation that one can deduce that he will be dead in three years" (3:356). The comparisons are not flattering, even if the last symptom, pronunciation errors, tends to refer the reader not to some nineteenth-century medical paradigm but rather to the literary paradigm engendered by the Verdurin circle. Still, the important point is the certainty of diagnosis. Paraphrasing Freud, we might translate his "remains of the day" that find their way into the dream into the remains of the text. This comparison evokes two kinds of discourse on homosexuality, as well as certain theorizings on enunciation expressed earlier and certain key events vaguely remembered by the unconscious of the text at this point. Thus Swann's prediction of his own death is recapitulated in the deduction of a patient's future death; the stroke that fells the grandmother is echoed as well. The pronunciation errors—or dysphasia, for lack of a better word—that characterize numerous members of the Verdurin clan and are metonymically repeated in the way its patriarch mislaughs are recapitulated, as are all the characters' endless pronunciation errors: those made by Françoise, Aimé, and Bloch, among others. The narrator also recapitulates the discourses of medicine and jurisprudence that have been attached to homosexuality. The revolution is in the complete dissociation of content and sign or signified and signifier. The totally arbitrary relation here between the two parts of the sign does not prevent the expression of desire or the situation of that desire from being understood. Somehow homosexual desire inserts itself—is inserted—and exists at the bar between signified and signifier: "But there is a more direct relation here between the revelatory sign and the secret" (3:357).

Charlus's discourse gives away his homosexuality, regardless of what he is saying; the discourses of others, especially Mme Verdurin, show at least an unconscious recognition of that homosexuality. In a pointed passage Mme Verdurin is given to be understanding while attempting to preserve the appearance of normative, heterosexual society, although this is done not for psychological reasons but rather for the benefit of the reader as a function of narration, signs, and meanings. Sexuality, or at least the implication thereof, is made "innocent" in her remarks. The whole passage is telling, because Mme Verdurin moves from a comment suggesting female virginity or innocence to a bedroom farce posing as a concert:

> Yet what astonishment M. de Charlus would have had if, one day when Morel and he were late and, never having taken the train, he had heard the Patroness say: "We are waiting only for those young ladies!" The baron would have been even more stupefied, given that, barely moving from La Raspelière, he gave the impression of being a chaplain or local priest [abbé de répertoire], and sometimes (when Morel had a two-day pass) spent two nights in a row there. Mme Verdurin then gave them two adjoining rooms and, to put them at ease, said to them, "If you want to make music, don't worry, the walls are like those of a fortress, there is no one on your floor, and my husband sleeps like a log." (3:431)

Of Algebra and Voyeurism; or, the Geometry of the Brothel

Like any couple, the Charlus-Morel household has its ups and downs (3:447–58), but my concern here is less with the psychological or sociological dynamics of that relationship, as if Charlus and Morel were "real people," than with the novel's encoding of homosexuality around the figure of Charlus and subsequently around the figures of this couple, which Jacques Dubois has explained (139–44). The final step in the encoding of the couple occurs in the introduction of the last element, the bedroom farce with the Prince de Guermantes. This farce will be turned into a somewhat pathetic version of itself in one of the novel's more scabrous scenes, Charlus's whipping, which will also recall the scene in which Bloch escorts the young Marcel to the brothel where he meets Rachel, thus making the final brothel scene echo both previous ones.

Can a brothel be a secondary or tertiary modeling system? This may seem an odd question at this point in the study, for the vocabulary is distinctly out of place. Soviet semioticians considered language to be a primary modeling system, the essential communicative substrate onto which all other structures must be mapped and the means by which all other systems of thought are coded. A secondary modeling system, such as science or literature, can then use that basic substrate to develop a set of codes and protocols. A brothel is a social and economic institution in which various secondary modeling systems function: a code of exchange, codes of gender, codes of biopolitics, and so forth. Thus a brothel is a locus at which various modeling systems communicate and whose representation can be seen to be a figure, perforce ideological, of one or several of those systems. Later, in what will come to be known as postmodernism, another version appears in Jean-François Lyotard's concept of the *différand*—specifically, in the intertranslatability of discourses and modeling systems. Lyotard's greatest concern was justice, which he pursued by asking about being just in the face of competing models, but his inquiry and its consequences are not limited to that matter and can be used more generally to understand how various modeling systems communicate with one another, how they are translated, and how they compete.

The exchange of epistemological information—that for which language, as the primary modeling system, would be a vehicle—is accompanied, although not necessarily in a parasitic sense, by an exchange of ideological information. For example, as David Bell has shown in his studies of French novels, the translation of a scientific discourse into literature is accompanied by an almost blind transfer of the ideological presuppositions of science and the general permeability of literature—admittedly a limit case—to such ideology. Unconscious, implicit ideological structures may come in through the back door or even the front: literature's permeability to other discourses, its self-reflexivity due to its materiality, and its endless capacity to assimilate make it the most welcoming of institutions.

In the United States recent critical trends, perceiving some of the excesses of deconstruction as a refusal and even denial of contextualization—especially in the wake of the de Man scandal—have returned to historicizing literary discourse. Quite often this rehistoricization creates a history with a capital H, as if it were the purveyor of truth against which the literary object is measured or by which it was framed.[17] The truth of the literary object is thus always derivative. This position is a ultimately a reactionary one, for on the one hand, it ascribes truth of and in representation to some extratextual moment, and on the other, it categorically rejects the insight from formalists through Roland Barthes that the literary text has a semiautonomous position relative to other discursive, ideological, and cultural productions. This is true not only in the sense that literary objects have a historical line that does not necessarily coincide with the line of history but also in the sense that the translatability of discourses, the exchange of epistemes, can happen according to laws of form that scarcely resemble those effective in other realms.[18]

In the latter two brothel scenes of the *Recherche,* the locus becomes insignificant as a place for the exchange of women. In the first of these two scenes women are an excuse; in the second, set in an exclusively (homosexual) male brothel, women do not even appear. The former, in which Morel has an assignation with the Prince de Guermantes, arguably uses the brothel merely as a cover, excuse, or convenient locus; other locations would be equally plausible without changing the story significantly. One could imagine the assignation taking place in a hotel room rented by the hour, a room in a country estate, or, were the action set in the city, in studio apartment.[19] What makes the brothel the locus of choice is the possibility of multiple exchanges, misunderstandings, and voyeurism that might be absent in a more domestic or more restricted environment. In the case of the male bordello, one could exhume, although undoubtedly without much interest for this novel, a history of male prostitution and show how the bordello functions as a locus of economic and gender-bending performances.[20]

Such a reading ignores the semiautonomous nature of the literary work. Any literary work constitutes a locus in which the exchange of epistemologies and modeling systems takes place; in which an economy of representation functions (especially in a so-called realist novel); and in which, for that representation to work, the means and mode of representation must appear realistic. The literary work also has its own codes: the secondary modeling system that is the gradually evolving canon of literature or even its rule-breaking noncanonicity. Here the two scenes primarily manifest the literary codes of homosexuality, specifically as they relate to and emanate from Charlus. The brothel also functions phenomenologically as a convenient site for the exposition of these codes, precisely because it is a locus of exchange in which, although regulated by the marketplace—and there is certainly an amusing mercantile subtext in the last scene—an extraordinary amount of freeplay remains possible.

Proust frames the comic scene of Morel's assignation with two secondary modeling systems: algebra and music. Both are part of a flimsy set of excuses for Morel to have some freedom from what might be termed Charlus's possessiveness. Desiring some free time, Morel is purportedly giving violin lessons, which makes psychological sense, especially since we know the extent to which the character is motivated by money; as he himself says, "I can make 40 francs doing it. That is not chicken feed" (3:463). If not giving violin lessons, he is taking a course in algebra whose utility is murky and whose efficacy is limited.

Both music and algebra are specific modeling systems, neither exactly primary nor fully secondary, for although neither is directly predicated on language as a system of meanings, both are predicated on writing. The Derridean distinction is not without importance. For developing their own archives, music and algebra have their own systems of writing and annotation. The annotation system for music is basically nonalphabetic. Written language, in the most commonly used sense of the term, is present only as either a set of instructions and labels or a parallel text, as in vocal music.[21] Algebra, too, uses written language, doing so predominantly in equations and functions by assigning letters to variables (and sometimes constants). In both of these forms certain letters can stand for any number. Moreover, algebraic equations often involve "unknowns"—*x* and *y*, for example—whose values must be found: meaning comes afterward, the signified follows the signifier at a distance, and the arbitrary relation between the two was never more clear. So music and algebra both have codes that distance the modeling system from meaningful written language. The context is estranged from the world of material exchange, a distancing that the author willfully creates to help the reader recognize the utopian nature of this game, even if it is ultimately dystopic for all involved. Moreover, the players become signs who signify not according to the rules of language but in an arbitrary fashion, as in the case of algebra. Any of the players can be entered into the paradigm or the algorithm.

Here it is the Prince de Guermantes who initiates the encounter, ultimately more geometric or trigonometric than algebraic. Morel encodes the matter differently, for the homosexual liaison with the prince is the excuse not only for gain—as is the case with the pretense of violin lessons—but also for heterosexuality: "the sensuality of being entwined [entouré] with a woman whose brown breasts were clearly visible" (3:464). For the homosexual encounter is set against what is normally and nominally a heterosexual background. From the point of view assigned to Morel, this encounter is an intermittence—not of the heart but of the genitalia—set against the permanence of heterosexuality. The prince's money is the means by which a homoerotic space is carved out, banishing the heterosexual for a time. Even within the confines of the brothel the same formula applies: "In reality, Morel was at that time with the Prince de Guermantes; for the sake of appearance, he seemed to have gone to the wrong room, having entered one where there were two women who seemed to be in a hurry to leave the two gentlemen alone" (3:467). And finally, because the means of communication is always bivalent, the episode of homosexuality is clearly replaced, again by a counterdiscourse of heterosexuality: "Morel had been warned that two gentlemen had paid quite dearly to see him; the Prince de Guermantes had been made to leave, metamorphosed into three women. Poor Morel trembled and was paralyzed with stupor, so that, if M. de Charlus saw him badly, he, terrorized, speechless, not daring to take his glass for fear of letting it fall, saw the baron fully" (3:467).

Heterosexuality, which now takes the form of family relations and family values, multiplies ad infinitum in the endgame of the scene, for when, in a follow-up assignation at a villa rented by the prince, Morel sees a collection of family photos, including one of Charlus, he believes he is in a trap set by the latter and flees. The point of vision is reversed. In the earlier scene Charlus wants to see Morel but ends up seeing him badly, while Morel sees the baron fully. In the epilogue an absent Charlus, as if a gorgon, effects a fixation on Morel: "The baron seemed to immobilize on Morel a strange and fixed stare" (3:468). The picture of Charlus has a magical and chastening effect. As Stephen Infantino (67) says, the photograph of Charlus "does not simply hamper activities[,] it precludes their very possibility." Thus once again a homosexual encounter is prevented.

The relation of these incidents to the two modeling systems and to an encoding of homosexuality can be seen in the way in which homosexuality is manipulated to preserve heterosexuality. In both cases Charlus—once in flesh, once in a photo—is used, despite his own proclivities, as a means of preventing a homosexual encounter. Music and algebra are exact correlates. The figure of the baron becomes an empty sign into which heterosexuality can be poured. Operating in a major key, the episode prevents any reading of a sharp or flat note—that is, minority sexuality; operating as an equation, the text precludes any answer other than the one determined by the simple linear equation, the quadratic equation, or the function.

The language of the brothel is the same as those of capitalism, theater, and pedagogy. The exchange of words among the boys, even when talking about certain sexual activities—whipping, bondage, and discipline—that would not be considered appropriate conversation in bourgeois society, takes on the most banal tones (4:391). In their closed sphere the local vocabulary is as neutral as any other trite conversation. When the closed world opens up—when there is a client—the language changes to show the move from the everyday world to the world of a ritualized vocabulary of criminality. In a typical example from the last brothel scene, Proust moves the text of Jupien's hawking his boy from a somewhat bucolic setting to a wild one in which the populist east side of Paris, the neighborhood of Belleville, is transformed into the wildest hallucination of the American West: "'He is an apprentice milkman, but really he is one of the most dangerous Apaches [i.e., hoodlums] of Belleville' (one had to see the lusty [grivois] tone in which Jupien said 'Apache')" (4:396).[22] Again, in a remark that betrays what he himself perceives as a theatricalization of the discourse, the baron notes how the vocabulary is itself meaningless but implicitly has a value as part of a scenario, a personal theater in which masculinity and outlaw status are aligned: "His face pleases me, but he calls me a scoundrel [crapule] as if by rote" (4:396).

New language puts truth into question: "Jupien had recommended them to the baron's better judgment, swearing to him that they were all Belleville 'pimps [barbeaux]' and that they would sell their own sister for a louis. Moreover, Jupien was lying and telling the truth at the same time" (4:403). Even the baron recognizes this, and the old truths of which he is the standard-bearer in the real world have nothing to do with the performance of truth and falsity in this one: "And how well he says it. One would say it's the truth. After all, what does it matter if it is the truth or not, since he gets me to believe it?" (4:404). The truth of homosexuality and criminality becomes a theatrical truth that will be echoed by Jean Cocteau and eventually by Jean Genet. There is no language that says what it says for homosexuality, because all language is inscribed heteronormatively. In other words, only a deconstruction of the dyadic couple of heterosexual and homosexual, or their language, can show the presumptive nature of the ordering. Such a deconstruction being necessary, however, homosexuality does not stand on its own without that strategy. This theatricalization is the ironic reversal that results from hiding the ideological status of compulsory heterosexuality behind heterosexuality and heteronormativity, letting it parade as the truth. The statements themselves—the supposed criminal behavior—have nothing outrageous about them: "M. de Charlus was struck only by how the smut was so limited"(4:406). In all this, it is perhaps only Jupien who maintains, in his own petit bourgeois fashion, the silence of middle-class morality: "Jupien did not want to speak only of scenes of sadism like those I had witnessed and of the very practice of the baron's vice" (4:409).

Structurally this brothel scene in some ways mirrors the scene in the hôtel de Guermantes, for it involves another case of espionage, or better yet, voyeurism. In Balbec the younger Marcel, in supposed ignorance of what Charlus is and is up to, attributes his eccentric and erratic behavior to a wealth of possible antisocial causes, including espionage. In the hôtel de Guermantes the narrator becomes a spy as he oversees and then overhears what transpires between Charlus and Jupien. Thus the figure combining spying and homosexuality, with both its own prurient overtones and the overtones associated with policing, is transferred to the narrator in a schizoid realignment of the Balzacian model concerning the various incarnations of Vautrin. No longer is the homosexual the equivalent of a spy; the furtive looks have a completely different meaning from what Marcel initially attributed to them. The position of the spy is thus also a sexualized one: caught not only in transmitting military and political secrets but also in transcribing sexuality, the observer takes a position only hinted at in the scenes in Balbec. There the triangulated position is also a participatory one, because the three are caught in a common set, in the mathematical or logical sense of the term.

The question of espionage comes up again, as if to remind us of the previous association: "Did this hotel serve as a meeting place for spies?" (4:389). But the role as "the spy of homosexuality"—and one could, in that expression, read a double genitive here that once again implicates the narrator as homosexual—is so thoroughly internalized, as is the gaydar, that his sleuthing is as unerring as it is unsaid. Instead of going into the room, he is "taken by another idea" but does not say what it is. Only then, from an isolated room, does he hear "muffled complaints" that he understands through gaydar or prescience. He knows or can predict the instrument of torture that is eliciting these cries of pain: "I heard the sound of the slap of a strap probably sharpened with nails." Sure enough, this "gay" Sherlock Holmes has foreseen the exact situation: "There, chained on the bed like Prometheus on his rock, and receiving the blows of a strap which was indeed studded with nails inflicted on him by Maurice, I saw, already completely bloodied and covered with bruises that proved that the torture [supplice] was not happening for the first time, I saw, in front of me, M. de Charlus" (4:394).[23] This comparison to Prometheus is not without its own interest, for it follows shortly on another classical reference, which is the writing on the wall at Pompeii that says "Sodom, Gomorrah" (4:386).

For what is Charlus being punished? Obviously, on the most basic level of psychology and plot, Charlus is being not "punished" but rather rewarded, having his masochistic desires fulfilled. Some might certainly associate that masochism with the eternal self-loathing ascribed to those who are victims of internalized homophobia. Yet Charlus's endless pride and self-lionization make the masochistic act his own sexual pleasure, which need not be pathologized, especially as it is limned with biographical overtones and a mixture of theatricality and money. More important is the simile, for as we remember, Prometheus is punished for having given fire to humankind. Charlus is being punished for having given the gift of homosexuality to the novel in general and the narrator in particular. Charlus's gift is a good thing, as is fire for humans in the Greek myth. It is that which, like Promethean fire, warms the novel, but is also that which, when pathologized by the imposition of Judeo-Christian moralizing, as mostly pagan Pompeii was, provides not only knowledge but also a loss of innocence and the concomitant gift of the danger of knowledge. Charlus has gradually made the narrator immune—the French would say "mithridatized"—to the perils of homosexuality, but the baron has also given him the gift of such well-honed radar that he can now seek it out unerringly and even know what scenario will take place. Finally, Charlus, in a projective sense, is receiving the blows that Marcel cannot receive—not for having touched the veil of the goddess, to paraphrase the last line of Flaubert's *Salammbô,* but rather for having lifted the veil of "the goddess H" (Barthes, *Barthes* 68).

Again, the translations from previous scenarios are palpable as Proust reminds us of previous episodes. Thus Charlus and Jupien recall Mlle Vinteuil and her friend: "'We cannot be heard?' said the baron to Jupien, who affirmed that they couldn't'" (4:394). Because vision is no longer necessary, the concern is with being heard. But how does the narrator affirm their safety, with a nod of the head or with a word? If it is a word, it is supposedly unheard, although it is overheard, and vision, such as that the narrator would have, is superfluous. Significantly, the remark is made not to the partner in the dyad but to someone who functions outside the sexual pair: Jupien. Jupien thus doubles Marcel's position by this re-placement, and Marcel comes to occupy a position like Jupien's. How should we read this? A psychobiography might project the real Proust into the novel, for he had given his own material and financial support to the establishment of such a brothel in the real world. In such a reading Proust would be seen to divide that support between an alter ego in the form of Marcel and, shall we say, an alter id in the form of Jupien, who fulfills that part of the event that cannot be ascribed to the narrator, who must remain literally and figuratively above all involvement with male homosexuality. Proust makes the pairing of Jupien and Marcel even more specific, for Jupien is "intelligent, like a man of letters" (4:394). Structurally the scene is made more complex by the association of Marcel as a character and Jupien. Jupien continues to treat Marcel deferentially: his place is "not there" and he does not belong to this world, even if he does belong to the current ruling classes. In other words—and this is significant—as much as the narrator is co-opted into a position of homosexuality by the textual dynamics he sets up, the social constraints of the novel's world force him away from that position and establish a sphere in which he has no control, sway, or power. Thus has Charlus participated in such a world by submitting to it.[24] Charlus's assumption of the masochist position is required psychologically: what is known in French as "the English vice," that is, being whipped or caned, is associated with the upper classes. It is also necessary textually: to enter this world, a gay version of the demimonde, he must submit to its laws. Although Bakhtin might call this a carnivalization of the real world, where everything is topsy-turvy and the lower classes rule, it is not exactly that, for the power structure is the same as that of legitimate power in the real world; it is just that there are different people in the position of "players" or operators.

Proust goes even further and has Jupien open the transom, which he "had invented so that the baron could see and hear without being seen, but he would turn it the other way [retourner] to my benefit against him" (4:402); Marcel can see and hear Charlus without being seen. Thus in passing do we learn from Jupien that Charlus shares Marcel's/the narrator's inclination toward voyeurism, overhearing—auditory voyeurism, for lack of a better term—or sexual espionage. If not the spy Marcel once thought him to be, the baron is certainly a spy in a sexual sense, although he is never observed being a voyeur, because doubling the position of the voyeur might look ridiculous or point to the narrator/author. When we do see the baron looking with concentration at an object, it is a matter either of cruising, as in Balbec, or else, in almost a parody of a Gidean position, of pursuit at a distance. There is nothing untoward in saying that Charlus is like the narrator; what is implied is that the narrator is like Charlus. Again, we cannot say that the narrator is homosexual, but Jupien's insistence here on the reversibility of positions leads us necessarily to pursue that thought, even if it remains foreclosed by the novel.

The final comparison along these lines of this scene puts Charlus, Jupien, and the narrator all in the same position of exchangeability. Given the comparison of Jupien to a man of letters and the eventual profession of Marcel—

not to mention the author's profession—the last comparison is striking. It starts out as a negation, and in such a guise it begs the reader's righting of the remark: "If M. de Charlus had been a novelist, then the house that Jupien had set up would have been a misfortune for him, because it would have greatly reduced risks—at least the danger from a stranger picked up in the street (for a police raid was always to be feared). But in art, M. de Charlus was merely a dilettante, who did not think of writing and was not gifted for it" (4:410). If it is too far back to Balbec to think of Charlus's fake writing, we may remember it nevertheless and also remember that, like Marcel in Combray, Charlus is capable of writing, at least insofar as writing impassioned letters is concerned.

Narrative Closure and the Boys in the Back Room

Framed by the *Arabian Nights,* the brothel scene is influenced as much by narrative orientalism as by the stay of execution that those tales imply. The narrative starts with the narrator thinking about Haroun al-Rashid, "in search of adventures [aventures] in the forgotten [perdus] neighborhoods of Baghdad" (4:388). So already the complicitous and implicit identification between the narrator and the character in search of a contact—adventure or accidental sexual encounter, for the French *aventure* can mean both—marks this part of the novel. That Marcel will not have an *aventure* as such will be compensated by the sexual thrill of voyeurism that is a trademark of the novel. The stay of execution is double; by telling stories Scheherazade avoids both deflowering and death. Marcel remains a virgin in the forests of homosexuality, endlessly spinning tales to avoid his own sacrifice on that altar and his own death as a heterosexual narrator.

Invoked again in the final conversation with Jupien is the tale of tales, which, in a passing reference to several of the stories, provides a segue not only to Ruskin's work and Proust (the narrator's translation thereof) but also to the total chaos that will follow. The narrator states what we have already come to know as the theatricality of these performances: "This house is something completely different, more than a madhouse, since the madness of the insane who live there is put on stage [mise en scène], reconstituted, visible. It is a real pandemonium" (4:411). Yes and no, one might say, for to the extent that the madness—to use the narrator's term—is theatricalized, it is not a true pandemonium but a false one, a copy of pandemonium from which the demons are exorcized. The true pandemonium will follow, but there is nothing demonic about it.

In a seldom-commented episode occurring in a dark world between the theater of the brothel and the safety of the home, the narrative enters a mysterious space almost completely enshrouded in darkness, a darkness that means liberty: the night, the darkened streets, and a city engulfed by blackness. During a bombing raid the brothel's clients flee into the streets and scatter in various directions. Some go out into the dark streets, but others descend into the safety of the metro, a haven beneath the earth's surface and far from the bombings by German planes.

How does the narrator set the scene? As if fleeing a tidal bore [mascaret], the narrator briefly recalls a double destruction: the lava spewing from Vesuvius that engulfs Pompeii and Herculaneum and the cities of the plain themselves: "I sped up to flee him [the god of evil] like a traveler pursued by a tidal bore[;] . . . I thought of Jupien's house . . . on which M. de Charlus could have prophetically written 'Sodom,' as had, with no less prescience, or perhaps at the beginning of the volcanic eruption and that catastrophe already begun, the unknown dweller in Pompeii" (4:412). First of all, this imagined scene of writing recalls the scene in the brothel itself (4:386), fresh in the reader's mind, where the writing is on the wall. Again the narrator has vacillated in his inscription of Charlus's writerly skills or potential, thereby underlining the labile nature of these positions of writer and sodomite and once again inscribing the act of narration—and the narrator himself—into the "scene of homosexuality." Beyond that, will there be confusion between the referent—the flow or destruction that is visited on these cities—and the inscription of that act as graffiti, written by someone about to die, or at least someone who has foreseen death visited on cities in which wayward behavior takes place? So is this a condemnation of homosexuality? Hardly likely. Rather, the narrator inserts himself into the paradigm through the act of inscription where he cannot do so directly. His voyeurism is translated into the writing of homosexuality, a kind of graffiti, pornography, or sexography recapitulating the possibility of vulgar sexual couplings.

In this bombing of Paris the narrator finally takes the last step, at least hypothetically, into the darkness that he has previously only sensed. I say "hypothetically" for the narrator does not explicitly say that Marcel follows the characters into the bowels of the earth. He indicates that Marcel continues to flee (4:412) and that some of the people fleeing the brothel went down into the "hallways of the metro, black like the catacombs" (4:413). Yet the narrative itself follows in a temporary version of Balzacian omniscience. With or without Marcel, the metro scene moves to the fulfillment of this whole scenario in what would be called a back room in modern gay parlance. A back room—a locus that enjoyed its heyday during the gay sexual revolution before AIDS—is a dark room, usually in a gay bar (those in gay saunas are usually called "orgy rooms"), in which indiscriminate sexual contact can occur. Specifically, the contact is indiscriminate in the sense that visual clues are few and far between, because the room is barely lit at best. Auditory clues being taboo—one doesn't chat in these areas—the only shibboleths for discrimination are tactile. The back room is one of the purest incarnations of a space for Deleuzian desiring machines or a Lyotardian multiple libidinal band.

Instead of the marketplace that is the brothel, this space is one in which there is a free-for-all in both a literal and a connotative sense of the term: it is free for all involved—one does not even need the usual metro ticket to get into the orgy—and it is a chaotic, ill-defined orgy, with the roles of subject and object, passive and active, and the like no longer pertinent. The first stage is the insistence on the tactile, for in this world whose hallways are "black like catacombs" (4:413), the sense of touch is all that remains. The first part of this singular quotation sets the scene for what will happen in the metro, but also is testimony to a shift in pronouns: "Yet the darkness that bathes everything like a new element has, as an effect, irresistibly tempting for certain people, the suppression of the first stage of pleasure, and it makes us completely enter a realm of caresses to which one does not usually accede until after a while" (4:413). The first-person plural *nous* ("us") sits uncomfortably between *certain people,* which would call for *them* as an object, and the following *on* ("one") which, as a defective pronoun without its own objective forms, does call for *nous* as an object; the *nous* could also refer to humanity in general, for the present tense of *bathes* could indicate an atemporal, universal truth. The narrator's position is ambiguous. Like the light and dark playing with the curtains in Balbec and like the magic lantern, he is both the brightness and obscurity of the scene, in it and yet in the dark, away from it, imagining it where he cannot allow himself to be.

The scene continues in full force:

> Whether the coveted object is a woman or a man, even supposing that an approach is simple, and that the flirting that would occur in a drawing room (at least in daylight) would be useless, in the evening (even in a street as dimly lit as possible), there is a preamble where the eyes alone count their chickens before they're hatched [les yeux seuls mangent le blé en herbe], where

> the fear of passers-by, of being the one sought after oneself, prevents one from doing more than looking, speaking. In the darkness, this whole game is abolished, and hands, lips, and bodies can make the first move. The excuse remains of darkness itself and the errors it begets if one is rebuffed. (4:413)

In this extraordinary passage, followed by what is an even more remarkable set of comments, the narrator has not only fully dissociated sexuality from vision, sight, and light but also completely dissociated it from social behavior. Sign systems as such are abolished, and a sign appears only as an aftereffect, the "excuse of darkness" that otherwise would not have any sign. Signs of sexuality are therefore associated with what the narrator calls a preamble, in which the eyes possess what they do not yet have.

In this free-for-all humans return to a state that one might call prelinguistic or presemiotic were the entire situation not framed by technology and the whole set of encounters not based on an elaborate game of acceptance, acquiescence, pleasure, and will. Better to say that it is postlinguistic and postsemiotic. Here, then, is the moment after the initial acceptance, the rebuff having been dealt with by a return to the semiotic:

> If one is well-received[,] that immediate response of the body that does not pull back, that advances, gives us of the woman (or man [celle (ou celui)]) we are silently addressing an idea that she is without prejudices, full of lust [vice], an idea that adds a bonus to the happiness of having been able to eat the fruit without having coveted it with one's eyes or asked permission. Yet the darkness persists; plunged into this new element[,] Jupien's regulars thought they had traveled, had come to see a natural phenomenon like a tidal bore [mascaret] or an eclipse, and instead of tasting an already prepared and sedentary pleasure, taste one of a fortuitous meeting in the unknown; they celebrated, in the volcanic rumblings of the bombs, at the foot of a bad Pompeian spot, secret rights in the shadows of the catacombs. (4:413)

In this postsemiotic moment socially imposed divisions between homosexual and heterosexual are completely gone. No longer do the visible signs on a face or the audible signs of a voice indicate the invert, the courtesan—for the aging Charlus and the aging Odette are the same—or the cryptosapphic. Anyone can participate in this game, and the player's gender means little. As if refugees from the world pictured by Aristophanes's speech in Plato's *Symposium,* the split halves will know how to find each other: gay men will seek their other halves, just as straight women will seek theirs. In any case, gaydar has been turned into a sonar system.

For gay men in particular, the contrast is striking: the once paying clients of Jupien's brothel can make the most of serendipity and enjoy themselves in an active sense. Thus all these gay men, whatever sexual roles they play, become active rather than "sedentary" as pleasure itself changes from an already manufactured, prepackaged commodity to something fresh, new, and exciting. In that, it moves from the theatrical, now viewed as the delivery of something canned or represented, into the realm of the fresh and present. Gay men become primitive men, proto-Christians in a sacrilegious metaphor that compares their sexual encounters in the darkened subway to the rites and masses performed by early Christians—or celebrants of any repressed cult—in the catacombs. Thus does homosexuality itself take on a religious status. The comparison to primitives is reinforced by the awe ascribed to them when faced with natural phenomena such as an eclipse or a tidal bore.

Nevertheless—and this is where the entire scene becomes extraordinary—that tidal bore appeared barely a page before, when the narrator indicated that Marcel fled "like a traveler pursued by a tidal bore" (4:412). The gay men taking refuge in the metro do not flee before that deluge, the volcanic flow that becomes the music of their night, but stand in awe of it. Is the narrator so different from his horde of characters? Or does he protest too much? The connection of the two sentences by two similes involving the relatively uncommon word *mascaret* cannot be avoided. Seemingly there is a contrast between the narrator's own position and that of the sodomites. And yet in this dark world, if he were there, how could he see? How could others see? How could the narrator, caught in this darkness, avoid being touched even if he keeps his hands to himself? He has taken a moment to insert women into the picture, but it is highly unlikely that they represent any significant part of the underground population, for we already know that most stores are closed and most people from the daylight world have gone to the country (4:388–89). Indeed, not only women are absent; people from the nontwilight world are as well. The only people in this world are those entering and exiting Jupien's brothel. Only they are there, plus perhaps the narrator and the imaginary woman he hypothesizes to keep things straight.

So this exclusive population enters the metro, making the brothel itself a kind of movable feast and transforming the Parisian marvel of mass communication into Sodom-sous-Seine. And what then of Marcel/the narrator? He may have entered Jupien's world as a voyeur, but there is nothing to see here. If he is here—and we must assume that he may be because of the ambiguous scene setting—he cannot protect himself through invisibility, for everyone is invisible here; everyone has the advantage that he alone once had.

He is not separate; he is not an observer but a participant. Perhaps everyone who comes and cops a feel from Marcel/the narrator winds up having to make an excuse. Does he reach out and touch someone? We never know. Silence.

A sudden segue to the world of light, a room where everyone can see one another and where he can narrate again, returns us to the world of signs, of separation, of observation, of faults in pronunciation, and of errors in tact, judgment, and socialization. After a night in a brothel, after having finally lost his homosexual virginity, there is nothing left for Marcel/the narrator to do except to go home. Or is there? A few pages later the narrator seems irresistibly drawn to comparing Charlus once again to himself, implicitly and explicitly: "And [Charlus] pretended to fear the German bombers [gothas], not that he felt the slightest fear, but in order to have the pretext, as soon as the sirens went off, to hurtle into the shelters of the metro where he hoped for some pleasure of brushing up against someone in the night, with the vague dreams of medieval undergrounds and dungeons and of *in pace*. In sum his desire to be chained, beaten, betrayed in its ugliness, a dream as poetic as, in others, the desire to go to Venice or to keep dancers" (4:419). The metro becomes the new "Merovingian night," the locus for a desire to go to Venice or entertain women. And Marcel/the narrator, fresh from his group grope? He can say no more.

3 Figures of the Homoerotic: Gide and Cocteau

Of Latency and Homoeroticism in L'Immoraliste

Clearly Proust offers the most extensive and complex depiction of male homosexuality in modernist literary fiction. No other novelist has described its range of situations or has given such a discursive analysis of its various aspects. Other canonic writers, including André Gide, Jean Cocteau, and (later) Jean Genet, have treated various aspects of male homosexuality in their writing, but no one comes close to Proust's tour-de-force of the signs, discourses, and semiotics of homosexuality. This chapter will be devoted to two matters: the figures of homoeroticism in André Gide's groundbreaking work *L'Immoraliste* and the constellation of figures of homosexuality as expressed by Jean Cocteau in key parts of his works.

There is no single, unified, and noncontradictory view of male homosexuality in any of these authors' works or, a fortiori, among their works. Rather, the various statements, situations, discourses, uses of rhetoric, and enunciative structures bring to life a discursive field and an evolving image of homosexuality through which certain statements can be made and against which male homosexuality can and will be articulated. Proust might, for example, have recognized Cocteau as a kindred spirit, for to some extent they shared an aesthetic vision of what male homosexuality might be, but Cocteau's idealization of younger male beauty is also somewhat consonant with Gide's ephebophilia.[1] As is well known, moreover, Gide was not at all pleased with what he perceived as Proust's reduction of homosexuality to inversion, and he criticizes Proust in a famous footnote to *Corydon,* a book in which he proposes classical pederasty as the model of choice, a model repeated in the post-Proustian novel *Les Faux-Monnayeurs:* "Some books—those of Proust in particular—have accustomed the public to set less enraged and to dare to consider with *sang-froid* what it tried to ignore or preferred to ignore at first. [. . .] [Proust's work considers] only certain cases of homosexuality, those with which I precisely do not deal in this book: cases of inversion, effeminacy, and sodomy" (*Corydon* 8). In a very complicated scenario, moreover, Gide refused to publish *Du côté de Chez Swann* when it was first proposed; the refusal came in 1912, the year after *Corydon* had been privately printed. He later regretted his decision and recommended publication of the remaining volumes of the *Recherche,* even if, in *Les Faux-Monnayeurs,* his writing seems pre-Proustian in its classicism and in its many attempts to maintain a kind of objectivity seldom seen in Proust. Although these authors' approaches to describing, narrating, and treating male homosexuality can never be fully reconciled with one another, they coexist in the discourses of the era and especially in the patrimony that we have inherited from those literary inscriptions of homosexuality.

What interests me here relates to my earlier comments on gaydar as it appears in Proust's passage where the narrator describes Saint-Loup and Charlus and their individual interactions with Marcel. In specific, the matter relates to what the Proustian narrator cannot say: he cannot truly describe male beauty from the point of view of a male admirer, for there can be no suspicion that the narrator might have a homosexual penchant. Saint-Loup may be elegant and handsome; one of Proust's talents as a novelist is that he is able to suggest Saint-Loup's elegance, handsomeness, and attractiveness to women without letting the text consciously move toward homoeroticism. Thus are the descriptions mediated through various safe gazes. Later, presenting Morel through Charlus's eyes or through a sympathetic reading of Charlus's position, the narrator can again allude to the attractiveness the older man might perceive in the younger. It is safe, too, to present the somewhat portly, middle-aged Charlus, for there would be no suspicion of homoeroticism in that description. What Proust cannot have his narrator do, however, is establish an unmediated discourse on male beauty, for that would tilt the narrator toward an uninscribable homoerotic gaze. Indeed, Proust's famous remark to Gide, recorded in Gide's *Journal* (1:1124), sums this up: "You can tell anything, he exclaims; but provided that you never say 'I.'" Proust says "I" and says everything except that one thing that might conflate the real I and the fictional one. As early as *L'Immoraliste* Gide says "I" in a confessional mode but manages to say what Proust cannot. And later, in works such as *Si le grain ne meurt,* Gide will say "I" in the hope that the reader will understand that there is no difference between the writer and the real individual saying "I."

I take pains to distinguish between the homoerotic and the homosexual here, for *L'Immoraliste* is not about homosexuality, even though, as Naomi Segal remarks, "homosexual desire is not absent but repressed to about an inch beneath the surface, from where it shapes everything in the text" (169–70).[2] The story is rather simple: Michel, confessing to his friends, tells of his voyage toward understanding himself, his marriage, his trip to North Africa, his discovery of his interest in adolescents, his wife's death, and his return to life in North Africa. Nothing untoward happens; there is no sexual contact between Michel and another male. Rather, using an old-fashioned term that is tinged with medical and psychiatric overtones, one could say that Michel is a "latent homosexual" or that the confession is an inscription of latent homosexuality. Latent homosexuality would remain an unconscious and preconscious structure that produces symptoms, such as (to be stereotypical) "sissy" behavior or an interest in matters presumed to be of interest only to gay men, without the latent homosexual's ever being conscious of same-sex desires or acting on that desire.

As early as *L'Immoraliste* André Gide can and does do what Proust cannot, and he does so by filtering the appreciation of male beauty through the confession of a seemingly latent homosexual.[3] He could not do this without taking some precautions, because it was not clear how a direct exposition of homoeroticism would be received. These precautions start with Gide's own preface, written so as to distance the author from the narrative while insisting on the inevitability that such a narrative occur, despite the most inhospitable conditions: "I am giving this book for what it is worth. It is a fruit full of bitter ash; it is like the colocynths of the desert that grow in sun-baked [calcinés] spots and present one's thirst only a more atrocious burn, but are not without beauty on the golden sand" (*Romans* 367). Long before the botanical imagery of *Corydon,* Gide offers a complicated image of the colocynth, a fruit-bearing vine that manages to thrive in hostile, difficult environments. So the first aspect to notice about this growth is that despite a perceived metaphoric hostility, this fruit/flower must come out. No amount of hostility will prevent it from emerging, and doing so, it turns out to be something beautiful.

Gide indicates that the fruit (otherwise known as the bitter apple) will not slake the thirst of the traveler who discovers it, and we thus might take what will eventually be known as a kind of innocent—or not so innocent—

flirting with homoeroticism to be be an ersatz love. This is partly correct, but the trope is also a way for Gide to make a comfortable, rhetorical move, for he is suggesting that this homoeroticism is situational: if, for one reason or another, heterosexuality is not working, then, given that things need to come out one way or another, homoeroticism might be a solution. In implying that hypothesis, Gide is merely following the model of nineteenth-century medicine and public health: prostitution was evil yet necessary for protecting the bourgeois marriage and bourgeois women.

The real interest of these opening words lies in what Gide neglects to say, for the colocynth is a quite poisonous fruit that can nevertheless be used in small doses as a powerful cathartic. Tasting this fruit, which offers a burning sensation when one is trying to slake one's thirst, leads inevitably to a catharsis through a powerful purging of the bowels. The story must come out, as it is spewed from a body that drinks in through one orifice and expels through another. Although I would not characterize the homoeroticism that is infused throughout *L'Immoraliste* as being particularly oral or anal in nature, for homosexual congress is not the issue in this work, Gide nevertheless invokes one and represses the other in this initial phrase.[4]

Entering the fictional frame provides a second safety net for the confession that follows. Gide offers four interlocutors for Michel, three who visit him in a group and the fourth, the brother of one of the listeners, to whom the transcription of the monologue is addressed. The three interlocutors present show sympathy, understanding, and signs of friendship, in direct opposition to the hostile environment evoked in the author's preface, where he distances himself from Michel: "some wanted to confuse me with him" (*Romans* 367). The interlocutors, however, can get close to him without being confused with him; his homoeroticism will not be infectious: "We remain with Michel; we do not want to leave him; you will understand if you are willing to read these pages; it is thus here, where he lives, that we await your answer; don't dally" (369).[5] The message is clear: one can confess to one's friends, who will be supportive and understanding and who will be loyal to a member of their class. Indeed, the transcriber tells his highly placed brother—the "President of the Council" (369)—that they must find Michel a position in service to the state, which Bersani somewhat theatrically translates into, "Should a homosexual be a good citizen?" (113). We should remember that even though these pages precede the confession offered by Michel, they are logically and chronologically situated after it. Thus the transcriber has heard what Michel has said, and yet he still seeks a normal position for him, one in service to the state.[6]

What is not clear, however, is how these pages relate to the final pages of the tale, in which, having returned to Biskra, Michel indicates that he seeks to remain where he is, that he wants to get rid of what remains of his fortune, and that he has strayed well beyond the bounds of bourgeois, moral heterosexuality. Perhaps he has not yet had sex with another male (we can never be sure), but he has caressed Ali, kissed an Italian coachman, and made numerous remarks about the beauty of the adolescents and boys who have come into view. So the recommendation that a position be found for Michel is made in full knowledge of Michel's actions and somewhat egregious behavior. Beyond that, however, the logical order is not clear. Does the interlocutor want to remoralize Michel by putting him in service to the state and thereby making him an upstanding, straight citizen again? In that case, the immorality will have been an episode easily corrected by what we might quickly call a Protestant work ethic. Or does the interlocutor fully expect that Michel will continue his immorality once back in France and that this is all right as well? The interlocutor is careful not to pronounce judgment; Gide is careful to leave the ambiguity.

That ambiguity coupled with this double frame is what allows the exposition of homoeroticism to take place. From our perspective at the beginning of the twenty-first century, it little matters that the homoeroticism is tame and that the latency is inconsequential. Nor does it matter that as early as 1943, in his analysis of the third form of bad faith discussed in *L'Etre et le néant,* Jean-Paul Sartre seems to be criticizing this confessional mode. Troped under a rhetoric of sincerity, Sartre's model is of a gay man confessing his homosexuality to his straight friend, who then accepts the homosexuality of the former. For Sartre, both men are acting in bad faith: the gay man in thinking he needs to confess and to be pardoned and the straight man in believing that he has the power to pardon the (im)morality of the other (*L'Etre* 100–104). In the face of all this anachronism—Proust is profoundly more of our times than Gide is—what is important is that Gide introduces, through his framing, the possibilities of discourses about male beauty, innocent same-sex flirting (which is distinct from Charlus's aggressive cruising), and latency.

Michel's narrative actually starts under the aegis and within the structures of heterosexuality, and specifically with the blessings of normative heterosexuality: "The last time we saw one another, it was, as I remember it, near Angers, in the little country church where I was being married" (*Romans* 372). This powerful opening phrase establishes the standard against which the rest of Michel's confession will be set. It develops both a ritual and an observation of that ritual by the current interlocutors. Michel is inserted into the heterosexual structure as if it were compulsory. We quickly learn that this is not a romantic marriage, for it is not based on love: "I said that I did not love her at all—at least I felt nothing of what is called love for her, but I loved her, if you want to understand that as tenderness, a kind of pity, great esteem" (373). Not all marriages need be based on some sort of romantic love, of course, but this is *also* not the traditional bourgeois notion of a marriage based on uniting the two spouses' worldly goods. Michel is rich—although he does not know how rich until the day of his marriage—and he does not need any dowry from his future wife; in fact, she brings very little (374). Rather, the marriage occurs to please Michel's dying father, who is concerned about Michel's being left alone (372). As Michel hastens to add, moreover, at least he had never loved another woman (373). What he does not yet say is that he also has not yet loved any member of the male sex, but this will soon become apparent, and he will love a boy long before he loves his wife.

The structures of paternity and those of church and state—a civil marriage is obviously implicit—mark the space in which Michel, emotionally, psychologically, and physically a virgin, is placed. And there is an implicit recognition that only form need be observed. Again, although one imagines a kind of modesty in the newlyweds, more remarkable is the way in which the hollow structures and empty forms are there for others: "The very evening of our wedding, we slept in my Paris apartment, where two bedrooms had been prepared for us" (*Romans* 374). We do not know whether the orders have been given for two separate rooms. We do know that this continues to fulfill the model already laid out, that this will be a sign of conformity perhaps bereft of any content of conformity; it may be mere hollow convention. To use Apter's felicitous phrase, this is "a grotesque travesty of a conventional wedding night" (114); this is a honeymoon in drag. There are no shivarees here and no blood-stained sheets. Even when Michel and Marceline are on the boat from Marseille to Tunis, when the "marriage really began" (Gide, *Romans* 376), this is merely a recognition of a developing emotional bond, not a physical one. Gide not only insists on Michel's physical separation by indicating separate beds and, more important, by marking Michel's bed as his, not theirs, during his illness; in addition, the marriage is not physically consummated until after their stay in Africa: after Michel's encounters with the various young men, after Michel's discovery of his body, after he has shaved, and after the struggle with the drunken coachman. It is only when all these transformations have occurred—when he has become himself and unconsciously assumed his homoeroticism—that he can actually play a heterosexual: "It was that night that I possessed Marceline" (405). Again, it is a kind of drag show in reverse: the nonheterosexual can now play the role of a heterosexual.

Whereas the structures proffered by what could be called the patriarchal order—the father, the church, and the state—produce the conservative conformity of what looks like a reproduction of that order in the marriage of Michel and Marceline, it is ironically the result of that conformity, Marceline's being with him, that introduces the homoerotic. Although this might seem strange to some, heterosexuality does not fully become itself until it occurs as an event. The space in which homoeroticism is about to occur does not consist in the transgression of heterosexual rules but is instead nonheterosexual in nature, what we would now call a queer space.[7] And it is in this space that Marceline comes to procure for her husband in name only, for it is she who, without any necessary consciousness of what she is doing, introduces the object of homoerotic desire; it is as if she telepathically shares Michel's latent homosexuality: "'I am bringing you a friend,' she said; and I saw a little, dark-complected Arab enter behind her. His name is Bachir and he has large, silent eyes that look at me. . . . I notice that he is completely nude under his thin white gandoura and his patched burnoose" (*Romans* 381).

No sooner has Bachir been brought near the slowly recuperating Michel than the latter immediately focuses on the nudity of the body he sees before him. The remark about nudity is seemingly unexpected, yet it is the only logical and appropriate remark in this queer space. Certainly the nudity can be read in a variety of ways. For example, it can be seen as a sign of innocence or of poverty, the latter reinforced by the fact that the burnoose has been patched. This perceived innocence and the object's economic modesty are among the first instances in Gide's writing, whether fiction, autofiction, or autobiography, of an attraction to an object of desire precisely because of those qualities. Gide's objects of desire are organized through a colonial sexual tourism, as I have indicated elsewhere (*Alcibiades* 113–30). Beyond that, the presence of the word *completely* is key here: Bachir is completely nude. Without saying it, Michel has seen everything, has remarked the young man's private parts, and has, perhaps for the first time in his life, espied a circumcised penis.

This remark might seem an extreme overreading were it not for remarks a few lines later, as if there were a Freudian displacement through language from what cannot be said or seen to what can be mentioned: "His hair is shaved in the Arab style; he is wearing a poor fez [chéchia] which has only a hole where the tassel [gland] would be. The gandoura, having slipped a bit, shows his cute shoulder" (Gide, *Romans* 382).[8] The fez is missing its tassel, having only a hole in its stead. Significantly, however, the French word for the glans, the head of the penis, is also *gland.* Michel has just looked through a hole in Bachir's clothing—Barthes would have said a gape—and seen Bachir's *gland* and his hole(s). That language is displaced to his head, to other hair, to another *gland,* and to another hole. Michel fully possesses Bachir and caresses him or even rapes him with his eyes as he immediately recognizes his attraction to the boy and uses a language that he has not—and could not—use about his wife. Bachir's shoulder is cute, he says: we have left neutral language behind as Michel moves into an affective language that a straight man does not "normally" use when talking about another man, except perhaps in a parody with well-marked distancing quotation marks, even in spoken language. Nor would he, as a straight man, feel compelled to touch the "cute shoulder" were he in full heterosexuality: "I need to touch it. I lean over; he turns around and smiles at me" (382).

The basic structure of Gidean homoerotic attraction is already in place. The envisioned nudity of the body of the desired other is a natural, unfettered beauty—which will be repeated by Cocteau in *Le Livre blanc*—and it is completely unself-conscious. The nudity is reinforced by a set of references to the falling apart and falling away of clothing: the burnoose has been patched, the fez has a hole, and the gandoura gapes to reveal flesh or droops to reveal a shoulder. Thus nudity is complemented by the movement toward the natural, the removal of that which civilization has added to the purity of nature. All this appears in one of the most famous passages from *Si le grain ne meurt:*

> He did not spend too much time with the complicated knots of the laces that served him as a belt; taking a little dagger out of his pocket, he cut through the mess with one movement. His clothing fell, he threw his jacket far from him, and he stood [se dressa] there naked like a god. For an instant he raised his thin arms skyward, then, while laughing, let himself fall against me. His body was perhaps on fire, but seemed as refreshing as the shade to me. How beautiful was the sand. In the adorable splendor of the evening, in what rays was my joy clad. (Gide, *Souvenirs* 279–80)

Thus does Ali become the anticolocynth, the refreshing oasis in the desert, the means by which the whole truth of what happened in the desert is finally told. As with the colocynth, there is a purgative effect, but in *Si le grain ne meurt* the effect is to purify the system and make Gide—if not his fictional Michel—healthy by finally telling the whole story.

In *L'Immoraliste,* however, we are not yet there, and that beauty and nature are almost immediately displaced into a nonerotic form, even as Michel silently reeroticizes it: "The next day Bachir came back. He sat as before, took out his knife, wanted to whittle some wood that was too hard, and managed to stick the blade in his thumb. I shuddered in horror; he laughed about it, showed the brilliant cut, and was amused to see his blood flow. When he laughed, he showed very white teeth; he licked his wound with pleasure; his tongue was pink like a cat's. Oh, how healthy he was! It was that to which I took a fancy in him: his health. The health of that little body was beautiful" (*Romans* 382). In a double move that Gide will repeat in *Les Caves du Vatican,* although without the unconscious element noted here, Gide marks the parts of the body, fetishizing the piercing of the body or the homoeroticized body of the other and penetrating the body with a knife. In *Les Caves du Vatican,* with no audience but the invisible narrator and the observing, prurient readers, Lafcadio sticks a small blade into his thigh several times as a punishment for having had his life penetrated. Here Bachir remains innocent of Lafcadio's queerness, but the scenario is the same. Gide has the erotic other penetrated by his own hand, just as the words used to describe him mark the flesh and just as Michel would wish to penetrate him. Because this cannot be said, however—for we have moved quickly from presumed heterosexuality to scopophilic homoeroticism—the eroticism is replaced with health, which Bersani (119) strangely seems to take at face value. Nevertheless, that health is immediately considered "beautiful"; it is remarked as erotic, just as the shoulder was "cute" and just as the voice will be exquisite: "'Sick?' he said kindly; the tone of his voice was exquisite. Marceline returned" (Gide, *Romans* 383). It is certainly not a question of health.

For the homoerotic gaze to continue, the other must be a surface or set of surfaces. Or rather, the other must not demonstrate a subjectivity different from his body: "However pleasant Bachir appeared to me, I knew him too well now, and I was happy to change" (*Romans* 389). Bachir becomes less interesting and less appealing homoerotically as he becomes more familiar. The word *appeared* is accurate here: the homoerotic attraction depends absolutely on appearance, and as soon as some depth interferes with surface appearance, the attraction is diminished, precisely because the other is manifesting a subjectivity that Michel and the Gidean persona in general do not want to see in the other. The rest of the stay in Africa is thus marked by a series of adolescents: "a tall fourteen-year-old boy, black as a Sudanese" (389); a twelve-year-old shepherd named Lassif, who is "almost naked" and "handsome" (392); Lassif's elder brother, Lachmi, who is less handsome (393); and of course Moktir, who is handsome (394) and who steals Marceline's scissors as Michel complicitously looks on (393–94), a complicity to which I will return.

Even Michel will attempt to make himself into an object of his own homoerotic glances as he tries to convert his own body into that set of surfaces: "I shall speak at length of my body. I shall speak about it so much, that it will at first seem to you that I am forgetting the role of the mind" (*Romans* 386). Becoming healthy means constructing the self based on the model of the other, rejecting his own past, the life of the mind, and shaving his beard (402–3) so that he can find his own smooth skin, so that he too can be "shaved in the Arab style." Aside from revealing what had been hidden, being beardless is also a way of imitating the beardless adolescents Michel admires. He is becoming one of them as he discovers, to be trite, the adolescent within whom he had abandoned: "And I compared myself to palimpsests; I tasted the joy of the researcher, who, under more recent writings, discovers, on the same paper, a very ancient text that is infinitely more valuable. What was this hidden text? To read it, was it not first necessary to erase the recent texts?" (399).

While the image of the palimpsest is obviously a fascinating one within a literary work, for my purposes I will focus not on the "textuality," which would have been the object of study during the heyday of critical theory in the 1970s, but on the opposition that distinguishes Michel from his objects of homoerotic attraction. The boys are interesting to the extent that they are beautiful, handsome, or good-looking. Once there is the manifestation of a singularity, they are less interesting. They are attractive as well to the extent that they show the natural or the instinctive, as when Moktir steals the scissors and steals Michel's heart in the process. But Michel can never fully go back to the natural; there is no complete turning back no matter how hard he tries. Even if he tries, his skin can not be white or tanned, for it is discolored (*Romans* 401). Civilization has used and abused him. The only way to free himself from it is to go beyond it and recognize that in feigning, faking, or lying, he can imitate the natural position but never return to it. This, then, is the sense of the palimpsest: once there is writing, there will always be writing; one can never return to innocent illiteracy or a blank sheet of paper or parchment. Thus can Michel feign reading while watching Moktir's theft; thus can he lie to Marceline, telling her some made-up story—a "fable" (395)—to explain the fact that the scissors are missing.

The recognition of this impossibility will take a while to develop, and Michel seems to believe that he can renew himself by changing his outward appearances and behavior. On returning to Europe, as I have already indicated, Michel shaves his beard and has heterosexual relations. The reader, after having thought about the episode of the theft and seen that this theft is essentially the last act in Africa, recognizes that a change is occurring. Immediately thereafter Michel indicates that their African stay is coming to an end. How can Michel explore his own liberation if acts such as shaving or heterosexual intercourse will not fundamentally help? He can and does reinscribe the "instinctive" theft in the realm of the civilized, and he chooses to flout the law as the newly marked position of homoerotic desire.

The next real instance of homoeroticism interrupts what appears to be a return to a life of conservative, traditional, bourgeois behavior that is modified by these seeming acts of liberation, which are anything but that. Like so many other moments in Gide's writing, the event seems to develop naturally from a set of circumstances. Here it comes from that resumption of Michel's previous life: he takes up his work as a historian again and gravitates toward the sixth-century Goths. Yet there is one figure in particular who seems to draw his attention: "But, I shall confess it, the figure of the young king Athalaric was what attracted me the most. I imagined that fifteen-year-old child, secretly [sourdement] excited by the Goths, rebel against his mother Amalasuntha, balk at his Latin education, reject culture as a whole horse does a bothersome harness, and, preferring the society of the uncivilized Goths to that of the too wise and old Cassiodorus, taste for several years, with uncouth favorites his own age, a violent, voluptuous, and unbridled life, to die at the age of eighteen, completely spoiled, drunk with debauch" (*Romans* 407). Opening with a confession, Michel therefore repeats the structuring rhetoric of the beginning of the work. At the linguistic level Gide extensively uses verbs that repeat, react, or undo. That conscious stylistic move makes it clear that a return to innocence is not possible and that the only possibility for someone like Michel is to revolt against the harness of civilization by going beyond it. Yet it is not clear whether Michel learns the lesson of what he confesses here or even whether he recognizes this to be the solution to his dilemma. Arguably it is a pact made between Gide and his rhetorical readers without the character(s) recognizing the construction of a new kind of homoeroticism. This homoerotic figure, rather than being that of the innocent, pure, native adolescent, will appear in a modern incarnation in the character of Charles, the son of the Normandy groundskeeper Bocage. Through Michel's visions and behavior, Gide develops Charles as one possibility for a healthy, modern homoerotic subject.

Gide carefully structures a Rousseau-influenced universe on the property in Normandy but fully marks it as space where civilized humankind constructs and controls nature. Unlike the desert, the wadis, and the general environmental situation, all encoded as natural, nature is marked here as controllable through knowledge and technology, as in the draining and repairing (*Romans* 412) of a pond. Whereas the relation to nature in North Africa has been direct or pastoral, here in Normandy it is mitigated by a hierarchy, an order, and a technological and social structure. Instead of a herd of goats (392) or even several peasants whose shirts are unbuttoned [quelques paysans débraillés] (401), placing them somewhere between the pure boys who are naked even when they are wearing clothing and the clad people of the civilized world, in Normandy there are anonymous, nondescript workers. This forms the background of codified civilization against which Gide sets the new object of homoerotic desire, Charles: "He was a handsome strapping man [gaillard], so rich in health, so flexible, so well built that the awful city clothes he had put on in our honor did not make him too ridiculous; his timidity hardly added to his beautiful natural flush. He seemed to be only fifteen years old, so much had the clarity of his look remained child-like; he expressed himself clearly, without false shame, and, unlike his father, he did not speak in order to say nothing" (412).

Charles is obviously not fully citified and retains some of the allure of purity that Michel tends to seek in others. His natural health shines through, despite all the trappings of civilization and its orders. At the same time, he is nothing like the adolescents whom Michel has encountered in North Africa. Instead of being completely at one with nature, Charles has the possibility of a kind of atavistic return and can alternate between two positions. Moreover, that health and the possibility of return mark even his chronological age: although he is seventeen years old, he looks younger. He also lacks the corruption and decadence of false language, the possession of which would be an unpardonable fault according to the Gidean concept of sincerity: language and truth are intertwined for Gide in the essentialized and essentialist world in which his good characters must reside.[9]

Once the Arab boys manifest their subjectivity rather than their beauty, they become less interesting, but the case for Charles is different: the manifestation of his subjectivity makes him more interesting. He becomes a teacher, helping Michel learn about his estate, a metaphor for Michel's body. Charles teaches Michel a model for a return to nature after the corruption of civilization: Charles "suddenly removed his shoes and socks, put down his jacket and his vest, then pulling up his pants and shirt sleeves very high, entered the mud resolutely. I immediately imitated him" (*Romans* 413). Let us leave aside the all too obvious symbolism of a return to nature through a return to the primordial mud. Far more important to recognize is that in imitating Charles, Michel is following him and following his lead as well. The more he can be like Charles, the closer he can get to him. Distance melts into a proximity to the desired or desirable other: "I soon called him to help me encircle a big eel; we united our hands to capture it . . . Then, after that one, there was another; the mud splashed our faces; sometimes in sinking in suddenly, with the water rising to our thighs, we were soon completely soaked. In the ardor of the game, we exchanged but a few yells and sentences; but at the end of the day, I realized that I was saying 'tu' to Charles, without really knowing when I had begun to do that" (413). Much like the tryworks scene in Melville's *Moby-Dick,* Gide's description is filled with homoerotic overtones. The two male characters join hands to encircle what can be described as an phallic object par excellence. Seeking to trap the eel, they become ever more excited, alternating language and yells. They are covered in a gooey liquid, and at the end of the process, in what Gide calls "the ardor of the game," Michel realizes that he has used the familiar *tu* with the younger man. In fact, between eeling and poaching on his own land understood as his body (447–48), is Michel not becoming intimate with himself in repeated acts of what amounts to masturbating himself as he is also masturbated by the other?[10]

The Gidean construction of the homoerotic implies a kind of ecstasy in the action of bonding. Michel loses his conscious self and his self-repressive functions—the superego or the name of the father—as he slips into this event. The physical limning of this homoerotic act onto sex itself is, as before with the discussion of the *gland,* readily apparent. Here, however, the displacement is itself by contiguity. As long as the two can complicitously focus on an exterior/external object, anything can happen. It is only when there is no third to mediate that there is a displacement. We cannot be sure whether Michel is supposed to be aware of this distinction; I believe he is not, and perhaps even Gide himself does not fully recognize it as he constructs this work. After all, Gide is basically constructing a vocabulary of homoeroticism as he goes and, it is not always a coherent and consciously structured discourse. At a point such as this Gide is consciously or unconsciously looking backward toward a heavily Protestant-influence literature, of which *Moby-Dick* and other Anglo-American novels are the best examples. Perhaps more important, he is also looking away from French literature and the characters of Vautrin and Lucien de Rubempré, for example.

The episode with Ménalque adds nothing to the structures and images of homoeroticism proposed or invented by Gide in *L'Immoraliste,* although that character presents a sense of existential openness that has not yet been seen in *L'Immoraliste,* as well as the possibility of standing out against society, marching to a different drummer, or simply provoking bourgeois outrage by one's behavior. In this work Gide offers only three more scenes in which he further articulates homoeroticism. The first is set on the farm in Normandy, when Michel is captivated by the beauty of one of the workers: "One attracted me: he was rather handsome, tall, not stupid, but solely led by instinct; he never did anything that was not sudden, and he gave in to every passing impulse. . . . One night I went furtively to see him in the barn; he was sprawled in the hay; he was sleeping a thick, drunken sleep. How much time I spent watching him!" (*Romans* 442). Perhaps ironically, there is no really new element in this object of desire, for the worker combines the beauty of the Arab boys with the implicit strength of Charles. In addition, the negative qualities of impulsiveness and drunkenness fall in the same category as Moktir's theft of the scissors: there is no relation in this work between inner and outer beauty, and a character need not exhibit moral values to be considered attractive. Gide thus lays the groundwork for certain characters by Cocteau, such as Dargelos, the fallen angel; in essence, Gide predicts the entire output of Jean Genet.

The new element here is the admission of attraction, a strong word that goes beyond simple homoeroticism or even latent homosexuality. Even if not acted on, this attraction is a move toward a phantasm of nonlatent homosexuality. Michel never specifies the possible results of that attraction, nor would we expect him to do so. Nonetheless, it is difficult for his listeners and the readers not to see the shift from homoeroticism to homosexual desire—that is, the move from latent homosexuality, which was classically considered to be unconscious or preconscious behavior, to Michel's recognition of his homosexual desire. Another novel element is the way in which that desire plays out: not acted on, the desire is turned into a voyeuristic gaze that lasts quite a while. Even if he does not say what thoughts are crossing his mind as he looks on the sleeping worker, he recognizes that he is gazing for quite some time and that he is lost in a kind of rapture or sensuousness.

The scene of Michel complicitously poaching on his own land (*Romans* 447–48) is duly famous, but it is little more than a reinscription of the scene with Charles at the pond, even to the extent that both involve a removal of animal life for the purpose of eating. The only difference is that whereas the first scene is a constructive one whose values are predicated on repair and legality, this one inverts the values because the law is undermined. The construction that Gide offers thus repeats both the scene with the scissors and the scene just discussed. All this introduces modification in the consciousness of self and in a rejection of projecting such behavior only into the past: "Now, if young Athalaric himself could rise up from his tomb to talk to me, I would no longer listen to the past" (457). Flouting the law can occur in the present, at least here and now in *L'Immoraliste,* although Gide will, in *Corydon,* for example, try to capture the past of history and science as a justification for the present. In *Corydon* there is no break between past and present, for the former is recuperated for the latter. In *L'Immoraliste* the situation is not so fluid: the past must be distinct from the present, and when the element of rebellion occurs in the present, it does so at the price of losing the past.

We should not expect Gide or Proust to give us explicit descriptions of the male body or specific descriptions of homosexual sex. In the famous scene in the male brothel Proust devotes some attention to the whipping that Charlus receives, but the description is anything but graphic. Except for allowing one explicit line (discussed later), Gide tends to restrict himself to recognizing male beauty and vaguely alluding to what might happen. In *L'Immoraliste* Gide offers one additional element that he does not develop at length: a quick flirtation. Gide does not develop any of the vocabulary of homoeroticism, for to do so would force Michel to recognize what he usually does not see. Had this been a third-person narrative, matters could have been developed; at the same time, that would have lost the narrative's confessional nature.

Just as Michel possessed Marceline for the first time during their initial trip to Italy, he now bridges the physical gap between himself and the other in yet another trip there: "I had stood up in the car to speak with the coachman. He was a short Sicilian from Catania, handsome as a line from Theocritus, splendid, sweet-smelling, tasty [éclatant, odorant, savoureux] as a fruit. 'Com'è bella la Signora!,' he said in a charming voice, as he watched Marceline become more distant. 'Anche tu sei bello, ragazzo,' I answered. And as I had leaned over, I couldn't hold myself back, and soon, pulling him next to me, I kissed him. He permitted it, while laughing. 'I Francesi sono tutti amanti,' he said. 'Ma non tutti gli Italiani amati,' I replied, laughing as well . . . I looked for him the following days but never managed to see him again" (*Romans* 462). Many of the other elements remain the same as well: the innocence and natural way of the other, the attraction that is both emotional and physical for Michel, with the emotional attraction complemented by a literal physical pull and the impossibility of self-control. What is added here, in this quick moment, is the insistence on the innocence of the act, as both participants laugh about it. The coachman's remark ("all the French are lovers"), along with Michel's reply ("But not all Italians are beloved"), indicates that innocence but also implies a discourse of sexual tourism. Given that Gide himself participated in a kind of sexual tourism and that Michel implicitly participates in a kind of voyeuristic sexual tourism, this exchange remarks a common knowledge: Northern European men travel south for sex that is frowned on—if not actually illegal—in their world.

What has Gide wrought in *L'Immoraliste?* Earlier than Proust's massive textualization of male homosexuality and earlier than Thomas Mann's association of such behavior with sickliness in "Death in Venice," to be written in 1911 and published the next year, Gide offers a beginning vocabulary and semantics for homoerotic encounters. Even though it bears a confessional aspect that will be quietly rejected in French discourses but retained in the Anglo-American world, Gide underlines the naturalness of such behavior. By focusing on a few encounters and by framing the tale with a discourse of acceptance, Gide offers, perhaps to himself alone, years before *Corydon* and *Si le grain ne meurt,* a language in which he can articulate "the love that dare not speak its name." Elements particularly central to his concept of homosexuality, including sexual tourism and the differences implicated in classical pederasty, are also already in evidence. As I have shown, Gide's version of pederasty can be based on chronological difference, social difference, ethnic difference, or some combination thereof, but that difference is necessary and essential to the Gidean universe, something that will not be the case for Proust, Cocteau, or Genet and will be rejected wholesale in the arguments of queer theory a century later.

One final note. In 2002 Gallimard brought out a previously unpublished, very short story that Catherine Gide had discovered in her father's papers. The edition included a foreword by her, a preface by Jean-Claude Perrier, and a very well documented afterword by David H. Walker. Written in 1907, the autobiographical tale itself runs a little over ten pages and relates a one-night stand between Gide and a young man named Ferdinand. It has all the elements of *L'Immoraliste,* although it entirely eschews the confessional mode and is fully explicit. In this work, situated between the latency and homoeroticism of the earlier work and the apology that will be *Corydon,* Gide lyrically describes a sexual encounter. What he adds, however, is an explicit remark:

> His tanned skin was soft and burning and I covered it with kisses. For an instant, he could be mistaken; completely amused: "That's it; we're going to give one another b[low] j[obs]," he said. From his tone that was a bit trem-

> bling, I was persuaded that he said that to swagger [crâner], not out of "vice," but out of shame for his innocence and will to go through with it. "Have you ever done that?" I asked him. "No, never. But I've been told what it is." I held him back in his gesture, little given to vice myself and loath to ruin through some awful excess the memory that this night would leave in both of us. (*Le Ramier* 30)

A passage with no consequence, for it remained unpublished until almost a century after it was written, and no one would bat an eye at publishing something so explicit nowadays. Nevertheless, it is intriguing to think what might have happened to the discourses of homosexuality after 1907 had Gide somehow published it at the time. It is something that we shall never know.

Astonish Me

One Paris night in 1910 three men were walking across the Place de la Concorde after a late supper. Walking ahead of the other two was Vaslav Nijinsky, who was then considered the greatest male ballet dancer in the world and whose name would eventually come to symbolize ballet. Behind him was his lover, Sergey Diaghilev, the director and motive force behind the incredibly influential Ballets Russes, a troupe of dancers from Imperial Russia whose mastery of classical technique set the dance world on fire. With him was a twenty-one-year-old Parisian, a jack-of-all-arts named Jean Cocteau. As Cocteau recounts the event in *La Difficulté d'être*, the mood was rather quiet, with Nijinsky brooding, as was his wont, and Diaghilev both bemused and restrained (Cocteau, *Romans* 880). "Accustomed to praise" and perhaps hurt by its absence, Cocteau questioned Diaghilev about his reserve. Diaghilev stopped, and out of the blue he gave Cocteau a command: "Astonish me."

Cocteau was taken aback, in part because he had never thought of the idea of surprise, which, although "enchanting in Apollinaire" (*Romans* 880), was not part of Cocteau's bag of tricks, for he was then still caught up in aestheticism and a sense of measure. What Cocteau means is the idea of calculated surprise, a surprise not to the artist but to his audience. So Cocteau revised his whole approach to his art and to himself as artist. He was willing to build in surprise and astonishment, in somewhat of a calculated fashion, although he continued to take great pains to indicate that some of the surprises in his work are surprises to him, too. Cocteau set to work, and with *Parade*, which premiered in 1917, he accomplished what he had been ordered to do: "I astonished him" (880).

I have taken this version of the anecdote from the relatively late work *La Difficulté d'être,* written between 1945 and 1947, but other versions would have served just as well. I have chosen this one in part because I will return to this volume in the last part of this chapter. The volume is key to understanding the figures of homosexuality in Cocteau's work, because, as I will make clearer in what follows, it marks a certain end of productivity with the completion of the film *La Belle et la bête.* Although I will not read Cocteau's works chronologically here, some of them may be assigned to an initial period that includes *Parade* and novels such as *Le Grand Écart, Potomak,* and his great early masterpiece *Thomas l'imposteur.* This period coincides with his exploration of various media and the love affair, perhaps the most important of his life, with Raymond Radiguet.[11] Several years later, after Radiguet's untimely death at the age of twenty in 1923, Cocteau entered what would be the most feverish and important period in his artistic production, a five-year stretch that saw him write various important works and create his first film. *Le Difficulté d'être* corresponds to another important creative moment: it comes between *La Belle et la bête* and *Orphée,* arguably his two greatest and most accomplished films.

Choosing one version of an anecdote is always an arbitrary act when reading Cocteau, for like Gide, he tends to repeat certain incidents, phrases, and events that in part form his public mythology. The Diaghilev story comes back a number of times, as does his reflection on his famous line "I am the lie that tells the truth [Je suis le mensonge qui dit le vérité]" first appearing in *Opéra* but oft-repeated and even used as an epigraph. When Cocteau is concerned with a character who is part of his personal mythology, he comes back time after time. Thus does Dargelos, a bad boy or would-be Lafcadio, return: he is in *Les Enfants terribles* and appears as well in the anonymous *Livre blanc* and *Opium.*

Cocteau's return, be it obsessive or calculated, to a nexus of "events" is a way of creating this mythology and reminding readers of his wittiness over the years. In this iteration, however, it is a way of being anything but astonishing. What if we were to read the situations anew, say what Cocteau does not say, and be reductive? For the lie that tells the truth could be, *pace* all the queer-studies critics in North America and its colonies, the most transparent door to a noncloset ever invented. Dargelos, the studly kouros-like boy with whom Paul is hopelessly smitten in *Les Enfants terribles,* is a homoerotic angel who is the stuff of gay adolescent and not so adolescent fantasy.

What if someone were reading that story from the outside, simply looking at the available information and reading with neither judgment nor guile?

What would he or she read? After a late supper, three gay men are walking across the Place de la Concorde and heading toward the Tuileries, a famous gay cruising ground.[12] The physical star of the group, a famous athlete long admired for his prowess and shocking exhibitionism, walks alone. His older lover, who is also his boss—for this is an unequal relationship, ripe for what the later twentieth century, in its charmingly eccentric manner, would come to call sexual harassment—is more taken this evening with the mind of another man, who seduces with his tongue and talent, if not his physical presence. Jaded, the eldest of the three seeks a new thrill and asks the budding artist to astonish him.

Reductive and perverse? Of course. But not wrong. For the stories that Cocteau tells and the anecdotes that he repeats about himself and his production always have a visible homosexual subtext right below the surface. This remark will come as no surprise to any reader of Cocteau or to anyone familiar with Cocteau's life; his well-publicized relationships with Raymond Radiguet, Jean Desbordes, Marcel Khill, Edouard Dhermitte, and Jean Marais are no secret. What is astonishing about Cocteau's personal life is the extent to which these relationships were out in the open and, perhaps even more amazing, how "normal" they seemed to be, how unneurotic they were, and how little is to be made of them. Cocteau is thus the totally normal gay man. Let us not be tempted to associate his drug use—opium being his drug of choice—with some badly lived homosexuality. Let us not force him into the straitjacket of compulsory homosexuality or heterosexuality; there were relationships at various points with women. Let us just say that this is a fairly uncomplicated, extremely sane, and well-lived homosexuality that provides little if any fodder for a neurotic symptomology of Cocteau's art.

To say this, however, is to deprive Cocteau neither of his figures of eternal return, be they Dargelos or Orpheus, whose returns are both intra- and extradiegetic, nor of his pet projects. To say it is rather to allow an unusual freedom to textuality wherein the poetry of homosexuality is not tempered by some superstructure. Proust and Gide construct homotextualities that are far more imbricated; Genet constructs a far different one, but at a price: the freedom to be Genet. Cocteau creates a poetics, but it is of so little interest to him and he has so little subjectively invested in it that the resistance—of the text and of interpretation to it—simply slides away.

Cocteau's art, for example, includes hundreds of erotic drawings, explosions of good humor and male homoeroticism in which the simply drawn lines speak volumes and in which the representation of male sexuality and homosexuality is done with abandon, freedom, and obvious joy. In Cocteau's entire œuvre there is perhaps only one sticking point, a decision, a caprice, and a blank all at once: the production and publication of what was to remain an anonymous work, the single piece that is specifically, overtly, and clearly about homosexuality, *Le Livre blanc.* It is Cocteau's one written work where the subtext becomes complicated by the fact that the work itself is about homosexuality and that it appears to be, from many aspects, a fictionalized autobiography.

The remainder of this subsection follows a straightforward trajectory, for I examine the three figures constitutive of Cocteau's inscription of homosexuality in his writing. I will not, however, say much about the effect of astonishment: the superficial, the camp, or the surface elegance that twentieth-century society decreed an acceptable mask for the gay man of letters, one that started with Wilde and his wit, that was epitomized in *The Importance of Being Earnest,* and that Wilde destroyed when he went looking for gay content rather than a gay gloss on life. It is a position seen in Cocteau's performance of self, as well as in writers such as Noel Coward—again, someone involved in several arts—or, in slight variants, in the archness of Clifton Webb and his performances (Edelman 201–8). Nor will I consider the drawings, and I will only tangentially discuss the films. What interests me here is the use of language to create a figurality and discursivity of male homosexuality.

Let me briefly contextualize *Les Enfants terribles* with other texts of its kind. One of the common topoi of early twentieth-century Western literature, although by no means limited to that time or place, is the homoerotic relation of two adolescents. The schoolboy crush, as it is often known, falls not on a person of the opposite sex but on one of the same gender, often someone perceived to incarnate true or ideal masculinity. The figure was especially prevalent in German literature: not only Robert Musil's *Young Törless* but also numerous works by Thomas Mann fit the bill, as does a work such as Hermann Hesse's *Demian.* The figure is more romantic in the sense of literary romanticism, and less romantic in the sense of erotic overtones, in American buddy works (think of Mark Twain), and it is more subtle and more perverse—because often inverted—in Henry James, whether in the rather explicit (for James) novella "The Pupil" or in a work such as *The Ambassadors,* which is strongly marked by an unenunciated latent homosexuality. Repeating it in a later incarnation and—for reasons of religion if not of state—in a revisionist mode, Evelyn Waugh, in *Brideshead Revisited,* has Cara, the worldly consort of Lord Marchmain, consider such relations a passing phase of a man's existence.

In *Les Enfants terribles* Cocteau sketches what seems to be another version of this homoerotic crush. He strikes out into new territory and casts the relations that this crush implies as something far from a passing fancy. Cocteau takes a classic mytheme relating to the wounds of love and gives it a homoerotic twist as he modernizes it. The initial presentation of Dargelos merits the readers' attention, not only because it serves as the initial impetus for the development of *Les Enfants terribles*, but also because it forms the kernel of Cocteau's future references to the character, most importantly in *Le Livre blanc*. In addition, to the extent that the figure of Dargelos comes to "symbolize" or serve as the archetypal figure of "homeros" for Cocteau, it is important to examine this presentation up close.

The narrative presents three characters in a staggered fashion, appearing out of a melee. The battle is a snowball fight undertaken by the adolescent students at "le petit Condorcet." The first character, Paul, appears initially as a questor and questioner: "Have you seen Dargelos?" (Cocteau, *Romans* 110). We do not yet know who is asking the question, nor do we know of whom he speaks. The answer comes from an adjuvant, helping both the interrogator and another: "Yes . . . no, I don't know" (110). Thus the presence of Dargelos is immediately cast into a phantom, flickering state of presence and absence, even if the answer's vagueness—not willful ambiguity—is due to the anonymous interlocutor's role as an adjuvant in the material world, for he is helping a wounded student seek shelter from the fracas of the battle: "The wounded student, a handkerchief around his knee, hopped away, grabbing on to shoulders" (110). The fact that the anonymous interlocutor lends a hand to a wounded comrade in a display of human kindness and sympathy in some measure guarantees his reliability as a witness: material and verbal reliability go hand in hand.

Before turning to this phantom or phantasmatic scenario for Dargelos, I will focus on the remainder of the scene preceding his appearance, for Cocteau introduces important elements in this passage, which might otherwise seem to be a banal episode serving only to present the beloved. The figure of the wounded student follows naturally from the snowball fight, but it also presages the congealing of various traits in the person of the lover, Paul. There are two components to this foreshadowing. The student has been wounded, something that will happen to Paul a page later, although the wound occurs to his leg, whereas Paul will be hit in the mouth. The leg wound and the consequent limp prefigure the next paragraph, which presents Paul himself: "The questioner had a pale face and sad eyes. They must have been the eyes of a sickly person; he limped and the poncho [pélerine] that reached the middle of his legs seemed to hide a hump, a protuberance, some extraordinary deformity. [. . .] One saw that his pace and that sick hip were simulated by a way of carrying his heavy leather book bag. He abandoned the book bag and stopped being sickly, but his eyes remained the same" (*Romans* 110). Against the real wound producing a real limp is a simulated limp produced not by battle but by books. A figure of Oedipus, the figure of the swollen foot, Paul takes his wound from the epistemological part of the myth, the story of the sphinx, and not from the material or etymological part. The transmission of knowledge destroys his purity; Paul will suffer, as will all the figures of the novel, from the text's insistence that they become adults all too soon, that they walk on two legs earlier than the afternoon. His limp will return not only as the wound to his mouth, a displacement discussed later on, but also as a permanent crippling of the mind or soul when the characters enter the closed theater of the apartment in which they all limp around.[13] This knowledge and weight of the past can perhaps be cast off as easily as putting down one's books, but the weight will soon return, never to be shrugged off again. Despite Paul's return to health, moreover, his eyes—the "windows to the soul" that will reflect outer and inner worlds—remain sad; the release from infirmity is merely a reprieve and perhaps only a fiction.

Relieved of his physical burden of books and thereby of the weight of knowledge, Paul can become his natural self. With a scenario that Cocteau will replay in *Le Livre blanc,* the author creates an adolescent homoerotic sexuality that is both chaste (i.e., without sex, without the implication of the sensual, the corporeal, or the sordid) and natural, for the desire is mitigated neither by self-awareness—and thus distance and alienation—nor by knowledge: "He looked for Dargelos. He loved him. This love was ravaging him all the more as it preceded knowledge of love. It was a vague, intense pain, for which there is no cure, a chaste desire without sex and without a goal. Dargelos was the big man on campus [le coq du collège]. He liked those who stood up to him or supported him. But each time the pale student was faced with his twisted hair, his wounded knees, his vest with interesting pockets, he lost his head" (*Romans* 111). Sexuality without sex: a vague pregenital set of images, a cloudy love for the homoerotic other, the male illustrating the almost stereotypical features of the bad boy, the homoerotic chthonic angel, without that love being translated into body sports. The love is spiritual; no sense of the physical need interfere with that spirituality. Physical proximity brings about a disturbance in the air and in Paul, as if the other's unruliness—his ruffled hair and wounded knees—which is also a sign of rebellion against adult norms, created, through echoes or wavelets, a tremor in the adorer.

This confusion of limits and insistence on defining the position relative to the other as one of love—an insistence that appears often in Cocteau's work, and not merely out of some false modesty—produces the real mark of physical danger. The danger is coupled with an act of speech, for both characters must break the confines to which they have been consigned. As in the initial presentation of Paul, there is a double marking, both physical/material and epistemological/linguistic. The wound on the physical body is doubled by a wound to the mind created by knowledge, specifically, the knowledge that one never comes first. This is part of the Oedipal crisis: there has always been a male—the father—there before the individual.[14] He (for this is a question of male sexuality) can never be his own progenitor; parthenogenesis of the self is forbidden to men. The individual is always hobbled by the impossibility of his own originality. Even in the scene with Diaghilev, the astonishment is created by the command to astonish, a kind of double bind wherein obeying the command automatically limits the astonishment. For Diaghilev could have said (and undoubtedly did not): I commanded you to astonish me, and you did, but as it was my command, the astonishment is that much less, so you did not astonish me.

The physical and the spiritual-linguistic play out in a reinscription of a wound like that of King Amfortas in *Parsifal,* but one displaced from the flank of the always guilty king and from the innocent limp of the previous page's battle-scarred victim and of Dargelos himself, with his wounded knees:

> A hand indicates the pale student who is teetering and who is going to call again. He has just recognized, standing on a stoop, one of the acolytes of his idol. It is this acolyte who condemns him. He opens his mouth: "Darg . . ."; immediately the snowball hits him in the mouth, penetrates it, paralyzes his teeth. He has just the time to perceive a laugh, and next to the laugh, amidst his staff [état-major], Dargelos standing up [se dresse], his cheeks aflame, his hair in disarray, with an immense gesture. A blow hits him square in the chest. A dark blow. A blow of a marble fist. A blow of a statue. His mind goes blank. He guesses that Dargelos is on some sort of rostrum, his arm at his side, stupid, in a supernatural light. (*Romans* 111)

Wounded midword, the hapless and ardent Paul cannot say the name of his beloved. The oral offering, be it the name or something else, is never fully realized. Willing to be subservient to this beloved other, Paul never has a chance. The snowball stops the word, penetrates his mouth, and paralyzes his teeth. It is as if Paul has become passively, orally sodomized by Dargelos: the word *penetrate* is unmistakable. Standing erect with flushed cheeks, the phallic angel that is Dargelos stops the action and the talk of love to thrust a silencing phallus into Paul's mouth from afar. Staking out an intersubjective position relative to Dargelos is muted for Paul. He cannot call the other; the other becomes Other, dominating physically—as well as mentally—in Paul's mind.

The first blow is seconded by a strong physical one, the second snowball, which hits Paul in the chest so hard that it may have a rock hidden within it (*Romans* 112). Even Paul's own explanation when he revives is weak, for he explains, "This snowball was a snowball. I ran, I must be having a stroke" (114). The figure cannot be decided; that is, we cannot tell whether there was a rock at the heart of the snowball. It matters only because it suggests both a material foundation to Dargelos's power and a malevolence on his part. This seems far from Cocteau's intent, however, and far from the way the figure plays out in Cocteau's work, in which Dargelos's actions, which have unleashed the development of the story, will also lead to Paul's death. Rather, Dargelos is invested with brute force on the level of fantasy, a masculine power to which all sorts of strengths are imputed but that finally is rather banal in its incarnation. The snowball has a power because those who are not Dargelos believe him to be invested with a power to which evil and violence are ascribed: "In the iron hands of Dargelos, a snowball could become more of a criminal force than his nine-bladed knife" (116). The figure is invested with power as he takes on a life separate from who he is. His real presence shortly disappears from the text, even as he is about to haunt not only this novel but also other works as an archetypal Coctelian figure.

The figure of Dargelos begins to separate from the individual as he first becomes a fetishized image, but not as a classically or psychoanalytically defined fetish, in which desire is invested in a metonymical sense relating to Oedipal trauma. Rather, there is a gradual separation of image and reality; the image of Dargelos becomes its own constellation in Paul's imaginary universe, purer than any of the other images that remain directly representational, albeit ripped from their context. Dargelos is the origin not only of Paul's original physical ailment but also of his psychological ailment: "Paul closed his eyes. An awful discomfort showed him Dargelos, a Dargelos who continued to live elsewhere, a future in which Dargelos had no place" (*Romans* 126). The future splits into two distinct worlds, one in which the investment of desire has an immediacy and the other in which that desire is mated by an absence. The coexistence of these worlds—the noncommutability of one image to another—creates separate universes, one in which the beloved lives (this will come up again in *Orphée*) and one from which the beloved is absent. Cocteau will offer, at least initially, a *reworking* of the developing image by presenting Dargelos in two guises. In one he continues to polish his bad-boy image (127) by showing his techniques and talents as a bully. In the other a greatly overdetermined figure of possession, power, manipulation, and control combines with gender bending: "The other proof shows him in Athalie's costume. The students had put on *Athalie* for a Saint-Charlemagne feast. Dargelos had wanted the role that served as the play's title. Under his veils and finery [oripeaux] he seems to be a young tiger and resembles the great tragic actresses of 1889" (128). Dargelos thus incarnates the aggressive side of masculinity and the male animal's propensity toward control and domination, but this is refigured in the desire to play Athalie, to play a woman, the power behind the throne, and the manipulator of all Rome. Travesty means not a weakening but rather almost an insidious incarnation or apotheosis of power in the form of the phallus cloaked in silk and velvet. In his physicality Dargelos becomes the bad angel of homoerotic desire: the ineluctable attraction of the bad and even evil to the lover.

Dargelos is invested in a fairly modern way, as an image of himself. But he is not alone in this; there is a pantheon of votive images, for the bedroom shared by the two children houses a heterogeneous collection of fetishes: "On the middle of the mantle reigned a plaster bust to which one had added eyes and a mustache in ink; thumbtacks pinned everywhere pages of magazines, newspapers, programs, representing film stars, boxers, and assassins" (*Romans* 118). The images are fetishistic not in being likenesses but in being parts of a whole, decoupages of a body part or even a whole body whose picture was cut from a magazine. The fetishized image differs from the fetish object because it involves a relation of semiotic verisimilitude: this image looks like the person it represents. Some amulets in a traditional sense and some objects invested with desire require no relation of iconicity or verisimilitude; rather, there is a metaphoric amulet or a metonymic shoe (to choose a common example of a fetish) whose relation to the original object is mediated by an investment of desire.

With this imagery the desire is invested in the likeness of the image. A brief excursus into classical portraiture will help illuminate the significance of what Cocteau is proposing. A classical portrait given as a keepsake—the traditional form of iconic fetish—differs from the fetish here in at least three ways. First, the portrait is mediated by a kind of direct artistic production: an artist makes a picture of the beloved, and somehow the possessor of the object is deemed to be the proper or improper owner of it. He has been given the picture by the beloved, or she has it as a token of remembrance and love. Such is the sense of the portrait of Jeffrey Aspern in James's *Aspern Papers.* In fact, the narrator's ultimate possession of the portrait signals his impropriety, his desire to acquire that which is not rightfully his. In the end, the portrait stands as a reminder of propriety. The fetishized picture thus evokes a sense of rules that determine who may have such a fetish. Second, the fetish portrait often recalls its more "primitive" past, the fetish without verisimilitude: a keepsake or locket quite often held a lock of the beloved's hair. This synecdoche is a throwback to a system of "primitive" amulets that fetishize desire. Third, the fetish portrait has a frame; it remains distinct from the world around it. That is, the fetish has its limits, as if fantasy had a protective guardrail to safeguard proper thinking and behavior.

What Cocteau proposes differs categorically from such primitive and classic fetishes. Writing at the same time as Walter Benjamin but far from deploring the fate of the work of art in an age of mechanical reproduction, Cocteau celebrates the possibility of ripping things from context and removing frames. This is one of the profound senses of his mirror worship, for Orphée can walk through the mirror, the last figure of realist reflection imaginable. With this mechanical version of an artist's studio, Cocteau takes a shortcut. He gives us a decontextualized, unframed, ready-made object in a constellation of representations over which the origin of the image never had any control. In short, Cocteau gives us tabloid fetishes. There is no investment of propriety or impropriety. The image belongs to anyone who wants it, and the image can be ripped from its frame with nary a thought.

The possibility of a bifurcated or bicameral universe allows the further possibility of a normal fetish, for Paul wants to put a photo of Dargelos in the "treasury," a votive hiding spot that he and his sister have for their prized possessions (*Romans* 128). Soon, however, the angelism that Cocteau is developing—the all-possessing figuration—goes beyond merely fetishizing Dargelos:

> Moreover, Dargelos's prestige began to change registers. Not that he diminished. On the contrary, the pupil grew, took off, rose to the sky of the room. His beaten eyes, his curl, his thick mouth, his wide hands, his crowned knees, began to take on the form of a constellation. They moved, turned, separated by the void. In short, Dargelos was going to join his photograph in the drawer. Model and photograph were identified with one another. The model became useless. An abstract form idealized the beautiful animal, enriching the accessories of the magical zone and Paul, delivered, voluptuously enjoyed an illness that represented nothing more than a vacation to him. (129)

Dargelos is idealized into an erotic figure of power and might whose exaggerated features loom so large that he becomes the star of their room—indeed, a constellation. As a figure of stars forming a pattern in the sky, the constellation of Dargelos is invested with desire and an almost animistic vitality. No longer is Dargelos merely a bad boy or even a fetishized photo of himself. He takes on the power of a heavenly god, a guiding light to those below. As a constellation, however, he is also a collection of stances, things thrown together to stake out a territory, much in the way Mallarmé constellates figures on the page in "Un Coup de dés."

In this double sense Dargelos as constellation in an apotheosis of self increasingly marks the space as controlled by him, someone to be worshiped, whether or not the corporeal form exists. This is a founding moment of Cocteau's angelism: the model is no longer necessary, having been replaced by an idealized abstraction and fulfillment of the investment of desire. The hovering presence of the abstraction is not without erotic overtones in other realms. Once we have moved beyond the synecdochic economy of the fetish—part to part, part to whole—to a constellation, even feigned illness can be tinged with the figure of "the beautiful animal."

This double decorporealization allows the figure of the beloved to hover and undergo reincarnation, inhabiting or haunting different forms, bodies, or avatars. A previous passage has already evoked this process in a kind of mimetic behavior before the fact, for it shows Gérard's relationship to Paul to be the same as the latter's relationship to Dargelos: "Paul beaten by Dargelos, Paul victim of Dargelos, was not the Paul of whom Gérard was the slave" (*Romans* 121). But the figure of mimesis and adoration is not adequate for Gérard, because he cannot distinguish exactly that which makes Paul Paul: his adoration of Dargelos. What makes Paul an individual is what Gérard cannot abide. Later, the possibility of rediscovering the beloved other in totally different others, as long as they are under the same constellation, allows a change of sex from male to female: "And the secret taste of Paul, his taste for a special sort [un type spécial] had played no role here, for it was change, that, among a thousand girls, had made Agathe Elisabeth's companion" (164).

Only at the end of the novel, when Cocteau returns to the stories of the beginning, does he expand on Dargelos's power. Dargelos is not only the beloved; he is also the dark angel of destruction, but in a way that is as subjectively innocent as it is objectively dangerous: "Paul saw himself in class again, aping Dargelos, speaking only of savages, poison arrows, imagining, to astonish him[,] a massacre by a system of poison on the glue of stamps, flattering a monster, not thinking for one minute that poison killed. Dargelos shrugged his shoulders, turned away, treated him like a helpless girl. Dargelos had not forgotten this slave who drank his words and now crowned his jests" (*Romans* 177). Cocteau reinforces the mimetic parallel between Gérard-Paul and Paul-Dargelos by repeating the word *slave.* Because Paul does not willingly recognize this slavery, the narrator must make a point of telling the readers: "'Of course,' yelled Paul aggressively. 'Poison is marvelous. In class I dreamed of having poison' (it would have been more exact to say, 'Dargelos dreamed of poisons and I copied Dargelos')" (176).

Dissociating consequence from a kind of extremist behavior, Cocteau paints Dargelos here as an avatar of Gide's Lafcadio, among the most powerful homoerotic images of the previous years. Cocteau takes the introspective Lafcadio, who also exemplifies physical prowess, and turns him into a complete phenomenon, a surface, and a constellation of figures without depth. Whereas in *Les Caves du Vatican* Gide muses both on interiority—allowing Lafcadio to stab himself as self-inflicted punishment—and on bloodlines, Cocteau turns everything about Dargelos into a surface. As in the *acte gratuit,* there is no rational motivation to the action, but Cocteau goes further than Gide in separating reason from surface behavior. Whereas Lafcadio's random act of throwing someone from a moving train lacks a clear consequence and rejects responsibility, Dargelos's talk of poisons, a schoolboy game that ultimately solidifies into a banal—because bourgeois—adult habit, has no relation to what poisons actually may be.

In that shift to an adulthood of the practico-inert, Dargelos becomes far less than he once was. He is now merely the realization of a rather infantile, escapist dream: "'Dargelos,' continued Gérard, 'showed me poisons from China, India, the Antilles, Mexico, poisons for arrows, poisons for tortures, poisons for vengeance, poisons for sacrifices.' He laughed, 'Tell Snowball I haven't changed since school [bahut]. I wanted to collect poisons; I collect them'" (*Romans* 176). Strangely, reporting the behavior involves a desacralization, a deritualization, a demythification, as if the poisons, separated from their ritual categories, were nothing more than an inventory. The adult, a mediocre figure who can no longer be a model, is the one who can no longer astonish, no longer impress, even with surface beauty.

As an adult the "real" Dargelos is a disappointment. But nothing is ever lost in Cocteau, for he reconstellates matters in different ways. In his first admission of love for Dargelos, Paul allows that it is "chaste" (*Romans* 111). By calling this homoeroticism chaste, the narrator is at least positing the possibility that there might be other, nonchaste forms of love. Can these be named, or must we remain within the realm of the homoerotic that can be named as long as it remains unfulfilled? Naming the beloved, signing one's name as a testament to the act of love: this is what cannot be said. To name Dargelos is to love him in a world beyond chaste homoeroticism. This naming must be cut off, for it is "the love that dare not speak its name." Cocteau illustrates what he already knows: the naming of homosexuality is the impossible situation. He was certainly aware of the phrase in question, for in "Le Dieu nu," a poem in the 1910 collection *Le Prince frivole,* Cocteau chooses this very line as an epigraph (Christensen 33). There is thus a physical illustration of the interruption of representation and naming that takes on a phantasmagoric quality associated with penetration, with the role of a dentist boring into the teeth and penetrating the mouth of the patient or subject. The name is interrupted so that homosexuality will not occur, yet homosexuality occurs as the interruption of the name. The graphic image of the act folds over the naming of the act itself.

Portraits-souvenir (1935) gives us another version of the mythic snowball fight, one that starts with the following statement: "To tell the truth, something like the story of the snowball did take place" (Cocteau, *Romans* 783). In this version Dargelos is not the teachers' favorite but rather the worst student in the class. What is appealing is his natural beauty, like that of an animal, a tree, or a river (783), an enchanting beauty that operates like witchcraft (784). He is frankly described as the "vamp of the school" (784). Dargelos has a power others of his age do not, the power to make things hard: "I have always thought that the very touch of a Dargelos is sufficient to change snow into marble, to harden it to the point of murder. . . . This snowball, origin of a scandal whose ramifications form the plot of my book [*Les Enfants terribles*], glows with phosphorescence. It hits Paul's chest like a statue's fist. After, the statue stays still and no one would think of accusing it" (784–85).

Before proceeding to the "blank book," I propose a brief final glance at fallen angels. In *Mon premier voyage,* the tale of a Phileas Fogg–like trip around the world, with Marcel Khill serving as Passepartout, Cocteau wonders: "Should not the fall of angels be rather 'the fall of angles'? (In Hebrew, there is only one word for expressing the two things.)" (198).[15] It is a strange and false remark, for Hebrew has separate words for angels and angles, and no speaker of the language would confuse the two. Late Cocteau believes his myth, but his younger avatar explains it better. In an earlier work, *Le Secret professionnel* (1925), Cocteau explains this bizarre etymology as "an ideal sphere, the disappearance of the divine force, the appearance of the conventional and the human" (*Romans* 500). The image of the fallen angel; the constant erotic fixation on "the fallen angel"; the mythology of "l'ange Heurtebise" or Dargelos, whom Pierre Macris sees as epitomizing the "angelic type" (78); the creation of a mythic other as part of a private mythology—all this has been replaced by the apotheosis of the poet. Ironically, however, the best example of the fallen angel is the fallen poet: "Arthur Rimbaud remains the type of angel on earth" (Cocteau, *Romans* 500). The fallen angel who is also a poet, the combination of the sought for object of love and the power to represent it, is ultimately Cocteau's angelism. In this angelism Cocteau seeks to merge the possibility of describing the other with that other himself, the Jean that reflects—not as a mirror, but as a means of absorption and angelic representation—with all the others: Jean Desbordes, Jean Marais, Raymond Radiguet, Marcel Khill, and so many other, unnamed ones.

The Transparency of Anonymity

During a period of about seven years starting in 1925, Jean Cocteau produced a corpus second to none. The collection of poetry entitled *Opéra* was written over a three-year period from 1925 to 1927. His monologue *La Voix humaine* was written in 1927 and first presented in 1930. *Les Enfants terribles,* perhaps his best novel, was published in 1929, and *Opium,* meditations on a cure that took place from 16 December 1928 to April 1929, appeared in 1930. The end of this brief span also witnessed his first film, *Le Sang d'un poète* (1932), the film that announced the invention of Cocteau as cinematographer. In the middle of all that appeared the unsigned volume *Le Livre blanc,* written in 1927, presented in a first edition of twenty-one copies in 1928, and published more widely but still anonymously in 1930. Although Cocteau did not acknowledge the work until decades later, no one ever seemed to doubt that he had written it, for much pointed to him: the style; the references to figures that are clearly his (such as Dargelos); and ultimately, in later editions, even unsigned ones, the drawings that he furnished to accompany the text.

Of all the things Jean Cocteau "wrote," what interests me the most is the absent signature on his homoerotic novella *Le Livre blanc.* This is perhaps a startling revelation, because I have chosen to write about Cocteau, and one cannot go far in writing about something that is not there. Similarly, one cannot go far in saying that this absence is more interesting than what is readable. Nevertheless, this blank where the author's name would be—this blank that matches the blank book in which he seems to tell all but his name—draws me to Cocteau and makes me want to read between the lines of his work. Unsigned by Cocteau, not signed by Cocteau, signed and erased by Cocteau: this is a book that makes the name of the author into as much a problem as the book is. Who signs where? Perhaps he can sign a book with contents, with a mythology, or with a drawing. Are Cocteau's lines—the lines that form a readable signature of his name—the only way of signing a work? Perhaps he can sign it later with his blood, as he will do in his first film, *Le Sang d'un poète.* Perhaps he can sign with tribute, signing a preface to Radiguet—a belated homoerotic love note to his dead first love—or signing the preface to Jean Desbordes's work *J'adore.* Or perhaps he can sign with an image. In "A bas la terre," part of *Opéra,* Cocteau asks the following three questions: "Does God sign his work with the lizard? Would the storm be his other signature? What poem does the zebra have beneath his stripes [ratures]?" (*Romans* 321). One can ask what poem Cocteau has beneath his stripes: are the invisible lines of *Le Livre blanc* perhaps not the best camouflage of all, not for homosexuality, but for Cocteau's poetic force?

Things are different toward the end of Cocteau's life, when signing his homosexuality would not matter, especially when it has always already been signed. On 7 October 1958 he wrote a postscript to a letter to one of his correspondents, Milorad: "Your mistake is in not understanding that sexuality makes the power of my work. People believe that the poet must speak of things. No. He must be them" (*Lettres à Milorad* 86). He seems to feel that he is the sexuality—arguably the constellated homosexuality—that he has created. Cocteau believes in his own mythologizing about sex, in his own figuration of sex, and in the transcendence of sex through a greater force. Writing to Milorad (15 Oct. 1958) Cocteau says that when he speaks of sexuality, it is as "of a dream that served me through its mechanisms and not through its *spectacle.* I speak of the sexuality of ink—a male force that erects the fountain pen and detests any surface, childish silliness [touche-pipi]—especially when it is transcended as Gide does. The childish silliness of the soul is the worst of all" (87). By the end of his life Cocteau had become a revisionist of his own sexuality, his writing, and his mythology. He came to believe that the "lie that tells the truth" is a superior form of the truth. In a spirit that predicts Foucault, moreover, Cocteau wrote the following quite late in life (6 June 1961): "Sexuality is a problem only in relation to the different police that disorganize our poor world" (167). Sexuality is problematic only when it is controlled; otherwise, the poet profits from his vatic freedom to be, to become, and to astonish.

Who signs what now? Cocteau signs his name, and indeed his name has preceded the poet and the poetry. As he says in a journal entry from 27 December 1952, "My name has overtaken my work. My work must catch up" (*Passé défini* 1:409). His relations with Radiguet and Marais have long ago entered into cultural history: there are no secrets. To sign or not to sign now is beside the point, for, as he notes on 29 January 1954, "a work is always the portrait of the person executing it" (3:30). Let us take Cocteau at his word. Let us look at that famous lack of a signature and see the portrait of the poet and the poetic process uncovered thirty years before, after Radiguet, during Desbordes, and before Marais.

Not signing a work about homosexuality seems precious for Cocteau, for it is not as if he has been quiet about homosexuality during the period in question; indeed, his work is rife with references, as his life has been. The open expression of love and mourning for Radiguet was well known, and his panegyric praise in his preface to Jean Desbordes's work *J'adore* leaves little to the imagination. In this preface Cocteau writes that he would have to be the Leopold of the famous and homosexually tinged Leopold and Loeb murder case to write about Desbordes (5). And he does not forget to praise Radiguet anew. As Peter Christensen remarks (33), even Cocteau's early works already contain scattered references to homosexuality, including the poem "The Archers of Saint Sebastian" in *La Danse de Sophocle* (1912) and a poem called "Le Dieu nu," in the 1910 collection *Le Prince frivole,* for which Cocteau chooses a well-known line from Lord Alfred Douglas as an epigraph: "I was the love that dare not speak its name."

Opéra contains the poem "L'Ange Heurtebise," whose title figure will become another of Cocteau's constellations. Also important in this collection is a prose poem entitled "The Red Package" ("Le Paquet rouge), which starts by equating blood and ink. The poem's speaker goes on to say that he has become a double, someone who stole papers from a certain "J. C.," someone who has a fake profile, and someone who must continue to astonish to be taken seriously. The work ends with what Cocteau will consider to be his most famous "thing to have said": "Let whoever understand this who can: '*I am a lie that always tells the truth*'" (*Romans* 349).[16] In the same period there is the nominally heterosexual but certainly gay-hysteric monologue of *La Voix humaine.* Milorad reminds the reader of an amusing anecdote with a profound message: "During the preview for *La Voix humaine,* 15 February 1930, Paul Éluard was not wholly wrong to yell to Berthe Bovy, the creator of the single role in the play: 'You are telephoning Desbordes!'" (*Lettres à Milorad* 129). After *Corydon* and *Sodome et Gomorrhe* and after his own production, can it be so shocking for a visible gay man of the theater to sign his name to a homoerotic work? I think not.

How exactly does he not sign *Le Livre blanc*? One cue comes from a letter dated May 1930: "People have said that *Le Livre blanc* was my work. I suppose that this is the reason for which you ask me to illustrate it and for which I accept. It does seem that the author knows *Le Grand Écart* and does not scorn my work. But however good I think that book is—were it even by me—I would not want to sign it because it would take the form of an autobiography and I shall keep the right to write my own, which is far more unusual. I shall be content to approve through the image this anonymous effort to clear a terrain that has remained too uncultivated" (*Romans* 224). In other words, he admits being the artist whose drawings are used in the book but cannot admit authorship of the words, as if readers would automatically take a gay narrative as an autobiographical confession. So he shall sign this work with an image, with pictures, and with lines that do not bring the author as close to the work as his name might; these lines do not confuse the distances and differences between the fictional and the autobiographical. Signing with images allows Cocteau "generously" to keep the fiction a fiction, to keep the blankness of the *White Book* (as the title is usually translated) in play without tying it up with his name, to approve the clearing of new uncharted territories—roughly speaking, a poetics of homosexuality.

The book is about homosexuality, about the possibility of homosexuality, and about becoming or being homosexual. The entirety of the problem rests there, assuming that a problem exists. The problem is not that Cocteau was homosexual, which is neither newsworthy nor interesting, even though he had sustained sexual relations with women at several points in his life. The problem is about homosexuality in writing, a representation of homosexuality, a representation of a homosexual being. These are not the same, and from the outset the great representational problem in Cocteau's work is the vacillation between representing homosexuality as some depersonalized, transcendental, abstract concept and representing a homosexual individual, or part of that individual, with a homosexual ethos that remains personal and a singularity that never quite fits the abstract.[17] Without being narcissistic (although the author is often given to narcissism in a sense of egocentric behavior), Cocteau is endlessly writing about the personal aspect of the performance of the self and the creation of a self as an ongoing production. It is a permanent impromptu that cannot accept the necessarily alienating relation that says to him you are that: homosexuality, which is in you, is some abstract situation in which you find yourself and over which you have no control.

It is certainly a case of nature versus nurture. Does Cocteau feel that homosexuality is given to him or constrains him even as it permits his freedom to be or to become Jean Cocteau? If homosexuality is there for him, before him, to what extent does this compromise his freedom? Cocteau is never completely satisfied with the answer he gives or those he gets. The beginning of *Le Livre blanc* sets up an aporetic situation between the givenness of the homosexuality and its accidental occurrence. The very first lines set up the problematic. The opening words show that the matter pre-dates the author. Homosexuality is something he fell into without choosing it; it is something given to him over which he had no control: "As far back as I go and even at an age where the mind does not yet influence the senses, I find traces of my love for boys. I have always loved the stronger sex that I find legitimate to call the beautiful sex [i.e., the fair sex]. My misfortunes came from a society that condemns what is rare as a crime and obliges us to change our penchants" (*Romans* 193). Homosexuality is there as a trace and as writing that seems to precede the writing of the subject as a subject. The traces of love precede the establishment of the self. They are there to be discovered and rediscovered in the construction of the self. From the very first, it is clear that there are two possible paths to take. The first is dictated by society, which tells us to be like others, to be heterosexual, and to conform to laws and morals. This point will surface over and over through Cocteau's writing, doing so from time to time in *Le Livre blanc.* It is also the note that closes the book: "In France this vice does not lead to jail because of Cambacérès's morals and the longevity of the Napoleonic Code. But I do not accept being tolerated. That wounds my love of love and freedom" (223). The state may have decriminalized homosexuality, and society may tolerate it, but that is not enough.

This closure reinforces the other version of the given: the aestheticization of homosexuality, the cry for freedom that can come only from coloring outside the lines. Cocteau goes one step further by making the lines himself: his lines are always outside the lines, going beyond the given ones. Cocteau will not accept being tolerated, nor will he accept that people allow him to color within the lines that ultimately would have formed a ghetto of well-placed behavior and channeled desire, a prison house, a closet, or a fabulously decorated prison cell. Cocteau is neither a revolutionary nor a deep thinker. His argument is visceral, an argument of creation and redemption through the production of an aesthetic that astonishes. Diaghilev says "astonish me," and that is all Cocteau ever intends to do. His solution to the question of homosexuality is not to stun people or astonish them by parading before an audience with his fly open. His solution is to define his own aesthetic, one of homoeroticism, beauty, and love, and a mythology of fallen angels that he invests in his every line.

From the very beginning of *Le Livre blanc* Cocteau redefines beauty: it is the male sex or male gender—the distinction means little here—that defines beauty. Cocteau defines the world according to his act of reinscription, for the question of homosexuality is endlessly recast as a question of reinscription and of the appropriation of signifiers by other signifiers. He produces a constellation of signifiers: dots form lines, and lines form an image. This reinscription is evident in those first lines: his present state is a retrospective glance at the past in which homosexual desire always looms large and forms the structures of that memory. Unlike the surrealists, Cocteau did not delve into the Freudian unconscious but created endless arabesques of signifiers born of that eternal preexisting homosexual desire. Whereas André Breton and his circle banned the mere evocation of male homosexuality because it conjured up an unspeakable signified, Cocteau focused on a question of a different order: how can he take the lines that are given, the initial lines—"traces of my love for boys"—and reinscribe them so as to spin a web of illusion, of theatricality, and of life?

Let us return to the opening pages of *Le Livre blanc*. Because the entire project is set under the sign of the aesthetic—for the issue is more representational than ethical—what transpires is an argument about the manifestations of a homosexual aesthetic instead of a symptomology or neurosis. The narrator (whom I would willingly confuse with Cocteau himself save for the absent signature) gives three reasons, which he calls "three decisive circumstances" (*Romans* 194). But decisive for what? For becoming homosexual? This is hardly the case, for he has already said that however far back he goes, even before his intellect became involved, he finds traces of that love. These traces are thus internal. These circumstances must be decisive, then, for the way in which his individual aesthetic will develop, not as a neurosis, but as a poetics. These lines, images, and visions may come from without, but they graft themselves onto the points within, the writing that is always already there—the inscription of a self even before there is a self—that is homosexual and in love with the beauty of "the beautiful sex." These three circumstances are accidents that occur, figures that are grafted onto a preexisting nexus of sign and desire. They are not what turn him into a homosexual but what figure his lines and ruses thereafter.

The book's first two figures are fairly simple images, one of a nude farm boy riding a horse and the other of two Gypsies climbing trees, the significant point of which is seeing "three spots of black" on these two bronze bodies; these images are scarcely different from Gidean homoeroticism. The third is a more complicated scenario. It is the story of a servant named Gustave. Having spent so much time playing and replaying those memories, the narrator says, "I wound up really wanting my hand to touch what my eye had seen." Gustave has "a meaningful lump [bosse] in his pants" (*Romans* 194–95). How to touch it? The protagonist proposes to draw a woman, make Gustave laugh at the drawing (Gustave has problems controlling his laughter), and then ask to touch his crotch. What happens? When Gustave bursts out laughing, the narrator goes straight for his goal and cops a feel. Gustave turns red and pinches the narrator's ear; "pretexting" that the narrator was tickling him and "deadly fearful of losing his job," he escorts the narrator to the door. But Gustave loses his job anyway for having stolen some wine.

The structures of sexuality include the division of the sexes, the fragments of the body, and questions of class. From the beginning of *Le Livre blanc* Cocteau represents sexuality as related to or pinned on a discourse of class structure. Each of the three "decisive circumstances" implies a class difference between the bourgeois autobiographer and the erotic interest, whether the farm boy, the servant, or the Gypsies. Nonetheless, his class superiority can be overturned by a homoerotic image of the freer farm boy or Gypsies, who are unfettered by bourgeois oppression. The third example is the most significant, because it moves from the impression of the homoerotic image in which the participants play no role to a dynamic in which the servant, Gustave, is an ambiguous figure. Clearly the narrator feels that, as part of the dominant social structure, he has some right to possess Gustave, to touch his crotch, and to realize his sexuality. At the same time Gustave has given no encouraging sign or indication that he might be interested in being felt up by the narrator.

Gustave's punishment, his dismissal for theft, is almost comic in its stereotypical drama: the servant who corrupts the young master must be removed from the household to maintain the scion's straight, bourgeois purity. Cocteau is turning the time-worn example on its head: in no way has Gustave led the narrator down the garden path; in fact, Gustave no more bears guilt for "perverting" the narrator than does a beautiful woman for turning men's heads. Gustave's only sexual crime is that of being well endowed. Nevertheless, fulfillment is impossible so early in this work, which is structured on a continued lack of fulfillment. Gustave is banished for the banal reason of stealing wine, not stealing innocence. The narrator himself has stolen his own innocence and will spend the rest of the novel trying to return to a position of innocence, but at a higher level.

When Gustave disappears, Dargelos appears. The initial presentation of Dargelos, the archetypal Coctelian incarnation of male sexuality and specifically of the attraction of the homoerotic, in that sense reincarnates Gustave.[18] Without doing anything and without being "gay," Dargelos inflames passion simply by the presence of his raw masculine sexuality. Dargelos reached puberty earlier than the others in the class, so while they were all still wearing short pants, "only Dargelos had *naked* legs" (*Romans* 197). In all his incarnations Dargelos disturbs and inflames by his very physical presence. Just as he had once wanted to touch the servant Gustave, the narrator wants to touch Dargelos, but the latter rebuffs his offer of friendship (199).

Significantly, this is also the moment at which the developing sexuality of all the students is brought to the fore. Sexuality starts with masturbation through holes in pockets and ends with semen being wiped up with dirty handkerchiefs (*Romans* 197). But this masturbation leads in two directions. Even though all the boys practice it—so much so that the classroom is perfumed with the mixed odors of "gas, chalk, [and] sperm" (*Romans* 197)—the boys view their own behavior as a vice because they have been taught that this is so. Masturbation is a necessary but fundamentally offensive prelude to their true sexuality. Over the summer, however, something happens to the narrator's classmates: "Onanism was giving way to bragging. Post cards were circulating. All this youth was turning toward women just as plants toward the sun" (200).

Heterosexuality therefore has a valid economy and a viable representational system. Dirty postcards can circulate like so much chattel: the women the boys may have had, the women they want, and the women whose sexual favors the boys can describe in their bragging. The heliotropism is a confirmation by nature. Emblematic of the world of masculine heterosexual domination, in which the object and its representations—or the object and its means of production—are controlled by men, the postcards neatly figure all the possibilities of economy, possession, and representation. They are the metonymy of the women, the representation of the women, and the figures of a system that needs such representations to function. This is where the narrator differs, but it is also where he has already gone wrong: in seeking to possess the image of the farm boy and the Gypsies and in seeking to possess Gustave, the narrator erred by thinking that these objects could be part of an economy of representation and a system of exchange. He later discovers that the system can exchange only women and their representations by heterosexual men; there is no place for the exchange of homoerotic visions. They may be his, but there is nothing to be done with them.

For the narrator, the act of masturbation, while repugnant when practiced by this group of future heterosexuals, is not intrinsically vice laden but merely the low parody of what he already knows to be a higher form of love. Because he does not masturbate in class, his classmates take him for a prude (*Romans* 197). This is far from the truth; he simply refuses to banalize his ideal of love by participating in a parody. Moreover, there is no way of representing this love. The "love that dare not speak its name" is a love whose essence, while recognizable, is certainly not speakable: "The pederast recognizes the pederast as the Jew, the Jew. He guesses him under the mask and I take on the obligation of finding him between the lines of the most simple books" (195).

What is this mask? At least initially, it is the mask of faked heterosexuality and its discourse: "It was then that, in order to follow the others, I began to falsify my nature. In rushing toward their truth, they dragged me toward lying" (*Romans* 200).[19] Thus this initial sexuality is a move toward normality, not for the sake of normality, but to continue both to belong and to believe in the possibility of representing one's sexuality. To belong, therefore, the narrator convinces himself that the lie he is telling the others will become his own temporary truth, and he drags himself toward a performative heterosexuality, first in the arms of prostitutes and then in a full-fledged affair with a woman named Jeanne.

Here Cocteau begins to elaborate a theory of sexuality that does not conform to an economy of production. I have already shown that the narrator believes in a certain essentialism among homosexuals. He has also begun to be aware of certain masks of sexuality and normality that hide one's true nature from others or even from oneself: "Just as there are women pederasts, women with lesbian aspects, but looking for men in the special way that men look for them, there also exist pederasts who are unaware of this in themselves" (*Romans* 195). With Jeanne it becomes clear that the narrator is truly attracted to her own homosexual nature, which is masked with a veneer of heterosexual behavior: "Jeanne was a boy; she loved women and I loved her with what my nature had that was feminine" (201).

The narrator's developing sense of sexuality is confusing, to say the least. We have been presented with an essential homosexuality on his part, a homosexuality that never forces him to deny his maleness—he is not a woman—but that definitely has a feminine side. The object of homoerotic desire can be a masculine male, such as Gustave or Dargelos, neither of whom evince any homosexual behavior but who embody some masculine ideal for the narrator to worship and adore. The narrator can mask his own developing sexuality with the veneer of socially acceptable (i.e., heterosexual) behavior. That veneer leads ineluctably to an unmasking, however, not so much of the narrator but of Jeanne, who is really a boy. Different from his own feminine side, Jeanne is given a male essence.

Cocteau is developing a theory of one-sex sexuality in which everyone is a boy at heart. It is a theory of autoeroticism and parthenogenesis that Cocteau will spell out a little more clearly in *Opium:* "A normal man, from the sexual point of view, should be able to make love with anyone or anything, for the instinct of the species is blind; it works roughly. . . . *Vice begins with choice*" (*Romans* 628). In *La Difficulté d'être* Cocteau distinguishes himself from the moralizers who see homosexuality as a vice against nature, and implicitly recalling Gide's apologetics in *Corydon,* he even presents an argument that depends on the observation of nature and the discovery of homosexuality within nature. Because it is natural, it is by definition normal: "What man calls vice is common to all species" (955). In a note Cocteau adds: "Bitches mount male dogs. Cows mount each other. This disorder is sometimes an order. Islanders made it a rule before the missionaries came. It was a way of avoiding overpopulation." So the noble savage, living closer to nature than denatured Europeans do, recognizes the normalcy of this activity and even justifies it as a rule and with logic. The Christian position and the act of civilization are themselves the perversions.

We should not confuse Cocteau's position with some phallic monster but rather think of it as a Peter Pan–like vision of the universe in which everyone is a boy, regardless of appearance. In that case, everyone can be an appropriate object of homoerotic desire, even if the desires of the individual in question do not carry him or her in that direction and even if anatomy points elsewhere. It is only when one chooses, when one forces a mask, and when one seeks a representational system unlike Cocteau's that the problems begin. Vice is nothing more than an act of exclusion.

Revising Gustave Courbet's famous painting *The Origin of the World,* one can say that this is also the origin of the work of art, which can be recuperated in a world where all roads lead to some fundamental masculinity: "Art is born of coitus between the male and female elements making up all of us, but which are more in balance in the artist than in other men. It results from a sort of incest, from a love affair with oneself, from parthenogenesis" (Cocteau, *Romans* 628). Although we all have male and female elements, in this universe we are all fundamentally men or boys. The feminine coexists but is not essential; femininity is that which the artist actuates to impregnate. What happens in the artist is clear by Cocteau's three figures of sexuality: the male essence fertilizes the figure of the feminine, coexisting in the same body and pushing incest to its limit of self-love. Instead of stemming from the usual female parthenogenesis, however, art is a product of male parthenogenesis that is somehow the same as the producer—for parthenogenesis produces offspring whose genetic makeup matches that of their progenitors. Yet it differs somehow, too: there is no confusion possible between the artist and his art, even if the art is the lie that tells the truth.

What is a woman for Cocteau? Perhaps the best answer comes in a book called *Reines de la France,* where it is clear that a woman is a construct created by men: "There are solid motives that push women to submit themselves to fashion with the passive obedience of soldiers. It is important to please, to prevent anyone else from getting ahead, to maintain oneself, even through absurdity, in a style that is against nature [contre nature], I mean to say contradicting nature [contredisant la nature] that plumes [empanache] the male and that obligates the female to wear the most modest uniform" (154). Cocteau's choice of words is significant, for he cavalierly slips in the expression "contre nature," an expression generally used to refer to homosexuality. He then "corrects" his error to "contradicting nature." That the "error" remains—after all, we are reading a book and not listening to a live speech—is as transparent a feint as is the absent signature on *Le Livre blanc.* Women are figures of the male homosexual, just a less aesthetic version thereof, because they are formed by some anonymous order, not by love. One should certainly be protean, Cocteau says, but for love or art, not just for the sake of some corporate fashion structure. In his early correspondence with Jean Marais, he is quite specific. In December 1938 Cocteau writes, "Paint me as you want me to be. I will figure out how to become it. Otherwise the por trait will take my place in your soul and in your bed" (*Lettres à Jean Marais* 14).[20]

In *Le Livre blanc* Cocteau elaborates a version of homoerotic parthenogenesis that rationalizes both art and the men who incarnate beauty for him. It will become a cornerstone of the sexual dynamic with which he interprets the universe, a sexual dynamic that depends on the priority of the gay male as lover and beloved and that marginalizes women as sexual objects except insofar as they are an index of the true male beloved. The next mistress, Rose, is merely an excuse for the creation of a male figure, ostensibly (but not truly) her brother, with whom the narrator will once again fall in love. Rose presents her "brother," who resembles both the farm boy and Gustave. "His name was Alfred or Alfredo and he spoke bizarre French, but I didn't worry about his nationality; he seemed to belong to the country of prostitution" (*Romans* 202). This time, however, the narrator is permitted a closeness that did not occur in the previous instances. The years of homoerotic dreams are finally actualized as the narrator discovers the truth: "I understood that I'd taken the wrong road. I swore to myself never to get lost again, to follow my right path henceforth" (204).

The actualizing moment is contact with the body of the other: Alfred's body is that of a pure man, and it tells the same truth as the truth that the narrator realizes for himself. Alfred's body itself is constellated as the body of a celestial angel, "a perfect body . . . whose parts seemed to spread out like a star around a thatch [toison] where something rises—while the woman is built to fake—the only thing that cannot lie in man" (*Romans* 204). A man's penis tells the truth, and the erection of the penis from its matted thatch is the truth of man's being, which means that it is the truth of being for Cocteau. No matter how many lies are told or how many masks are worn, this erect member can never be glossed over by a lie. Whereas a woman can lie with her whole being, this one part of man cannot, and it is that unerring commitment of man's body to the truth that makes the man, at least in Cocteau's eyes, superior to the woman.[21]

Although possessing a divine body, Alfred cannot participate in freedom, the gift of the self, and the acceptance of adoration. He thus falls into a banal economy of exchange: "In Toulon, I realized that Alfred had taken a little golden chain from me. It was my fetish. I had put it on his wrist and had forgotten this circumstance; he did not take care to remind me of it" (*Romans* 205). Cocteau's narrator needs to escape from a bourgeois-defined economy of desire in which the self is represented as having a transcribable value. As soon as there is material or linguistic exchange, the validity of the adoration of the homosexual other and the homosexual self is put into question. It becomes a matter for the authorities. In *La Difficulté d'être* Cocteau moves his reader from a sense of the sexual to the aesthetic: "Where does the sense of beauty, I mean what leads us toward beauty, find its origin? Where does it begin and end? What nervous center denounces it to us? The free use of sexuality haunts all great men, whether they know it or not. Michelangelo exhibits it to us. Da Vinci murmurs it. Their admissions intrigue me less than innumerable indices of an order considered as a disorder and which does not lead to actions. What do actions mean? They come from the Police. They do not interest us" (*Romans* 961). On the previous page of the same work Cocteau pithily relates writing to sensuality: "Writing is an act of love. If it is not it is only writing" (960). The move into the representation of sexuality is necessary if sexuality is going to be a foundation for art and its celebration. This move opposes any valuation of the body in an economy of exchange and instead celebrates totality by eschewing the reductive: it celebrates the aesthetic through the inscription of plenitude.

As I have indicated, Cocteau sees the world as a Peter Pan–like creation filled with bodies of beautiful young men; the next incarnation of his sexual aesthetic occurs where he can project this belief onto the world at large, in Toulon, which he describes as a "charming Sodom" (*Romans* 206). In this world everyone is a gay male, and everyone is there to admire gay masculinity, the ideal of beauty wholly absorbed by all, as each individual subject dissolves into a mass of others like himself: "From all over the world, men taken with masculine beauty come [to Toulon] to admire the sailors who stroll alone or in groups, who answer glances with a smile and never refuse the offer of love" (206). Sexual fulfillment and aesthetic pleasure mean dissolving the self without any concomitant loss or alienation.

What must be lost is that which divides and that which reminds the narrator of a world different from his own. That world eschews aesthetic and sexual pleasure, and it marks, divides, and separates with its lines. The emblematic reminder of this other world is a tattoo he sees on the chest of his new Dargelos. The narrator sees "the ghost of Dargelos. Dargelos as a sailor" (*Romans* 206). From sight to possession is just one small step, but the possession and the mutual exchange are celebratory. Rather, they would be celebratory were there not a reminder of the outside world, for this boy, whom the narrator says "represented luck" for him, has "no luck" tattooed in blue capital letters on his chest (208). Such dystopic division must be removed, and the narrator boldly sails forth, creating another angelic, constellated astronomy of the male body: "With my pen, I crossed out the nasty tattoo. I traced a star and a heart beneath it" (208).

At least for now, this sailor is the incarnation of luck and the epitome of the beautiful male body given to fulfillment, sexual pleasure, and sheer joy. Again the body is constellated so it too speaks, not as a confessional murmur, but as a celebratory dance, a star-shaped line somewhere between body and representation, between prose and figure: "No luck! Was it possible? With that mouth, those teeth, those eyes, that abdomen, those shoulders, those iron muscles, those legs? No luck with that fabulous small sea plant, dead, wrinkled, aground in the moss, that unwrinkles, develops, stands erect and throws its sap as soon as it rediscovers the element of love. I could not get over it" (*Romans* 209). So "the only thing that cannot lie in a man" (204) again takes its primordial spot as the phallic center that defines pure maleness, the truth that speaks the truth, and the essence of manhood observed by the stargazing admirer.

Because Toulon is the Edenic paradise of homosexual encounter, moreover, it has a spot that seems to be the living, breathing apotheosis of the homoerotic world. The narrator finds a "clandestine atmosphere" in a public bathhouse that reminds him of the *Satyricon* (*Romans* 211). It is actually a male bordello with the boss showing off the merchandise. This is not the purity of homoerotic relations that the narrator desires. Rather, it is reminiscent of Charlus in a brothel, where sexuality becomes a performance instead of an honest, direct expression of self. The brothel incarnates performance and the lie: "One person would order that he be insulted, another that he be put in chains, another (a moralist) getting off only by seeing a Hercules kill a rat with a red-hot pin" (211). In a passage recalling the first pages of the book, the narrator reintroduces the class structure. Here those who can pay order the boys to do things, abuse them, or master them. The figure of the exchange is money, not pure lust, love, or adoration.

While refusing the imposition of the class structure or the hierarchies of social life, Cocteau still wants to make the magic, destroy the difference, and reconstellate the universe according to his vision. In a diary entry from 18 April 1942 he writes: "I'm always ready to use the familiar form, as long as one doesn't use it with me" (*Journal* 90). Cocteau's one-line philosophy is not without ambiguity; its sibylline nature comes from the absence of a future form of the subjunctive in French. Does Cocteau mean that he will address someone as "tu" rather than "vous" as long as it is he who initiates the familiarity? Or does he mean that he will use it as long as the other never replies in kind? One could argue the grammatical point and say that it is the latter; if Cocteau had meant the former, he would have used the past subjunctive in the dependent clause to indicate the temporal relation. Everyday French is not always that precise, however, and his failure to use the past subjunctive does not remove the shadow of doubt. There is a question of modeling, of hierarchy, here as elsewhere.

The only exception seems to be the situation of possession at a distance, but it, too, recalls the initial scenes. The boys, unhampered by their clients, can be observed through a one-way mirror (*Romans* 212), and the narrator watches the youth frolic and get off. Some of them "wiped off the tiles the sap that their blind stem had thoughtlessly thrown toward love" (212). This, too, is a performance, however, even if the performers do not know it. There is a Hobson's choice between a possession that involves the exchange values of the heterosexual world and an idyllic possession at a distance that seemingly can never be breached: "One time, a Narcissus who pleased himself, put his mouth on the mirror, kept it there, and pushed the adventure with himself to the ultimate point. Invisible like Greek gods, I pressed my lips to his and imitated his gestures. He never knew that instead of reflecting, the mirror was moving, that it was alive and that it had loved him" (213). Ultimately, there has to be a return to a position of truth and to a frankness that seems to surprise even Cocteau, a point when there are no more feints to be made. Having found a deserted beach, the narrator meets someone bathing nude. Having been asked whether he was shocked, the narrator replies, "My answer was so frank that it enlightened him about my tastes" (215). But can this be justified? It can be through grace, for in the confessional he is told that God's goodness goes beyond what one imagines (217), the implication being that God will forgive his tastes "against nature." Thus will Cocteau's seeming transparency always have been doubled or refigured by one-way mirrors that move one from one world to another, with torch-bearing hands that light the way and with the white light of an unsigned book.

4 Willy and Friends

WHETHER IT IS PROUST, with one magnum opus, or Gide, who by the 1920s had emerged as the grand old man of letters, even though he was to live over another quarter-century, the canonic gay-subjected author occupies a rarefied position. High culture places a premium on its own values and perpetuates its aristocratic marking of self and writing as a superior point incarnating superior values. Like any other cultural institution, high culture seeks its self-perpetuation. Despite all their revolutionary art and somewhat iconoclastic positions, Proust and Gide were rather quickly absorbed into the canon, thus becoming figures of the conservative.

The position of gay culture is unique, however, in that the fundamental thematic of "normal" homosexuality is anathema to the dominant culture and ideology. This anathema is not necessarily addressed to some specific individual who hypothetically may always be viewed as an exception, with the hysterical rationalization of a "yes, but" (Sedgwick 52–54). The individual homosexual may be included by that ideology and culture if it is strategic or pragmatic to do so. Rather, the position is anathema to heteronormativity's reproduction of its own cultural dominance. At the same time, the culture espoused by writers such as Proust and Gide is thematically not only within the dominant culture's view of its own values—with an exception made for the specificity of nonheteronormativity, the cultural positions of Gide and Proust also affirm the Keatsian adequation of truth and beauty. Whereas masculine nineteenth-century realism dissociates truth from beauty in a variety of ways, these two high modernist authors reassociate those values with each other, with high culture itself, and with its various incarnations.

For example, the nineteenth century offers readers the grotesque in the association of high and low in the novels of Hugo, the Brontë sisters, and Melville or in Stendhal's *Racine et Shakespeare.* As realism develops under the pens of Balzac, Eliot, and Flaubert, the extremes are made less severe. Quasimodo's excess of self is distinctly Hugolian and romantic. Balzac will settle for an ironic twist of the distinct mark, perhaps nothing more than a parody of an Alsatian accent or a stammer in a character's speech, and Flaubert will ironize the ironization: the detail is no longer distinctive but something that is completely mediocre and meaningless, nothing more than a clubfoot that is betrayed by even more mediocre science.

Proust and Gide seize this double position. First, they legitimize that double ironization by turning it into the negation of a negation. Homosexuality is neither ironic nor doubly ironic: it is completely unremarkable. Second, such a normalization allows for a reaffirmation of high culture as the apotheosis not of heteronormativity but of the unremarkable norm. As good middle-class citizens, Gide and Proust incarnate its values even if they do not bear the concomitant self-protection. With constantly reconfirming and guaranteeing its own existence no longer necessary, heterosexual culture seems suddenly to be higher: culture on a high wire without a net to ensure its survival.

Elsewhere on the literary spectrum we find some works that, while neither pulp fiction, potboilers, nor pornography, certainly lack the aspirations to high art seen in works by Gide and Proust. During and after World War I a number of popular writers turned their attention to describing parts of society that the period's high art often kept at a distance. Just as various pastoral or regional novels of the time received their own audience, a niche developed for novels about certain urban landscapes: not the rarified atmosphere of the Faubourg St. Germain or the Faubourg St. Honoré, or even the urban poor, whom Zola had sometimes championed, but an almost exotic group at the fringes of French society. The author Willy made a career of writing about soubrettes, small-time actors and actresses, as well as others in the "entertainment field." One portion of this market was concerned with sex and thus intersected the developing subgenre of novels representing male homosexuality. In this chapter I turn my attention to that intersection, where the popular novel deals with the eclipsed subject of male homosexuality. The first novel discussed, Francis Carco's epoch-making *Jésus-la-Caille,* focuses on the lower depths of society, but others put homosexual characters in every social stratum.

Carco and Miomandre

Francis Carco wrote *Jésus-la-Caille* between 1914 and 1917. As originally published the text included only the first two parts of the work as it now stands. Carco also published a separate work dealing with the relations of a prostitute, *Les Malheurs de Fernande,* whose title character appears in the story of Jésus-la-Caille. In 1920 Carco republished the definitive version of this material, an edition that includes both "the texts of *Jésus-la-Caille* and of *Malheurs de Fernande,*" for, as the editor indicates, the author had always considered the latter work as "the third part of *Jésus-la-Caille*" (vii). In so doing Carco removed some chapters from *Malheurs de Fernande.* The 1920 edition may more closely resemble a novel of suitable length, but there is a concomitant loss of focus. Although the combination of the two works does not affect the depiction of male homosexuality per se, it changes the balance of the novel and draws the reader's attention away from Jésus after the first hundred pages and toward this other character, Fernande, who takes center stage. The focus on homosexuality and bisexuality is thus changed, for the novel concludes with an extended examination of heterosexual relations.

The novel is set in Montmartre, and the characters are pimps, prostitutes, and gigolos, the last group taking money to participate in homosexual activities.[1] The depiction of female prostitution was already a long-standing practice in mainstream literature, not to mention pornography, where it was ubiquitous. The depiction of homosexual male prostitution, however, was rare: as recently as 1968 one critic wrote that this novel has a subject that is "difficult to treat decently" (Chabanaix 350). To emphasize the natural, popular, and nonliterary nature of the subject and to give local color and flavor while maintaining the privileged position of a literate narrator, Carco presents dialogue in often ungrammatical slang, marked by the argot of the streets and a decided lack of interest in points of grammar.

The novel focuses on Jésus's adventures as a gigolo; his relations with and love for his boyfriend, Bambou, who is in jail; and his relations with a woman, Fernande. In its final form the novel eventually turns to Fernande's life, leaving Jésus behind. At its the beginning the reader learns that Jésus's boyfriend, the one true love of his life, has been sold out by a snitch and arrested in a sting operation. Jésus's first entrance contains a brief description in which femininity is epitomized: "His pretty girl's face, barely made up, was strangely lively. He arose. The belt [martingale] of his overcoat bound his supple loins" (*Jésus-la-Caille* 2). Carco makes several points in this initial description. First, he equates the male individual and the female body. Jésus's look is feminine, as if the invert—or even one who plays the invert—is automatically less masculine. That femininity is accented by the makeup, barely present, that both remarks the femininity and leaves it as natural as possible. Thus, even as Carco marks the homosexual as feminine, he seems to distinguish him from the outrageous excess of the transvestite. Although it seems excessive to put too much weight on the word *strangely*, the narrator's position, while nonjudgmental and generally sympathetic to most of the characters, certainly differs linguistically, ideologically, and morally from those of his characters. This distance of the moralist will be used as a technique in many of the popular gay novels in the years that follow, as well as in Willy's more didactic work *Le Troisième Sexe*.

Finally, this initial description includes the French term denoting the back belt of an overcoat, *martingale*, which is itself polysemically evocative, calling to mind both equine dressage and a system of betting. The initial picture Carco paints, then, is one in which the homosexual protagonist is feminine, capable of being victimized, as his boyfriend has been; it is a situation in which, whether for his mere homosexuality or, more likely, for his marginalized, nonbourgeois homosexuality, he is subject to the will of another, as are horses, and gambling with his own life. More precisely, the martingale of dressage comprises straps that steady the horse's head. So again, that carefully chosen word lets Carco allude to possible activities for which Jésus may be paid, for his martingale "bound his supple loins." The word's polysemy thus marks both fellatio and anal intercourse, as the adjective *supple* remarks him as feminized.

Opposed to the creation of the homosexual as the one epitomized by his own acts of sexuality—the vice marks his body as his body reciprocally marks his vice—is the archetypal heterosexual, one who has an essence and can distinguish layers of behavior and whose signs do not necessarily mark his core but can be used as dissimulation. There are two such individuals portrayed in the novel, Pépé-la-Vache, who runs the bar, and "the Corsican," a pimp whose girlfriend is Fernande. Pépé-la-Vache "judged things soberly. He was aware of the Corsican's instinctive hatred for the equivocal couple [Jésus and Bambou], and like the Corsican, he detested Bambou, la Caille, and those of their ilk, but did not show it" (*Jésus-la-Caille* 2). Such "real" men as they, incarnating the hatred of the homosexual, remark that other less as an individual than as a typical member of a species or race.

The third category of character is the woman, generally the heterosexual woman, although there are passing allusions to lesbians. In the singular the woman is an individual who, like the homosexual, is somehow a victim of a male- and heterosexual-dominated society but whose natural pairing is with the real male. The Corsican pimp is named M. Dominique, and Fernande is "sa femme" (*Jésus-la-Caille* 7)—ambiguously his woman or his wife, albeit more likely the former than the latter—although she continues to ply her trade. Over a week after Bambou's arrest, Fernande, unhappy with the "bad luck" that weighs heavily on her, is reading her own cards. The following morning, while the Corsican is still asleep, she thinks of Jésus-la-Caille as she compares him to the cards: "Of the handsome knave/jack [beau valet], he had the graceful eye with long eyelashes, painted lips, and a rounded nose and chin[. . . .] Still, instead of the velvet hood [chaperon] where a feather grew, he wore the soft cap of gigolos. His hair nicely tousled in front was blond, his cheeks firm and pale, and his skin so white that the girl forgot that he was asking the cards to reveal to her the secret of his heart" (19). The epicene if not effeminate features of Jésus are thus universally appealing, exciting, and seductive, so much so that Fernande forgets her purpose as she falls into those features that inscribe desire. For Fernande, and in this general discourse of appearance, it is the surface resemblance and the typicality of the type that repeatedly come back. There is no singularity in the perception of the homosexual; he is the one who stereotypically resembles some previous iconicity. This is the case both for the narrator, who supposedly maintains an independent position, and for Jésus himself. First, there is the narrator's description of Jésus: "La Caille returned the discreet salutation of his friends. He was weighed down with a terrible lassitude, but his instinct armed him against himself. Driven crazy by the mystery wrapping Bambou's disappearance, he walked quickly, his eyes open wide under the cloth visor of his cap. He was no longer the depraved expert lowlife met at the Palm or at Bousse's. His shoulders stretched the fabric of his clothes; his delicate nape of the neck was rounded and his two meager arms, folded next to his body, lent him a driven look [une allure acharnée]" (3). Here are la Caille's thoughts of Bambou, given in *discours indirect libre,* followed by the narrator's completion of the thoughts and actions: "A small yellow photograph, stuck to the mirror, recalled the absent one to la Caille. Bambou was smiling in the picture. His hair pasted on his temples, the way he had his head, his way of looking . . . Ah! The kid Bambou! Everything was there . . . Even that fleeing, tender air, that sensual hardness, that equivocal languor that women adored. To complete the illusion, la Caille had even penciled in a beauty mark at the corner of his left eye. One could not desire better, and the trouble of the adolescent kept him propped on his elbows for hours in front of that moving and cruel spectacle" (8). A single process of eroticism and description is at work in all three descriptions at hand: Fernande's comparisons while looking at the playing card, the narrator's description of la Caille, and the latter's consideration of his boyfriend. The one who is desired is somehow both typical and artificial, singular yet typified. There is no natural beauty, just one that is marked as a general indicator: from the stereotypical image on a playing card to the fake beauty mark, nothing is generated by nature itself. Even the narrator's view of la Caille tends toward stereotypically marked beauty. In each case, however, something moves both the readers and the observer one step beyond, toward some sort of transfixed position or even ecstasy. Fernande is transfixed by the image she projects of la Caille, as is la Caille by the touched-up image of Bambou. And the narrator, if he himself is not subject to such a transfixing, marks the difference, the beyond of la Caille, who is no longer merely a "lowlife." The inscription of homosexual desire may somehow be triangulated by the socioeconomic climate that Carco has chosen for it; nevertheless, in a modest, quiet way, and despite the ambiguity with which such desire is inscribed, he lifts it into some other position that transcends the immediate surroundings and their "lower depths" nature. That elevation, however, will be increasingly challenged as the novel goes on.

This transcendence creates a problem, because this portrait of homosexuality is associated with both the artificial and the typical, leaving the reader to wonder whether there is something inherent, internal, or inner to that vision of male homosexuality. Thus, if the masculine, heterosexual male and the heterosexual woman are creatures who are singular and possess an essence, the homosexual is one of a type, created from the outside in. It is this phenomenological position that I will continue to follow in Carco's construction of a discursive network in which the popular image of the homosexual fits. Within that construction the hermeneutic problem is to discover whether the homosexual has an inside and is capable of real emotion or is only that surface, in what Willy and Ménalkas will call an "imitation of love." The subject comes up early as Fernande wonders about la Caille: "She wondered what his feelings about a woman could be. She didn't know if he detested women or not. His vice, which he made apparent [qu'il affichait], threw her into an extreme confusion [embarras] and seduced her" (*Jésus-la-Caille* 19).

As this plan is followed—and one suspects Carco is running a kind of laboratory of sexuality—he opts for one path of the two available. He chooses the more conservative, safer path, developing the relations between Fernande and la Caille to see what happens and, ostensibly, whether she can "convert" him. The path he does not choose—the more courageous one—will be the one chosen by Willy and Ménalkas in *L'Ersatz d'amour:* the exploration of the homosexual relation for itself. As I shall show later, Willy and Ménalkas hedge their bet by presenting Marc Renneval's homosexuality as situational: broken up with a woman and unable to find another, he accepts the ersatz situation of love with another man.

Carco explores the situation of the homosexual through the lens of heterosexuality. As the plot develops, Jésus and Fernande are dancing together one evening. Fernande allows that the Corsican was instrumental in the arrest of Bambou; she reaffirms that the Corsican cannot stand homosexuals and would do anything to be rid of them. Fernande is in love with Jésus, whom she undoubtedly sees as a sweet contrast to the brutality of her man. While admitting that he loves Fernande, he turns his head away, thereby making that declaration—really an answer to her inquiry as to whether he loves her—more than ambiguous (*Jésus-la-Caille* 30–31). Thus is the stage set as Carco looks into disambiguating the ambiguity.

One subsequent evening Jésus-la-Caille and Fernande are in a gay/drag bar near Place Blanche, replete with "gentlemen" (in English in the text): a couple of American tourists (husband and wife) who get a running translation, for homosexuality is different and so strange that it sometimes needs translation. There is also a "smart, agile, or tarty little hooligan [leste petit voyou]"—who gets up and performs a camp version of Zola's Nana, intoning, "I am a washed up [vanné] Eros" (*Jésus-la-Caille* 52). Even if she is in love with Jésus-la-Caille, Fernande reflects the opinions of others. She cannot fully break from the generalized discourse determined by a dominant masculinity that abides neither the effeminate nor the homosexual: "What low riffraff surrounded them. At the neighboring tables, she noticed in the paleness, accentuated by the warm swarthiness of their eyelids and their cherry lips, a tired, clownish, delicate breed [engeance]" (54).

This extreme version of male homosexuality has the classic signs of decadence as its signature; the use of the word *breed* reminds readers of the way homosexual men were often thought to constitute a separate group, a third sex, or a separate race. It is no wonder that Fernande, who represents the flowering of sexual desire, finds herself drawn to the standard antigay position taken by most of the "real" males of the novel: "She understood the disdain with which the males of the National [the club] could pour on these made-up teenagers, and her disgust made her heart sink [son dégoût lui remontait au cœur]" (*Jésus-la-Caille* 54). Instead of radiating a hale and hearty masculine attitude, these transvestites mark themselves with the signs of the feminine. There is a slippage between the feminine and the effeminate, whereas the "male"—solid, unshakeable, and biological—cannot be confused with any other essential position.[2] So part of the problem is that this slippage is possible in a world of the phenomenal, of the semiotic, a world where there is no essence other than that of the male. The semioticity of the transvestite becomes his essence, however; it is necessary only to adopt the signs. This then entails a phantom essence—an inversion of the sign by which the signs of the effeminate correspond to no real male essence that can be named—that corresponds to some unnameable essence of homosexuality: "She was especially distraught to notice how little la Caille differed from the others. His manners weighed her down with sadness" (54). Even at the margins of society, that propriety still marks Fernande.

The other problem is the association of the fallen angel's beauty with such improper manners. Whereas Proust and Gide associate truth with beauty and somehow elevate homosexuality in the process, Carco illustrates the problematic position of the generalized discursivity outside high culture. Here beauty and truth are associated, but that truth is nevertheless considered to be ugly not only morally but also ontologically, for it corresponds to no essential maleness. Here is a description of Jésus that reflects Fernande's point of view: "He was handsome, blond, thin, and his beautiful shoulders, flexible waist, and too wide hips made him the odious and tenderizing type of a race she now condemned" (*Jésus-la-Caille* 54). So the truth of Jésus's beauty gradually moves back toward a kind of Tardieu-inspired medical discourse that establishes correspondence between physical and psychological norms and, more important, between psychological aberration and physical anomaly. Thus do la Caille's hips become too wide, as if his vice were both preter naturally marked on his body and endlessly signaled by that body. Men whose hips are too wide are passive pederasts; this much is clear. And despite Fernande's love for him, Jésus is typical of that race. Whereas Proust comments at length on, for example, Charlus's hips and the "race of fairies," it is without a blanket condemnation of the individual or of the "race." Writing at the same time, Carco will not condemn his characters, even if Fernande's appreciation of Jésus-la-Caille is consonant with that of her peers. Still, the discourse that Carco presents, even as his narrator retains the distance and neutrality of a moralist, cannot ever fully undercut the condemnation implicit in the general discursive episteme.

Forced into each other's arms, Fernande and la Caille wind up in his bed. A search for solace turns into kisses, and then nature takes its course. Is this situational or compulsory heterosexuality? La Caille's own rationalization of his behavior—his own justification—is that contact with Fernande will get him more information about the Corsican's antigay behavior. It is a way of spying on those who might sell him out. Nonetheless, if itself a performance, this move toward playing the heterosexual has some unforeseen results in which la Caille cannot distinguish—at least for a while—when he is performing what. In this movement Carco is certainly illustrating two components of the generalized discourse. First, regardless of the individual's motivation, what a homosexual needs to make him heterosexual is a good woman. Thus is homosexuality conceived as a lack or an immaturity, a figure in a progress narrative whose natural conclusion is heterosexuality. Second, sexuality is as amorphous as the sign system itself, and beyond that, if it is a constant and repeated performance, there is minimal psychic trauma attached to some change along that line. So instead of progressing via a complicated Freudian mechanism, sexuality is produced from the outside in. Change the behavior; there is nothing more to it than that.

Thus in the next part of the novel la Caille becomes happily bisexual, if not a happy bisexual. He feels sad when he remembers Bambou, whom he still loves. But that does not conflict with his relation with Fernande. In addition, neither of those behaviors conflicts with his trade as a male hustler, which he continues to ply. Indeed, he plays that role better, for as a faithful figure of the actor's paradox, he becomes his role while maintaining his distance from it. His role does not really correspond to his heart; he can, therefore, without any ambiguity, hit all the right notes to be a better gigolo. He can pick up a man in what amounts to a singularly flirtatious dialogue between the adolescent and a "sprightly old man" (*Jésus-la-Caille* 72). Carco is quick to underline the performance of false naïveté of the heterosexualized—and therefore even more homosexual—la Caille: "'But what should I call you?' asked Bambou's friend innocently" (73). La Caille is far from innocent; his true homosexuality is drowned by a double litany, an anaphora of desire and the noise of the world that drowns all distinction. As he continues to work the streets, he meets an older man who will become a regular patron: "A cab stopped, received the couple, and as it slowly trotted off again, the old man, leaning over his companion, could no longer contain himself: 'I am called Mr. Pacific, but call me, call me,' he said. And the sound of the wheels covered the word" (73).

The word on the street soon has it that la Caille "wasn't like that [n'en était pas]" (*Jésus-la-Caille* 75). Once one is not homosexual, however, one must participate in the generalized discourse about homosexuality. Here I underline a distinction between some sort of poorly defined internalized homophobia, which does not appear here or anywhere else in these popular novels, and the generalized discourse about homosexuality, which if not "homophobic" is certainly disdainful. When la Caille is no longer gay, he becomes repelled by his own behavior, even as he continues to work the street: "There were days on Rochechouart that Jésus-la-Caille regretted such loves. Those from which he now got one louis after another made him sick at heart. Mr. Pacific, paying for the hotel, came twice a week, and he did not fail to notice the horror he inspired" (75). Carco does not disambiguate the possible causes, however, for he does not allow la Caille's position to be one in which analysis can occur. La Caille can be repelled because society rejects homosexuality, because he regrets turning tricks or being kept, because he is no longer homosexual, because he is now heterosexual, or because he is having relations with someone—a man or a woman—he does not love. Any or all of the reasons will do. Carco does not clarify matters, not because he does not have the talent to do so, but precisely because the complex of possible symptoms, reasons, or analyses is the point: in this world someone like la Caille cannot simply—or profoundly—be homosexual in the same way that Charlus can. Even the opportunistic Morel, far more bourgeois than Carco's figure of the lumpen, has a greater possibility of self-analysis and rationalization than la Caille does.

It takes la Caille four months and several episodes to work through this multiple performance; only at that point does Fernande realizes that he does not love her and that he has gotten close to her to help himself and Bambou. Carco does go on to make a singular point that may cause the reader to reflect on what may be performance, and in doing so he seems briefly and momentarily to have a kind of nostalgia for a bourgeois world in which matters were clearer: "In the great mottled hell of Montmartre, where disdainful and elegant Negroes, pimps, touts, street hawkers, bohemians, gigolos, and streetwalkers met, ran into one another, denounced each other, and mingled, Fernande was alone" (*Jésus-la-Caille* 84). So la Caille represents the whole. The figures that intermingle to form a collective world cannot be separated, for their lives are intertwined, as are their public or "professional" positions. They do not have the security to be independent subjects; their existence depends on or is parasitic on the classificatory schema of the bourgeois public.

The bourgeois individual can enter the demimonde or this marginalized world of trafficked sexuality; he—for the subject is by and large a male one—can also choose not to enter it. If the marginalized figure can be momentarily raised up, however (think of Nana in this context), that figure is fully dependent on the bourgeois for continued status as an appurtenance to that elevated position. Even when not raised up, a marginalized individual such as la Caille—whether walking the streets, hanging out in a bar, or being kept by a patron—still has his sexual position marked as being informed and mediated by money. The apposed artificial beauty mark that signals this world's falseness has never been more a mark of its sexuality: beauty and sexuality are created within the context of the social structure. Not that an individual does not have an expressible sexuality; rather, that sexuality is replaced by apposite signs instead of his or her own.

In *Jésus-la-Caille* all the characters are from the lower classes, really the *Lumpenproletariat,* with the possible exception of the mysteriously and fictionally named M. Pacific, who undoubtedly chooses an alias, as if he did not want his homosexual slumming known. This unique exception in the novel is a technique familiar to readers of Gide and Proust: a character with a certain social station takes a false name to pass in the lower depths. There are two elements to that disguise, though. The first, just mentioned, is the figure of self-protection that is also the figure that remarks class barriers. One crosses those barriers by pretending that one has not crossed them or that the social barrier is lower than it is. This itself inverts the figure that marks social ascension from Balzac to Proust: it is not necessarily a vague *arrivisme* that constantly marks the parvenu status of the individual but rather the possibility of changing class status or the perception thereof over time. The reverse movement of slumming—as shown most brilliantly in the screwball comedy *My Man Godfrey*—is specious to the extent that the slummer seeks to protect him- or herself, his or her good name, or his or her family's reputation. So the slumming is never complete, at least in this era, unless it is underpinned by some internal pathological state. The renaming then reminds the reader of the upper-class member's ability to change names while protecting his or her real name and access to the truth of consumption, whereas members of the lower classes can become a "cow" (*vache*) or a "quail" (*caille*) but never change names to disguise their true identities.

That name change is only one component of the slumming. The other component is the willful courting of ambiguity, as illustrated most emphatically by Gide in *L'Immoraliste,* where Michel poaches on his own land. Danger is courted, and that in itself is exciting to Michel. Ambiguous borders are erotic by definition. That ambiguity also marks a more classic approach to homosexuality in which the difference between the lovers is one of class, age, or both; again Gide illustrates this in his descriptions of good pederasty versus bad inversion in *Corydon.* Here I am interested in the ambiguity laced with danger. To explore that ambiguity and danger, I will briefly mention an episode in another forgotten novel, one that lends itself to a reading that interlinks homosexuality, class-barrier crossing, danger, and eroticism.

The novel is Abel Hermant's 1923 work *Le Suborneur.* Cast in a Gidean mode and in many ways echoing the Ménalque episodes in *L'Immoraliste, Le Suborneur* follows the vagaries of the very wealthy Lord Chelsea. The novel's single episode of interest here takes place after the witching hour. Accompanied by his younger friend Lord Roxwell, Lord Chelsea goes to a Turkish bath at 1:15 A.M., intending to sleep there instead of going home (74). The ensuing protracted descriptions follow Lord Roxwell through the course of the night he spends in the baths (74–87). While nothing is specifically described, there are suggestions that some of the men brush against or touch others. Again, the scene is marked, as are the brothel and metro scenes in the *Recherche* and the scenes with M. Pacific in *Jésus-la-Caille,* by the cloak of anonymity and by the mixture of classes.

The year after the definitive edition of *Jésus-la-Caille* appeared, Francis de Miomandre published a novel entitled *Ces petits messieurs.*[3] The plot in part parallels that of Carco's novel, although it differs markedly in the question of social class. Again, this is not a great novel, but Miomandre is adept at putting the available discourses into context, for the work reflects a popular conception of homosexuality. As Carco does in his novel, Miomandre posits a fluidity among homo-, bi-, and heterosexuality. Unlike Carco, however, Miomandre does not portray the social structure as depending on some inherent essential masculinity; rather, he assumes that people are capable of a variety of behaviors. Moreover, as the novel raises the protagonist into a higher social situation, there is no exploration, as there is in Carco's book, of society's lower strata.

Miomandre constructs a situation around the protagonist, Émile Roubert, who is nicknamed "Loulou," a vaguely feminine pet name as well as the name of the parrot who constitutes the divine figure of idiopathic repetition in Flaubert's tale "Un Cœur simple." Loulou is mostly heterosexual, but he is not above being kept by another man if it is convenient. He lives with Irène, his mistress, who exercises a trade similar to his own of a gigolo. All is peaceful until Loulou has an affair with the heir to the Albanian throne—Constantin, Prince de Samara—and Irène throws him out (93). Interestingly, the prince initially characterizes himself as purely homosexual—which will turn out not to be the case, for he conforms to the image of the decadent oriental man epitomized by the multiple references of his name: Albania, a Moslem land in Europe and until recently part of the Ottoman Empire; Constantin, which, while a Greek name, recalls the eastern city of Constantinople; and finally Samara, a city along the Volga in nebulous regions that have large indigenous, non-European populations. The prince is presented initially as the figure of the decadent oriental, given to sexual excess and the perversion of homosexuality.[4] In fact, the prince contrasts his own fixed sexual nature with that of Loulou, who can moved fluidly from act to act and bed to bed; he says that unlike Loulou, he is not "bilateral" (96): he does not have the possibility of such a movement.[5] Like Carco's Jésus-la-Caille, Loulou embodies a generalized eroticism and sexiness that appeals to men and women alike. That mutual appeal takes the forefront and drives the narrative.

Let me examine the plot before turning to an analysis of that universal sexiness. The prince has debts. He is living with the wealthy Baronne de Santa-Trinidad, who is married but separated from her husband. Already the prince's own homosexuality is skewed by this living situation, as if the decadent oriental cannot to his own self be true. Once the baroness is widowed, however, she inherits her husband's estate, but her widowhood changes the social situation. In a perversion of the social discourse, the baroness decides she has to leave the situation in which they share a household. She says she must leave for her honor. When the baron was alive, he could have answered any aspersions on her character relative to the fact that she was living in the prince's household. Now that the baron is dead, she has no one to defend her good name should someone say something. Because she serves as a kind of beard for the prince, however, her departure is not the best solution for him. Seeming to be generous, the baroness solves the prince's financial problems, but the generosity is a hollow gesture that hides her ambition to be a princess. To make everything acceptable socially, sexually, and financially, the baroness suggests a morganatic marriage with the prince; unfortunately, the prince is unfamiliar with the term and thus agrees to the proposed solution without quite understanding it.

The baroness is transparent in her ambitions, and the prince's innocence and gullibility figure heavily in them. Since the prince is the figure of the decadent easterner, he cares little that these actions will force him to get rid of Loulou. He does so, after which Loulou returns to Irène. When the prince finally realizes that the promised morganatic marriage is not merely a sham marriage of convenience but a real situation that compensates for a difference in class, he seeks to break off relations with the baroness. To do so, he uses Loulou's sexual appeal and sexual flexibility. The prince proposes to pay Loulou to sleep with the baroness, which will let him escape his commitment to the marriage. The prince "discovers" Loulou in the baroness's bed and gets rid of them both without paying Loulou. Loulou returns to Irène one final time, and in so doing he gives up his career as a gigolo.

Miomandre's construction of male homosexuality is interwoven with images of class and social structure, as well as the stereotype of the Orient understood as the geographic locus of generalized, endemic male homosexuality. The prince, who is the one real homosexual in the novel, is capable of betraying his own sexual interests for economic reasons. It is only when he realizes that his family's good name will be corrupted that he takes his own fate in hand and reevaluates his social position. Loulou's omnisexuality provides a solution to the problems created in his own situation. He will presumably go on to another affair with another gigolo. Thus are pleasure, sexuality, and social status construed as completely separable functions that can be added, subtracted, and especially, changed at will. Loulou's sexuality, however, is inseparable from himself; he cannot help appealing to all, and that generalized sexual appeal is considered nothing more than the incarnation of beauty.

For Miomandre, as for Carco, sexuality is not connected to a psychological situation. Rather, as if the matter were a criminal situation, it is connected to motive and opportunity or, more generally, to matters of economy and profit. Everyone is potentially omnisexual, as long as he or she is attractive to others. Both Carco and Miomandre associate the model of fluid homosexuality with a kind of fantasized bisexuality that Western popular culture often proposes for women. That is, at least in the pornotopic text, the woman is considered to have a capacity for bisexuality and is often given a scene in which that inherent lesbianism is played out. By constructing homosexuality on the feminine model and moving it away from the model of male heterosexuality, these writers create situations that feed the image of male homosexuality as effeminacy and of male heterosexuality as the rightfully dominant position. Not only is this the case in the effeminate features of Jésus-la-Caille or his use of makeup; the construction further appears in the appeal to the idea of beauty itself, always perceived as feminine. Thus does the woman mimic the straight man, himself seduced by beauty, when she is attracted to one of these homosexual or bisexual individuals.

Willy and Callias

Known more nowadays for being the husband of the brilliant Colette, to whose early work he added his name until she broke away and established herself as the individual and brilliant writer she was, Willy was a long-lived "author" of works quite popular in the first thirty years of the twentieth century. Although Willy (Henri Gauthier-Villars) was a well-known figure of the literary world, he was not a great writer. Far more clever than talented, Willy signed his name as a coauthor to works penned by upward of fifty ghostwriters (Caradec 303–4), of whom Colette was by far the most important and the most talented. Some other works seem to have been penned alone, often kinds of memories and souvenirs, but much of what was popular was written by someone else, with that person sometimes given credit as coauthor, sometimes not.

In the 1920s Willy signed his name to three books dealing with male homosexuality. Although he and Colette had not shied away from depicting the free-spirited Claudine as having lesbian sex, male homosexuality was far more daring a subject. Two of the books were novels coauthored with a certain Ménalkas, the pen name of the novelist Suzanne de Callias: *L'Ersatz d'amour,* published in 1923, and the much weaker sequel, *Le Naufragé,* published in 1924.[6] In 1927 Willy published a work of nonfiction entitled *Le Troisième Sexe,* a systematic view of the dominant cultural figures and institutions of male homosexuality. Although it is unlikely that Willy wrote this work alone, no collaborator has yet been identified. Before examining these three works, however, it will be useful to take a cursory glance at three other popular novels dealing with homosexuality, two written by Callias alone, *Jerry* (1924) and *Erna* (1932; published under her pen name), and the third coauthored with a certain Marc de la Roche and given the improbable title of *Metallo, mon ami* (1938; also published under her pen name).

Callias's open-minded perspective on male homosexuality is even more apparent in her own work than in those written with or for Willy, in which his more conservative—or more self-protective—hand is visible. In her own work Callias deals not just with homosexuality but with a freely assumed sexuality in general. For her, everyone should have the freedom afforded the male bourgeois subject, who can follow his interests without shame, guilt, or fear of being stigmatized. Thus in her novel *Jerry* Callias takes a perspective that likens her main character, Thérèse, to a man by rebaptising her as "Théo," the nickname by which everyone calls her. That assumption of the masculine is underlined by the manner in which we learn her name: she has received a card from a friend, Madeleine (known as Mad), addressed to her in the masculine: "Mon vieux Théo." The adjective here agrees with the gender of the name, not the gender of the person.[7]

Related in the first person, the story is intimate without bearing the slightest traces of Gidean confessions or apologetics. Callias strengthens the first-person narrative by semiotically marking the protagonist as an independent subject. For example, Théo is a sculptress working on the Ile St. Louis, and the story very pointedly begins on Easter Sunday 1918. These facts have significant implications. First, as an artist and a "bohemian," Théo makes her own rules. She creates, whereas other women, imprisoned in normative heterosexuality, are no better than slaves to the world that dominates them. Second, she has clearly moved away from her family and established an independent existence in Paris, where the rules are different. Third, starting the novel on Easter implies an iconoclasm on the part of the character—who is neither in church nor with her family—as well as her symbolic rebirth as an individual.

Callias edges the novel toward a notion of free sex when Théo, with a vague sense of discomfort, sees her physician, who is also a woman and who has therefore also broken through gender stereotypes. The doctor suggests that Théo may cure her vague illness by having a baby, even though she is not married (*Jerry* 20–22). A progressive discourse about sexuality thus combines with a more conservative one. The recommendation that Théo have a baby separate from marriage implies that marriage itself is not necessarily the woman's fulfillment. No stigma is attached here to the pregnancy of an unwed mother, although it is certainly not approved by society at large. At the same time, the text implies that a woman needs a man, perhaps not to combat some vague illness that is always a metonymy of hysteria, but at least to help her be fulfilled as a mother. Thus does Callias waver—or try to compromise—between a safe, traditional position and a progressive one of free love.

This is exactly the position in which homosexuality is presented as acceptable in these popular novels: it is made palatable by a combination of the progressive and the conservative. The middle classes, at least, embrace a literal conservatism that maintains the homosexual couple as a variant of the heterosexual dyad. Callias's *Jerry* underlines the paradigm in which the heterosexual couple and nuclear family constitute the absolute norm, for the author posits a variant of one position but not both. Théo can have a child without a husband or the equivalent, but she cannot fully abandon the marriage and motherhood model by eschewing both components: marriage and motherhood. In the gay novels on which I am focusing, we can dispense with the female member of the couple, but only if monogamy and romantic love are maintained. In addition, as I will show, the various peripeteia of one novel lead the gay couple to wind up with a child in a perfect imitation of the nuclear family.

Callias's novel continues to illuminate the situation as it provides the various components that figure into the popular construction of free sex, of which this imagined homosexuality is just one variant. Much of what follows involves Théo's meeting the right person to father her child. In Modane (Savoie) she meets the titular Jerry, a thirty-year-old captain in the American army (38). They meet and get to know each other in a few short pages; shortly the mechanism is set into motion, and they have only a lock sealing the door between their rooms, one that gives way under the slight pressure of compulsory heterosexuality: "And the lock proved that it was in fact not rusted at all" (43). The symbolism is heavy-handed, in stark contrast to the relative ease with which the ongoing plot is constructed. Théo soon gives birth, and the baby—named Francis but nicknamed Pouf—is happily swaddled in his cradle on 15 March 1919, roughly a year after the novel uneventfully started (31 March 1918). Jerry returns to Paris and bonds with his son; toward the end of the short novel (119), however, he returns to the United States, having served his function as doughboy and sperm donor.

This slight work is remarkable for the ways in which, having set up the situation, Callias places almost no impediments to her characters' actions. There is no time for mulling over a situation and no means of considering that an action may have consequences. The plot setups, the dialogue, and the narrative all agree that there not be any impediment to free sex. The narrative itself thus becomes a utopian accomplishment of desire: free sex can happen because a text says it can happen. Consequently, by putting no restriction on the implementation of desire, the narrative sets language, social structures, and cultural exchange as the means by which that desire is fulfilled and the context in which it can happen. Simultaneous with the construction of that sexuality, then, there is the construction of a social group in which the construction happens, as if there were already a group of people who had the same thoughts and whose existence would exclude the representation of any opposing forces. Although perhaps not wholly important for an eyebrow-raising variant of heterosexuality, it will be of fundamental importance in any consideration of homosexuality: homosexuality occurs not only as a sexual activity between two people but also within the construction of a social, linguistic, and cultural community in which it has already happened.[8]

In *Erna: Jeune fille de Berlin* Callias pushes the utopian aspect of fulfilling desire by setting the novel in a very modern Weimar Republic where everything is possible. This technologically advanced society functions as an incarnation of the modern: electricity is everywhere, travel is possible, and information exists for the having. Erna herself works in office where she "gathers radio information arriving from all over the world" (Ménalkas 10). This plethora of information marks a world where everything is available, and sexuality in general—and homosexuality in particular—are discursively describable objects accessible to those who have the information. Thus does Callias interweave a *scientia sexualis* with a generalized technology in which science, progress, and information are integrally linked. Whereas the very title of *L'Ersatz d'amour* equates homosexuality with the ersatz, *Erna* gives the ersatz a positive spin: technology means advancement. For example, margarine is used for cooking (27, 49), and this technological advance is interwoven with other values perceived as positive for a better world: nudism, vegetarianism, and sexology, with a thinly disguised portrait of Magnus Hirschfeld as Dr. Marcus.

Early in the novel Erna goes to a bar called the Silhouette, where "most of the couples belong only to the masculine sex" (Ménalkas 18) and the music comes from a record player: "The phonograph attacks a second tango" (19). Gay sexuality is neither exclusive nor isolated from the straight world; Erna, accompanied by her gay friend, Léo, is welcome to join this mixed world. Again, the interweaving of these various modernities includes homosexuality as one possibility among many. Because sexuality is related to the augmentation of knowledge, moreover, the rest of the novel is cast as a kind of progress narrative, if not exactly a bildungsroman. Erna undergoes a series of events that ultimately help her realize herself, but since Callias seldom places roadblocks between her characters and their accession to knowledge, there is minimal real development.

Erna's first step is to gather information for herself, just as she gathers information from the world at large, so she starts to read the nudist magazine *Freikörperkultur* (free-body culture) (Ménalkas 36). Consonant with the Weimar Republic's espousal of nudism as a way of life—an attitude common across the political spectrum—this position allows Callias to create a situation in which the positive aspects of this new culture are emphasized. Erna thus goes from reading about nudism to going to a nudist camp (43). At the camp she meets a Frenchman, Lucien Cardot, who serves as a mouthpiece to decry French hypocrisy about sex, contrasted here with Weimar freedom and knowledge. The freedom of the body means the freedom to use one's body, to become familiar with it, and to use it for knowledge and pleasure.

The next significant moment in this novel, which is given to long disquisitions, occurs in Berlin when Cardot and Erna are saying goodbye. Cardot sees Léo and remarks to Erna:

> "Useless to ask whether he is a member of 'the club' [la confrérie]."
> "The club? . . . Ah! Perfectly. I like that expression." (85)

We think that homosexuality is recognizable in this open world of Weimar Republic freedom, in which people bandy about words such as *confrérie* in a seemingly comfortable, favorable, or even familiar manner. Callias soon twists the plot, however, setting up a situation in which Cardot explains the apparent iconoclasm that he has heretofore manifested, for he reveals in this final conversation in Berlin that he was homosexual until age twenty-five (89). As much as he has previously seemed to be a voice of reason, Cardot now strikes a minor note in the general utopian discourse of sexual knowledge and freedom: "For if homosexuality is not a mortal weight [une tare mortelle] when it is occasional, it becomes so as soon as it is accompanied by a complete disgust for the opposite sex" (90).

Cardot's remark is the singular flaw in the general argument about sexual and bodily freedom. In distinguishing between kinds of homosexuality, he essentially divides what might be an occasional peccadillo from what might be perceived as exclusivity. At the same time, the statement does not amount to a logical opposition unless an implicit assumption is considered—namely, the assumption that totally exclusive homosexuality is automatically accompanied by misogyny. Yet this is neither explained nor argued anywhere. Perhaps one should assume that instead of signifying a minority position, Cardot's comment merely warns against separating homosexuality from the rest of the sexual continuum. Keeping homosexuality part of the community of sexualities will make it much more difficult for an individual to become the kind of bad homosexual disdained by Gide. The argument then would be that sexual exclusivity is not consonant with separatism, nor is misogyny or separatism requisite for being a good homosexual. This is not clear, however, for when homosexuality is presented again, the message is still a bit cloudy and contrasts both with the relative freedom argued in the rest of the novel and the final scene, to which I will turn shortly.

The reader follows Erna through various events, including a trip to France (Ménalkas 94), but only when she travels to Vienna to attend a congress on sexology (144) does the novel fully develop its position on homosexuality. The congress includes a day "consecrated to homosexuality" (153) during which Dr. Marcus, "a dignified, gray-bearded man" (154), knowledgeably speaks about the need for tolerance and acceptance of homosexuality, which he considers relatively normal. Marcus somewhat resembles the stereotypical portrait of Freud or the Viennese psychoanalyst as type, but as an expert in sexology, he also evokes the German Magnus Hirschfeld, whose campaigning for tolerance for homosexuality, as well as penal reform, marked Weimar life.

Marcus says that homosexuality has two possible causes. It may stem from an infantile complex, ostensibly analogous to the etiology Freud suggests, in which case "one must be able to extirpate it like a parasite." It can also arise from "a kind of internal hermaphroditism," however, in which case the only response is to "prevent it from degenerating into a morbid mania" (Ménalkas 154). Marcus's position thus modifies and explains the somewhat cryptic remark uttered earlier by the reformed homosexual Cardot. Given Callias's construction, in which knowledge, sexuality, and freedom are interrelated, Marcus's position corresponds to the official one for the novel. Thus, at least at this point in her understanding of homosexuality, Callias is reflecting perhaps a general "liberal" position in the process of evolving.

Marcus thus allows three possible configurations to male homosexuality. Consonant with the contemporaneous Freudian explanation of sexuality, homosexuality can be something that develops in early childhood and whose signs are visible. A connection can be made between the manifest homosexual behavior of an adult and a complex of nonsexual behaviors recognizable in an infant, behaviors that can be isolated and removed for the good of an individual. In such a case the child would do better to grow up as a heterosexual, with the protohomosexuality having been excised. There is no sense of trauma and none of suturing, but even beyond that, the psyche is treated as eminently malleable. This is a radical reinterpretation of the classic Freudian remark "Where it/the id was, there shall I/the ego become [Wo es war, soll ich werden]," but the ego is given as potentially always heterosexual. One need only extirpate the bad parts of the id, a decidedly non-Freudian approach.

Homosexuality can also relate to some psychocorporal disposition characterized as "internal hermaphroditism." Ostensibly this would be a natural condition within an individual's psyche, a natural construction that would be likened to the psychic conformations of heterosexuality. Implicitly the construction of homosexuality is the construction of bisexuality: homosexuality is perceived not as a psychic inversion or alterity (i.e., a woman in a man's body or something entirely different) but rather as the existence of a doubled or ambiguous psyche whose etiology is neither decadent nor parasitic. In this case homosexuality is as originary as heterosexuality and does not have to be replaced by it, as is the case for the infantile complex. Whereas the first type of homosexuality should be removed so that heterosexuality, the unwitting victim, can flourish, here homosexuality and heterosexuality are symbiotic. That one or the other manifests itself at a given moment does nothing to diminish the fundamental bisexuality of all individuals whose homosexuality is manifest without being a sign of illness.

Finally, the only danger is that the healthy manifestation of homosexuality may turn morbid in some sort of degenerative behavior. We never learn what this is, but presumably this perceived possibility of degeneration, which recalls the nineteenth century's general theories of degeneration, means crossing an acceptable line. This transgression may take the form of misogyny, as mentioned previously, or develop as some sort of obsessive behavior. Callias's interest rests in a normalized homosexuality that reproduces the heterosexual model of a visible monogamous couple who take their place in the community. She continues to associate sexuality and emotion and does not separate sexuality and sexual behavior from other social intercourse.

At the end of the novel Callias adds one final twist, with Erna finally being fulfilled by entering into a relationship with Billy (Ménalkas 165–66). Just as Théo is really Thérèse in *Jerry*, however, Billy is really a woman with the startling Valkyrie name of Brünnhild. And so they live happily ever after.[9] Erna's progress narrative has brought her to her own fulfillment in a lesbian relationship, which seems to have little need to be explained. Thus the end of the novel posits a final idyllic and utopian moment for its titular heroine, who, having learned, read, and studied, assumes her own homosexuality. Callias will approach the subject again in another novel in which she and her coauthor depict a male homosexual relationship, although one without sex.

This integration of homosexuality reaches its somewhat skewed fulfillment in a novel that Callias cowrote with Marc de la Roche, a book that bears the astounding title *Metallo, mon ami.* In *Metallo* the authors fashion a classic love story by combining the elements of heterosexual romance with certain fundamental aspects of the representation of male homosexuality, even though the two protagonists do not truly become romantically or sexually involved. As I will show, this is merely a technicality. Robert, the first-person narrator of the novel, is from a comfortable family, but to maintain his independence as an artist he moves into "a dump [une turne]" in Montmartre. He needs to have work done on the place, which is in severe disrepair. Robert then meets a twenty-five-year-old worker named Jean Pernet, whom he hires to install electricity (14).[10] In a spirit of solidarity with the working classes, Robert crosses class lines and soon lets Jean wash up in his house (20).

Their budding friendship develops through the solidarity of leftist, antibourgeois politics: together they attend a rally at which the attendees sing both the "Internationale" and the "Marseillaise" (24). Sharing a vision of the future, they join in the pursuit of a French socialism in which all men will be brothers and separations because of class or background will disappear. Again, without bringing up the question of homosexuality, the authors aim at including everyone. Because Jean lives in the far suburbs, he does not return to his parents' house that night and instead sleeps on Robert's couch.

The intimacy continues to develop as a result of an accident. Jean writes Robert a letter saying that his leg has been hurt in a fight. Robert goes to visit him and brings him home to recuperate; reversing roles, Robert serves as Jean's nurse (Ménalkas and de la Roche 49). As their intimacy develops, Robert invites Jean to go on vacation with him in London and Llandudno. As in other novels, the "other place" represents a utopian position freed from the weight of society. Their room in Llandudno has only one bed. They go out to draw and paint, and suddenly, as if the idea of the bed has inspired intimacy (although none is forthcoming), they begin to use the familiar pronoun with each other. At no moment does anything untoward happen. In fact, even the thought of homosexuality seems preposterous to Jean, if not to Robert. This becomes clear when one of the other residents in the boarding house, an older man—coded therefore as a suspicious bachelor—feels up Jean (92–93). Jean is indignant not that he has been felt up but that someone would think of him as a "fag": "'I am not a fag.' He is proud with conviction and indignant excitement. I admire him: 'You're right, sweetie [mon petit]. You are not at all what one calls a fag [une tante]'" (93). This is really the closest the novel comes to making the subject of homosexuality visible. Robert's comments are transparent to the reader, if not to Jean, who seems to remain blissfully unaware of the double-edged irony in Robert's answer. On one level Robert is agreeing with Jean's assessment: Jean's masculinity in no way matches the effeminate picture that the image of a fag conjures, the kind of figure described in *Jésus-la-Caille* and the stereotypical figure that some equate with the homosexual. At another level Robert, after having used the term of endearment of "mon petit" does stress the *vox populi* aspect of the situation: Jean is not a fag as the common image of the homosexual is presented, yet he is nonetheless homosexual in everything but name. It little matters that there is no sexual activity per se; everything else is there, including complete nudity during their last day in Llandudno: they go swimming, but because they have no swimsuits, they skinny-dip in total harmony with each other and with nature (98).

When Jean and Robert return to Paris after their idyllic vacation, Jean moves permanently into Robert's place. At this point they lack only a child to make a perfect nuclear family. And so, in a wonderful move that is nothing less than a *deus ex femina,* Jean gets his girlfriend, Yvonne, pregnant. At the same time Robert has to travel to the United States for a period of six to eight months (Ménalkas and de la Roche 132) in a surreal, gay version of the unwed pregnant woman's old-fashioned "*voyage en Suisse.*" In fact he returns after ten and a half months, and so the average mean between the promised trip and the real one is the nine-month period of gestation. In that time Yvonne has given birth to a baby boy who has been named "Bébert," that is, a diminutive of "Robert." Yet we are no closer to a happy ending until Yvonne conveniently receives a letter from her ex-boyfriend, who is inheriting money (145). She decides to go back to Brittany and leaves Bébert to be raised by Jean and thus implicitly by Robert as well. At the end of the novel Jean and Robert are happily raising Bébert, to whom Robert seems to have given both his name and his artistic talent.

Callias and de la Roche have fantasized a utopian homosexual relationship with neither impediments nor sex. At every turn class barriers are crossed, personal spaces are reduced, and proxemic distances are shortened, all without a hitch. Each accident serves to bring the lead characters closer together with nary a second thought. Most interesting, the entire telos of the novel reconstructs the heterosexual nuclear family, although the child comes about through a kind of virgin birth, with Yvonne's body, existence, and departure merely providing the means for the phantasm of a male-male couple having a child.

Whereas *Metallo* may go off the deep end in its quest to circumscribe male homosexuality, this is not the case with the first of the novels that Callias coauthored with Willy: *L'Ersatz d'amour.* (The second novel, *Le Naufragé,* is far less successful, and I will discuss it only briefly before turning to Willy's view of the world of male homosexuality in *Le Troisième Sexe.*) From its very title, *L'Ersatz d'amour* attempts to create male homosexuality as a lesser path, although one without ignominy. Homosexuality may be an ersatz love, but it is not without its own virtues; we already know that cooking with margarine will be an acceptable possibility, at least for Callias in *Erna.* So male homosexuality will be a kind of oleo of love, not devoid of nutritional value or taste, yet not quite as good as the butter of heterosexuality.

L'Ersatz uses many of the motifs typical of the other novels already discussed in this chapter, including an idyllic romp, the magic disappearance of many impediments, the artist as free spirit, and border crossings, much of which can be summed up in an "open sesame" or flying carpet found in the preface: "Let's cross the border" (Willy and Ménalkas xi). For example, the preface includes a long discussion on Germany as a kind of gay utopia where, despite the penal code's Paragraph 175, homosexuality has flourished since the war. Yet this novel differs from the others in several ways. First, class difference plays no real role in this novel. The Frenchman, Marc Renneval, is an artist, but he has the wherewithal to travel, attend concerts, and forgo work. The German, Carl, is of noble background and rich as well, and his family background and culture are extremely francophilic. Thus any social and economic differences are bridged by the fact that both men participate in the same high culture, although the reader is reminded at least once that the culture is an acquired one for Carl. They start talking about literature and the fact that Carl has lots of French books. Marc bets he can guess which ones Carl has. He guesses that Carl has books such as "*Claudine*—the whole series—the *Journal d'une femme de chambre*—*Aphrodite*—*Nana*—the *Demi-Vierges*" (53). Carl is astonished that he has guessed correctly. Marc guesses that Carl does not have "*L'Œuvre* among others by Zola; all Balzac; *En Route* and *La Cathédrale* of Huysmans—Jules Renard—Albert Samain; and the Jean Christophe of Romain Rolland" (54). Carl has the sensational or titillating "French" novels, but lacks those that might more adequately represent literary heights, even if they do not show the sordid or seamy side.

More important is the fact that the men are not from classes with opposing interests, so the rapprochement between them is unimpeded. Beyond the disappearance of class difference, the novel is much darker and more pessimistic than are the other popular novels. Even though some of the impediments magically disappear, readers realize from the outset that there will be a problem, for the novel starts in September 1913, just eleven months before the outbreak of World War I. Given that the relationship will occur between a Frenchman and a German, we recognize that there will be a problem sooner or later. Significantly, though, the problem will be external to the question of homosexuality: it would little matter at this point if the couple were heterosexual. Thus there is, at least in this depiction, nothing internal to homosexuality that is seen as a fatal or fatalistic means of destruction.

As I have already indicated, the novel's other departure is the way in it constructs homosexuality as a seemingly temporary solution to Marc's lack of a female companion. Marc lets himself go toward it almost despite himself, as if sexual need were basically undifferentiated, albeit preferential. He prefers heterosexuality, but if no woman is available, he will settle for the ersatz situation while remaining basically heterosexual. Need it be said that there is never any real questioning as to whether a sexual Rubicon has been crossed? Marc justifies his behavior from time to time simply by expressing it as a function of his physical needs. Thus at least one of the dominant rationalizations will be that sexual desire is not psychologically founded, or if it is, that the foundation or truth can be superseded by a physical need brought on by a specific situation or lack.

As Willy presents it in the preface, the novel's setup is more complicated than those of the other works, using a pattern reminiscent of the opening of *L'Immoraliste.*[11] To be discussed safely and rationally, homosexuality must be distanced at all costs, so that the readers, who are presumably open-minded heterosexuals, may look yet not fear contamination. The enunciative framework is mirrored in the closing of windows and doors as well: we see nothing improper beyond a bit of passing body contact from time to time.[12] Without such a frame we might be touched by it, and we might ourselves convert from heterosexuality to homosexuality, for the very presence of the latter may be enough to change someone:

> Last month, during one of my stops in Paris, which are always short for life has become too expensive there for me, I met an acquaintance, almost a friend, a true artist whose man-about-town snobbishness [le snobisme boulevardier] praises very highly, without loving it, the talent of a rather bitter originality . . . Painter, sculptor, or musician, let us not say . . .
>
> I did not exclaim: *quantum mutatus,* held back by the fear of being taken for a fake Latinist, but I could barely hide my amazement faced with the frightening change that this hale and healthy "jock" [sportif] had undergone, whom I found, after three years of absence, bent, sallow, and shaking with nervous tics. (Willy and Ménalkas, *L'Ersatz* vii)

L'Ersatz d'amour is presented as a multiply framed tale, but whereas Gide is content with one set of frames all relating to the same confession, Willy and Ménalkas set up an ambiguously defined double frame. The French protagonist of the novel, the artist Marc Renneval, has written his memoirs in the form of a diary that starts in September 1913 and continues for one calendar year. These memoirs have been brought by a soldier to Marc's friend and fellow artist, Simon-Pierre. It is here that the ambiguity arises. Did Simon-Pierre give these memoirs to yet another person who is himself a former acquaintance of Willy, doing so with the implicit challenge, so to speak, of turning these notes into a novel? "Here, since you are a novelist, if you want to see how the life of a man can irremediably derail after an absurdly unlikely set of events [aventure], leaf through this" (viii). Or has the acquaintance written his own diary, showing the depravity that can ensue from manifestations of male homosexuality?

Multiple distances are taken along an alternating chain to get to the transcription in novel form, the transcription that we do and do not read, for the diary is presented as is, as if Willy had never touched it. The truth remains what it is, untouched by the novelist's hand. This chain is itself a means of protecting both the truth of the text and the truth of the author: Marc Renneval, who has always been straight, goes to Germany after the breakup of his last relationship and meets a man named Carl, with whom he irresistibly and "unnaturally" falls in love. The diary that he keeps is sent to his erstwhile best friend in Paris, Simon-Pierre, who is not only heterosexual but also prejudiced against gays for their unnatural behavior. There the chain is broken. Either the manuscript falls into other hands, or there is a second manuscript, written by hands that repeat at a distance Marc's own conversion. This last, unnamed individual meets Willy on the street during a quick trip the latter has taken to Paris and gives him a manuscript. This chain of transmission is a way both of protecting the truth of the diary and of keeping the author's distance from possible contamination by the narrative of conversion. After all, in this world people spontaneously change from heterosexual to homosexual.

Finally, insofar as the preface is concerned, the chance encounter, from whose likes the readers need protection, is still the cause for an introduction of the literary as a privileged locus. Unlike the other novels already discussed, this one, which clearly shows Willy's hand, chooses high culture as a topos and a privileged locus in which greater thoughts can occur. Literature—and by extension art and music—is a spot where homosexuality may become acceptable. The friend met on the street confesses in oblique terms: "I am a washed up man now . . . existence ruined forever . . . me, who believed himself made for family life" (Willy and Ménalkas, *L'Ersatz* vii). This is immediate cause for the author's—Willy's—introduction of a compound motif: heterosexuality's superiority to homosexuality, the hetero-eroticized inscription of female homosexuality, and the function of the literary. "His confessions . . . caused that feeling of sadness that rises from masculine homosexuality for spectators whom the feminine does not shock; difference of appreciation motivated especially by reasons of superficial aesthetics in which morality does not have any role to play" (viii). Willy goes on to list all the exceptions to this feeling of sadness, for there are lots of authors who have treated the subject well, including himself, Colette (ix), and others whose writing may give rise to other feelings in the readers.

As I have already indicated, the novel starts in September 1913, a month after the breakup between Marc Renneval and his girlfriend, Rolande, who has refused a final meeting to explain her behavior. Unable to mend fences with his ex and hungering for a change in scenery, he gets the idea to visit Germany: "A sudden impetuous and unreasoned desire invaded my brain. I am going to go to Germany" (Willy and Ménalkas, *L'Ersatz* 28). Germany, however, signifies male homosexuality, as we already know from the preface, which is ostensibly written after the main text but is read before it. The preface alerts the readers that Renneval will be dealing with homosexuality, even if he remains blissfully unaware of it for the moment. Yet the readers recognize that this "impetuous and unreasoned desire" might itself be his unconscious speaking, his id screaming for him to be gay, to have a gay experience, or merely to test the waters across the Rhine.

This is only a possibility at the moment, but the space in which homosexuality can occur has opened. It will not happen, however, without one final stab at heterosexuality, notable because of the way in which Callias and Willy structure this sequence. In these novels, where the figure of the artist often comes into play (as happens with Willy's work in general, as well as in that of Colette), the artist usually encodes free-thinking in a kind of libertinage that is iconoclastic in all ways. For Renneval, this Willy-like libertinage is doubly marked, once by his profession as an artist and a second time by his avocation as a musician. As a musician, moreover, he is able to seduce women, who "fall for" his violin playing:

> I shall also take my violin; my violin that I use so *well;* this I know. I'll play it in the evening, in some corner of the salon at the hotel . . . It is generally a foolproof way of attracting women. And if I find a pretty German (or Pole or Russian) who starts to circle around my bow, I shall ask her to accompany me on the piano. A good beginning for an affair [*aventure*]. I would have to be really an idiot not to have my way with one woman there. And this is the most certain, infallible cure for emotional disappointments. In love, the only therapy is homeopathic; get rid of one ill with something like it. (Willy and Ménalkas, *L'Ersatz* 28)

Music seduces where words fail; the women see the soul of an artist and are ready to have an affair. Renneval cares little who the woman is; the multiple choice of nationalities essentially means that the world is wide open and that all women are potentially the same and available sexually to "circle around" his phallic bow. Music is thus a projection of his masculinity and a sign that he is ready to be a man. Moreover, this implied erection guarantees returned health: having been dumped by his former girlfriend implies a kind of impotence, but one that is easily cured. That the thinking is both demeaning and misogynistic changes nothing, nor does the fact that he is unsuccessful: he meets a young Polish woman, according to his plan, but she is leaving for Italy the next day (32–33).

What can we assess from this one failure? Not that his charm no longer works, but that the construction of the novel does not want it to work. He is still sexy and can attract another to his arched bow, but this will not happen without divine intervention. As any reader of "bad" novels knows, requesting the intervention of divinity usually brings about results, but often with a twist: Renneval goes into a church and makes a wish: "May the Lord God send me a woman and get rid of my memory of Rolande!" (35). The Lord God, however, sends not a woman but another music lover who is, of course, a man.[13] Seated on a café terrace, listening to predictable classical music (Lehár's *Merry Widow* and the overture to Wagner's *Meistersinger*), Renneval first exchanges glances with two women, but that soon ends, and he feels himself being penetrated by another glance:

> For a moment, I feel that there is someone looking at me with persistence; there, on the side . . . This time, it is not a woman. I notice that it is a very young officer, his torso cinched in a steel-gray dolman, his flat cap bordered in red, stuck on his dirty blond [blond glacé] hair. This young man is remarkably handsome. His profile looks like that of Carpentier, but finer; his chin more clearly limned. His skin has the color of a young English girl; his eyes, of a luminous blue, rather elongated toward his temples, are, for example, a bit dark [tannés] at the eyelids and remove the almost childlike look from this young face. (Willy and Ménalkas, *L'Ersatz* 36–37)

The person looking at him is a man, but the officer is nonetheless coded with mixed gender clues. Most notable is Renneval's immediate recognition of the other's good looks. Whereas the earlier, purely macho Renneval would probably not have noticed male beauty, this new incarnation remarks it immediately. The soldier's fine skin tone recalls the peaches-and-cream complexion of a fresh young woman; his eyes are typically Slavic and marked slightly by a stereotypical hint of orientalism coded in the heavy-lidded, dark eyes. He is marked as well by the removal of innocence. This penetrating glance with which the German officer persistently stares at Renneval is not an innocent act but rather the visual translation of the penetration that Renneval had previously imagined. The German officer initially takes the dominant position, that of the active searcher for the other, and Renneval is automatically feminized in the process, although without realizing it.

The officer gets up and approaches Renneval, who discovers that he speaks perfect French, for he offers to translate something. Marc asks him what the orchestra has just played (Willy and Ménalkas, *L'Ersatz* 37). Significantly, it is no longer *The Merry Widow* or even *Die Meistersinger* but Schubert's "Danse slave," yet another minor indication of the slight orientalism associated with Eastern Europe and ultimately with the German officer himself, who is part Polish and anything but Prussian: "This boy is nice and well brought up, nothing of the 'schneidig [pushy]' type of Prussian officers" (40). After a short discussion of the drawbacks of Fraktur, with each man criticizing his own people's shortcomings, and a longer discussion of some background, the officer tells Marc that there is to be a "Wagner evening" in the concert hall the following day (39). The officer indicates which seat is his and expresses his hopes that Marc will find a seat not too far away (40). Just as music was to have been the means by which Renneval would seduce a woman, it continues to be the means by which the unreasoned desire will find fulfillment. Thus are the authors proposing that there are universals to desire and that everyone is possibly seducible. Indeed, as a stereotypical remark demonstrates, Renneval is immediately seduced by beauty, a pleasure made bittersweet by an immediate regret: "'What a shame that he is not his sister,' I thought as I walked away" (40).

That Renneval can have that thought again marks the locus of beauty and sexuality as mutable through a kind of Proustian metempsychosis. Desire itself is mobile and can float from object to object or subject to subject. The other thus possesses qualities of desirability that are only tangentially attached to biological sex: if the officer had simply been a woman with the exact same features but a different hidden anatomy, everything would have been fine. The body is more social conformation than biological imperative. In other words, if the same features can be perceived on a man or a woman, it is only the social construction of the space in which sexuality occurs—the gendered body as exclusively heterosexual—that determines how desire is enacted.

Needless to say, they wind up in adjoining seats in the concert hall. Hearing the strains of Isolde mourning over Tristan's corpse, Marc is overwhelmed with emotion, but that is soon replaced by other thoughts: "What torture did I seek here? What recall of the mean, despotic, pitiless passion . . . Suddenly, I shiver, nonplussed [je tressaille, interloqué]. A hand has lightly grazed my own. What, is there a woman next to me? . . . I half turn, with precaution

. . . My companion, leaning a bit toward me, is gazing absentmindedly at the ceiling. Maybe his movement was involuntary? But the hand is steadily gaining ground. . . . Now it imprisons mine like a carapace; two, three, four fingers grip mine, their braid a living plait" (Willy and Ménalkas, *L'Ersatz* 41–42). The movement of desire is doubled here by the complexity of the situation. On the one hand, the desire is motivated through a sympathetic recognition of and identification with Isolde's position as she sings the *Liebestod* and apostrophizes her dead beloved. Whereas Isolde will ostensibly rejoin Tristan in the afterlife, there is no promise of that for the world-weary Renneval; heterosexuality is dead. Moved by fate into a situation, just as fate—in the form of a love potion—made Tristan and Isolde fall in love, he is suddenly shaken into a realization of his desire, as if the presence of her desire leaves him open for the first person who desires him. And that desire, of course, is from another man.

In that split second the self-righteous heterosexual returns and remembers, as often happens in such narratives, a previous instance of homosexuality. Homosexuality never happens for the first time. It has always already happened. In this case Marc remembers a fellow student from the École des Beaux Arts who had tried a similar maneuver that he had repelled with indignation. In this case, however, there is a "completely contrary" double movement. The first is of "instinct, the subconscious," as Renneval brusquely removes his hand (Willy and Ménalkas, *L'Ersatz* 42). The second is more telling, a movement of "reflection, of dilettantism, [. . .] leaving [his] hand where it was, and seeing what happens" (42). His reaction to the event thus reverses surface and heart, or conscious and subconscious/unconscious. Previously, seated at some unconscious locus, desire had no gender; it was poured into a surface structure created by mores. Here, however, the unconscious "instinct" is decidedly heterosexual or heteronormative, and it is the libertine conscious mind that seeks to play.

So the libertine consciousness is a way to queer imposed structures of gender and sex, whether they are imposed by nature as instincts or by society as learned behavior. By playing, by being a dilettante, and by abandoning his hand Renneval marks his sexuality as fully his own, a function of his conscious mind. He is able to choose his pleasure; he is not enslaved by instinctual desire or heteronormative society. By choosing to experiment, he is conscious of the choice. Fully recognizing the debasement that might ensue, Renneval will plunge in: "After all, I don't care; I am not a saint. There are moments in life, of total distress, of loneliness [esseulement], in which one starts to talk with one's concierge, in which one looks for the caress of a dog. . . . When one is dying of thirst, one would drink swamp water" (Willy and Ménalkas, *L'Ersatz* 42). Thus do the authors have Renneval's own behavior as a kind of recognized slumming, for desperate times bring desperate measures. The analogies are less than flattering, especially in the light of the Frenchman's previous admiration for the German officer.

Nonetheless, this rationalization carries the day. Renneval must first convince himself that this homosexuality, which does not amount to a real choice or even a real position of desire, is nothing more than the manifestation of self-abandon in a situation where it is the lesser of two evils, for assuredly nothing is worse than celibacy. What is excluded remains as interesting as this false choice, for it would have been easy to find a prostitute in any city of the time, and in Paris it would have been simple to hook up with a soubrette or music-hall singer. So Renneval's actions continue to beg the question, set as they are along a single line where there is seemingly no choice—no other woman in Paris, no woman in Germany; it's the German officer or nothing—but that is always a false dichotomy. There are other choices, but Renneval's actions continue to point him, rationalization or no, toward homosexuality.

After having rationalized his behavior as being something better than celibacy but no different from zoophilia, Renneval finds a second set of rationalizations brought about by higher ethical considerations. The officer invites Marc to his apartment for tea. Although he initially hesitates at accepting the invitation, even though it is only for tea, he then accepts with the following reason: "Oh well! I will take the leap. For once, I shan't die of it, after all. Pure curiosity of a dilettante, that is. When in China, it is completely natural to smoke an opium pipe. In Japan, you visit Yoshivara. I am in Germany, and Chance, that sneaky [cocasse] god, throws me into the arms of one of those followers of the Prince von Eulenburg and Kuno von Moltke, whose neo-Greek exploits delighted all the satiric newspapers five or six years ago" (Willy and Ménalkas, *L'Ersatz* 44).[14] So the process of having tea, in its natural course toward sodomy, is acceptable because it is part of the cultural climate, and going native is appropriate for a tourist, even if it means having sex with someone one would otherwise never choose as a bedmate. Moreover, because it is related not to any real specific desire but to a combination of horniness and curiosity, the behavior is acceptable. Nevertheless, there is something strange about evoking the cultural context, for the intermixed classical and contemporary references Renneval marshals to justify what he is about to do are potentially humiliating for him. Yet he will not be stopped in his exploration. It seems to be simply something he has failed to do earlier, which his memories of the generalized situation for adolescents from privileged classes suggest; he won't be hurt by this one experiment: "So many men did it in boarding school, and they returned to normal afterwards . . . It will make me younger, that is all" (44). Again, the rationalization is interesting, for it casts homosexuality as an innocent pleasure, totally unremarkable in an adolescent who, seeking some release, accepts that position only to return to "normal" heterosexuality when he returns to a sexually nonsegregated society. That homosexuality is an attraction for and to youth is seconded by what we already know: the still as yet unnamed German officer is youthful, and that aids rationalizing the events to come as a playing out of innocence.

Since Marc is a novice, "perhaps it would be better to define the program a bit, in order to avoid annoying surprises to one partner or the other," he thinks to himself (Willy and Ménalkas, *L'Ersatz* 45). After some "confused remarks" in which he beats about the bush, so to speak, giving various examples—ancient Greece and Oxbridge—he settles on Lesbos: "The students of Oxford, Cambridge . . . Their caresses always have something childlike, incomplete . . . Like those of friends of the feminine sex . . . Yes! The example of Lesbos is perfect" (45). Somewhat taken aback, the officer answers, ostensibly to reassure Marc: "'Of course,' he answered, pinching his lips with a prudish air. 'Only professionals and soldiers have such gross habits. Well brought up people know how to behave'" (45).

While it seems of little interest to speculate on exactly what is acceptable and what is not, note that the translation of male homosexuality into a kind of lesbian mutual masturbation is a way of normalizing it once again. The point of this translation is not to eschew vanilla forms of homosexuality that might involve some penetration but rather to make the activity more palatable to Renneval, for female homosexuality is within the realm of the representationally acceptable. Perhaps because Renneval is skittish at first, this way of claiming Renneval also makes things easier for the German officer, who, although clearly more devoted to homosexuality than this accidental encounter suggests Renneval to be, does not descend to the gutter level. Nonetheless, while acquiescing to Renneval's implication that their relations remain so much foreplay and mutual masturbation, the officer's remark is equivocal: saying that he would not do the unthinkable because only professionals and soldiers would do that is undercut by the fact that he *is* a professional soldier. So clearly he would do that had Renneval taken a position other than the very vanilla one he espouses.

Matters change immediately when they move from words to action—not the boundaries of acceptable and unacceptable behavior but reactions to the behavior. At first Renneval remains resolutely French and committed to his plan of pursuing the affair for a kind of release from what he will soon admit has been a thirty-two-day dry spell. He notices that the German has laid out two pairs of pajamas and has thus "thought of everything" (Willy and Ménalkas, *L'Ersatz* 46). After the first kiss he remarks that a Frenchman "would not have moved so quickly" (46). His caviling, however, soon gives way to a description of his own reactions to the events taking place. This confession clearly shows not only the change of heart and the rapidly receding importance of rationalization but also—and this is something never seen in Proust or Gide—a sentimental recording of reactions, feelings, and enjoyment implying that the actions constitute acceptable behavior because they are pleasing to a hedonist:

> I owe a complete [sans fard] confession here. Certainly, yes, for me, who lived in penitence of love for exactly thirty-two days, it was a fine, tasty joy, the hug of that young, lissome [flexueux] body, and the contact with that epidermis, delicate like that of a woman, whence came a rare perfume, and those lips of which one could not have said if they were hairless or shaved, intelligently ardent, and breathing out a fresh breath. All that was a harmless, admirable illusion . . . But there are moments in love in which you have to come down from the peaks a bit. For they are really whistling into the wind [ils nous la bâillent belle], in truth, those poets and novelists who always strove to idealize sexual caresses! In reality, certain parts of the human being have nothing pure or noble about them. It is a long atavistic training that has accustomed us to see them thus. The proof is that a virgin adolescent, faced with those realities, often freezes, put off a bit. But now, I was no more "trained." Thus, I swear that everything I was led to do along those lines was merely *politeness*, in order not to fall too far behind. Just as a well brought up man swallows, smilingly, a cup of tea that smells of artichokes and badly cooked cake of which he asks for a second helping, declaring it excellent. (47–48)

The passage has a way of softening the situation, feminizing the event, and thereby making it, at least in Renneval's eyes, less homosexual and more ersatz heterosexual. Thus the German has a young, lissome body, his skin is like that of women, there is a perfume, his face is "hairless or shaved," and so forth. This feminization is a way of rationalizing the behavior: Renneval is going to have sex not with another man but with an ersatz woman. At the same time, the generalized discourse of love, as proffered by poets, is itself a fiction, and sometimes other solutions will have to do, even if they are as distasteful as artichoke-smelling tea: one would not want to risk offending.

Thus does Renneval justify his own decisions. Moreover, the passage is quite an amazing one composed of the disparate elements of confession and admission, all guaranteed by the hedonist argument, which is itself clad in the Frenchness of being polite. To whom does he owe a confession, one might initially ask? To the readers or to himself? More likely to the latter than to the former, because within the construction of his own desire, he certainly has nothing to confess and thus nothing for which he can be granted absolution.[15] Rather, the confession is that things happened that did not remain at the level of the plan; Renneval was unsuccessful in his attempt to be a wannabe lesbian, and clearly, albeit implicitly, the German officer is both a soldier and a professional.

At first things remain on the surface: the evocation of surfaces in the prelude to a kiss and the implication that the act of sex will be caresses (like those of adolescents and lesbians) are underscored by the sensuality of the surface, such as the officer's lips and skin. But the body is not all lips and skin, all "papillae of pleasure," as René Crevel said. Rather, it includes excrescences and infoldings. A rhetoric of politeness values surface over depth, and so the body is perceived to be constructed along the same lines. Whereas the body of the woman may implicitly be seen to be entirely surface, as if invagination itself were no more than a continuation of surface pleasure and acceptability, this is not the case with a man, who has two body parts—genitals and anus—that can fall outside that category.[16] The text is carefully worded, and we are led to believe in something that hitherto seemed impossible: not that Renneval actively participates in anal intercourse but that, by dint of the adolescent's fear to which he alludes, the situation is reversed and his position becomes the passive one. Arguably the passage is ambiguous, yet by using that fear instead of priapism as the transition to the last part of the passage, the authors are at least implying the possibility of Renneval's being bottom.

The last part of the passage, too, is remarkable in its rationalized excuse making and especially its surreal simile. The rationalization returns us to the politeness that marks the episode's first section, the fact that a Frenchman would not have proceeded so quickly and would have begun by "offering tea" (46). Thus does Renneval cast his behavior, which here moves from the evoked act to some sense of reciprocity, as depending more on politeness than on desire. This may be explained biographically, for once: the mobility to the construction of sexual metaphoricity may result from the authors' apparent lack of experience at being a male homosexual. It is the passage's final comparison, however, recalling the earlier offer of tea, that is most interesting here. It points toward well-known references in *Du côté de chez Swann* where

Marcel eats a madeleine dipped into a cup of infusion and where a chamber pot is completely perfumed with the smell of asparagus Marcel ate earlier. Thus do the authors of this novel use literary allusion to combine oral and anal as they strive to imply that Renneval has given himself over to all kinds of homosexual activity, not just those promised at the outset of the episode.[17]

The next step in the process is some sort of acknowledgment of Renneval's new role. When they wake up the next morning, the two men still use the polite form of address, and it is not until Renneval is leaving that they learn each other's names. Renneval begins to justify his behavior yet again in an unexpected way. Earlier he was attracted to Carl (for that is his new acquaintance's name) because the officer could be confused with an imagined feminine version of himself and thus could be viewed—perhaps with squinty eyes—as feminine. Now, however, after this night of love, we learn that Carl is not feminine, or at least not effeminate. The night has brought counsel but also reoriented precisely what is attractive in the other: "Despite his inversion, his candidly sly looks, he is certainly less effeminate than the likes of him in the bars of Montmartre. Like British boys, the young men of Germany always keep something of full health and original male hardiness" (Willy and Ménalkas, *L'Ersatz* 48–49). So whereas Carco did not create a counterexample to la Caille or the slumming M. Pacific, Willy and Ménalkas imagine a reasonably well-adjusted homosexual whose behavior falls on the side of the healthy and the masculine. That attraction, which we now know to be mutual, turns Renneval into the figure that was denigrated only a few pages before: "Still, it is curious how one becomes a 'whore' [grue] as soon as one feels desired by another human being, of whatever sort [quel qu'il soit]" (51).

The evocation of the bars of Montmartre may recall Carco's novel, but it also sets the stage for a trip to a gay bar in Germany that is both similar to and different from the Parisian bars with which Renneval is familiar. They go to a bar called Nirvâna (Willy and Ménalkas, *L'Ersatz* 52), and even if he has some familiarity with such bars—for one can easily imagine him as a spectator/tourist in the bars of Montmartre—Renneval is new to all this and promptly mistakes a male dancer for a woman. "Jeez [Sapristi], it is true we are in Sodom here" (56). Yet all he need do, much like Emma Bovary, is take the position of the other. They dance: "Really, I feel Carl and I make a perfect couple. [. . .] The joy of the beautiful dance takes hold of me; our double image, returned by the high mirrors, gives me a passing feeling of aesthetic satisfaction" (58–59). Thus does being a spectator on one's own sexual position, as characters in nineteenth-century erotica and, in a more complicated way, in the *Claudine* series often are, guarantee the validity of the position: seeing oneself maintains the visual position of dominance, which is the position of the heterosexual male, whatever he may be doing. Thus, we may have moved from a fake lesbianism to Sodom, but Sodom is rendered less of a problem by the doubling of Renneval's position as performer and observer for whom the unique product of self-centered pleasure is Renneval himself. The dance and the observation thereof make the bond between the two men more intimate, for after the dance and the admiration of some around them, they magically change from the formal to the familiar form of address (60).

The relationship continues to develop during the various obligatory episodes. Renneval reflects that he can control Carl, misogynistically and "heterophobically" making the latter his woman: "[Even] with his vice that I don't fully understand [me dépasse], there is only a child, a baby, next to me. I could easily drag him into the basest stream; but I could also have him darn my socks" (77). As in the description of Carl, where Marc feminizes him to justify consorting with him as ersatz heterosexuality, this will to dominance and the refeminization of Carl as someone who can darn socks further rationalize Renneval's behavior: this is not really homosexuality but just a kind of heterosexuality in disguise.

The novel alternates between this refeminization and a normalization of behavior. For example, as befits this modern gay couple and consonant with the idyll necessary to all these novels, the two go to Heligoland on vacation (Willy and Ménalkas, *L'Ersatz* 83). Not for them is the previously mentioned trip to Italy, which as Renneval points out in another Flaubertian moment is passé: "But no, my darling [mon petit], you are behind the times . . . Italy is dated . . . It is a post card [chromo], a honeymoon" (70). Marc begins to get comfortable with the relationship: "I am getting used to Carl; that is the most appropriate expression I find for defining the situation. I am getting used to his social company [compagnie morale] and his physical company" (82). And so, despite some knee-jerk backsliding into the realm of the exclusively heterosexual, Renneval recognizes that he is also getting used to being involved in a gay relationship. Marc thinks: "What a pity after all that this pretty human animal is devoted thus to artificial and sterile love" (84). That night Marc goes to bed in his own room—contiguous to Carl's—and thinks to himself that he really has a feeling of "fraternal tenderness" (84) for Carl. Try as he may to fall asleep, he cannot, so he gets up, asks Carl whether he is asleep, and joins him in his bed (85).

The relationship becomes so intense that Renneval even becomes jealous of Carl's past. The jealousy may be Proustian, but the narrative frame is decidedly Gidean, a structure that seems to have been lifted from a mixture of *Corydon* and *Les Faux-Monnayeurs. Corydon* presents the reader with an emblematic portrait of Walt Whitman that marks the beginning of the apology and serves as the homofraternal sign under which the apology will occur. In addition, there is a letter found on a bed and written to Corydon from his admirer Alexis. In *Les Faux-Monnayeurs* Gide tightens the figure by inserting a letter into a book for safekeeping, but the letter is eventually discovered, and from it Bernard deduces a whole range of behavior. In *L'Ersatz d'amour* the authors combine the two parts of the figure. Renneval has been given free rein to wait for Carl in his apartment. This solitude—the orderly [ordonnance] is not there—allows the authors to create a marked framing, for Renneval can look through Carl's library. Carl is consistent in his literary taste. In addition to finding the French novels already mentioned, Renneval discovers semiotically loaded works such as *Frau Beate und seiner Sohn,* by Schnitzler, which is "the story of a mother who loves her son too much" (Willy and Ménalkas, *L'Ersatz* 87); the requisite *Death in Venice,* "where the feminine sex shines by its absence"; and even a work named *Bordello,* which has a "cubist cover," thereby marking the interrelation of progress on the sexual and artistic fronts. These are only a prelude, however, for the collection includes a beautifully bound edition of *The Picture of Dorian Grey* in which Carl has placed a photograph of a former lover as a keepsake. Renneval immediately becomes jealous of the ex, and his jealousy is appeased only when Carl rather theatrically rips up the picture along with one of another previous lover (90).

Having attained the intimacy sufficient to make him fully committed to this relationship, Renneval must leave. Nothing is to be gained by keeping the characters together, for as we know, this will not be a novel about the two figures facing an adverse society. One is a nobleman; the other is an artist. The die was cast when the novel began. By separating them the authors can create two series of episodes in which the audience will change for this developing relationship. One will transpire within the family circle; the other, in Paris. Each of these will modify the ways in which Callias and Willy propose that their readers understand and accept homosexuality. The series of events already discussed involved an acceptance of homosexuality by an individual for himself and within the structure of a somewhat isolated couple. The second series will mark that couple in relation to the family unit. And finally, because Paris is "society," it will be the locus in which the homosexual is marked by and for society as a whole.

Marc returns to Paris because of business obligations. He has already extended his stay in Germany far beyond the original plan. Once there he rediscovers, at least theoretically, the normalizing heterosexual environment that he had left. At this point in the novel the writers are unclear regarding the direction they want to take. Through some personal connections, Renneval gets his work exhibited in an art show at the Grand Palais. The narrator reflects on that, saying that "that year and those that followed" (Willy and Ménalkas, *L'Ersatz* 103) he was astonished to find his work hanging in such a place, and now it is he who has the power of helping others. Marc has less than a year to live, however, for he will die early in World War I.[18]

The depiction of homosexuality widens when the couple, having been separated, moves from the simple dyadic relationship to one that is both visible and invisible within the family circle. Most important, the return to Paris and its heterosexuality has changed nothing: Marc is resolutely involved in a gay relationship—this despite his repeated feminization of Carl—and not even the capital city of heterosexuality can straighten him out. Carl proposes that Marc spend Christmas vacation with his family near Koblentz. Marc meets Carl's mother, the Baroness von Rudorff, who in stereotypical fashion believes Marc to be a good influence on Carl, so she agrees to Carl's request that their guest stay in the room next to his instead of the nice guest room.[19] At one level the mother facilitates the situation, just as the various other works cast the idyllic spot as a locus in which proximity is somehow imposed. But a castle on the Rhine is itself already idyllic; it is a motive that the knowing and unknowing Mme Verdurin uses to allow Charlus and Morel to occupy a wing of her chateau, where the walls are so thick that they can make music all night without disturbing others.

At another level, however, this can easily be interpreted as what Eve Kosofsky Sedgwick has called "the epistemology of the closet": a double-bind between knowing and not knowing, where the secret of which no one speaks is still known to everyone, albeit unconsciously. Here the facilitator is the Oedipal mother: there is no father, she dotes on her beautiful son, the influence of the Frenchman must be a good one because he is the icon of culture, and he will not be a female rival for the mother. Nevertheless, theorists as different as René Girard and Gilles Deleuze might wonder at the simplicity of the Oedipal mechanism, homosexualized in this version of the epistemology. Girard, for example, would no doubt construe Renneval as a rival, consciously so or not, for the Oedipal mother. Deleuze would no doubt view the Oedipal trio as remarkably reductive. As Deleuze and Guattari show, the Freudian model is reductive in that it essentializes subject positions and eschews any social construction of the individual as the Oedipalized individual formed by capitalism. Sedgwick's model, too, is based not only on a reduction of the subject position but also—and much more problematically—on the reduction of that subject to an American subject. Girard's model has the advantage of not really formulating a theory of desire based on gender, even if all his examples were basically heterosexual. But here too, the reduction to a triangulated position reduces all the players to pawns and renders them incapable of judgment, decision, or choice.

This point of contact is not merely the product of a triangulation of desire or a bivalent closet but the intersection of multiple subjectivities, of the public and private, and of multiple discursivities. What Willy and Callias show, just as Proust shows in the scene with Mme Verdurin, is that a multiplicity of discourses determines the ways in which the public and private are negotiated. Conversely, the ways in which the public and private are negotiated help determine the discourses produced. The construction of a closet or the triangulation of Oedipal desire is less a factor—were we to assume, for the sake of argument, that this is a mimetic work of literature—than are the rhetoric of blindness and the possibilities of an discursive episteme in which occur multiple criss-crossings, or *traversées* (to use Kristeva's excellent word), none of which is reducible to a bivalent or trivalent situation.

This is recognized as even Renneval trivializes, albeit unconsciously, the unitary subject position that all these models require. After the midnight mass and the Christmas Eve meal, everyone goes to bed: "The door opens softly, just as I blew out my lamp to go to bed. Carl pads around in the darkness, in his bedclothes, and throws himself on me with stifled exclamations, and movements [transports] that are as unforeseeable as they are violent. I think I am dreaming when I feel this warm, burning, trembling body stick to mine, this body that not an hour ago was bent to receive communion in the old church" (Willy and Ménalkas, *L'Ersatz* 133). So what? one might wonder: there is nothing contradictory as long as one constructs the subject as multiple and fragmented, as being in the position of trying to master and being subjected to multiple forces of discursivity, social construction, triangulated desire, and so forth.[20]

The New Year's wishes for 1914 must ring hollow as everyone toasts a lasting peace between France and Germany (Willy and Ménalkas, *L'Ersatz* 134–35). This event not only serves as the transition to the next episode, which is life in Paris, but also sets the clock inexorably ticking as war approaches. Carl and Renneval become closer, both geographically and physically, for Carl gets transferred to Metz (137) and proposes a scheme for seeing each other: Marc will take the night train to Metz on Saturday and return to Paris on Monday mornings. Yet this physical proximity and the nature of a long-distance marriage are ironized by the historical events that will soon separate them: being geographically closer will shortly mean being further apart. If Marc cannot come to Metz, Carl will ask for a day's leave to go to Paris. This happens, and while Marc frets about where to set up a cot for Carl, the concierge just says, "Well, with a bed like yours, which would hold four, what is there to do but put the young gentleman there and you with him?" (142). Thus at one remove does the concierge repeat the mother's actions: common sense replaces rational thought and produces rhetorical blindness.

In Paris the group is constructed differently from what we have seen before. The couple's initial outings in Germany take place among strangers who might not know that a homosexual couple is in their midst. Although there are friends present at the chateau, the framework is fundamentally familial. In Paris, however, where artists go not only to become themselves as artists but also to be free of the family novel, the couple is surrounded by a heterogeneously constructed peer group consisting of other artists in similar situations: they too have sought to be independent subjects and muses to their own art and thought, free from the rules of family life. Nevertheless, some of these freethinkers strangely repeat the model with which they have previously been fettered. For example, when Carl meets Marc's circle, including Simon-Pierre, who suspects that Carl is gay (Willy and Ménalkas, *L'Ersatz* 144–45), Marc has to invent a whole scenario: he says that Carl is a young skirt chaser, the brother of his Hamburg girlfriend, and so forth. Simon-Pierre makes no secret of his dislike for or even disgust at homosexuals, and were someone of his acquaintance to be said to be one, he would either deny it or stop seeing that person (145).

Again, questioning anew his role as a man in a gay relationship, Renneval rebels against the version of himself that he has become. Although at first he thought he was heading toward a one-time fling that was just a quondam substitute for the real thing, his attachment to Carl has become so powerful that it puts his own identity into question. The plot dramatically or rhetorically underlines this questioning through the increasingly visible presence of gay men in his social group and the increasingly audible opposition to that presence by the group of friends of whom Simon-Pierre becomes the spokesperson. Renneval returns to his initial position, he thinks, by trying to refuse to become what or whom he has become: "It cannot really continue. I am willing to have had in my life, this strange weakness, once, which arose from a set of rare circumstances; I do not want to be a *pederast*. . . . 'No, I am not of the *confrérie*!'" (Willy and Ménalkas, *L'Ersatz* 152–53).

Nevertheless, this liberal position, which translates the German saying "einmal ist keinmal" (once is never), is betrayed by his own desire and his growing recognition that this desire is his. A few pages later, listening to Carl, he goes into a kind of revery in which he justifies his behavior: "So many superior men did not think that they were lowering themselves acting as I act, after all! . . . Yes, Michelangelo has right to write sonnets to Cavalieri if he wished; and Shakespeare to Lord Pembroke; and I was a dirty Jesuit to invent laborious lies to explain to my friends that I had taken Carl in because he was the brother of my mistress! . . . . Ah! So-called emancipated person [affranchi] who dares not go out unless masked" (Willy and Ménalkas, *L'Ersatz* 163). Playing the old game of naming names, Renneval begins to refuse the hypocrisy of the situation and to see his behavior as not a mere substitute but rather the expression of his own free will to be himself and to do so while remaining at a serious, superior level. Adopting an almost Gidean tone in justifying his own behavior by citing a genealogy of homosexuals, Renneval finally and fully commits to being who he has become, a commitment reinforced by a return of his essential definition of himself: he is an artist. For at this point, after this revery, Marc decides that he is going to paint a picture with Carl posing as the model. It will be a picture of "Balder, the young Scandinavian god, emerging from the sea, completely naked in a clear dawn" (163). Carl hastens to point out that Balder was the god of love.

If a negative side remains, it is in the exaggeration perceived among those who may not themselves be at that superior level. Incapable, perhaps, of thinking through who they are, these homosexual men—the men of the *confrérie*—are as captive and subject to the popular construction of the homosexual as a mincing queen, by which I mean someone who cannot choose to imitate Michelangelo or Shakespeare. These gay man are no less subject to that lack of free will than straight men are to the construction of the heterosexual man as a violent, macho, and misogynistic individual, a construction as stereotypical as that of the flame or fairy.

After recovering from a drug overdose, Carl spends a fortnight of medical leave in Paris with Marc (Willy and Ménalkas, *L'Ersatz* 165). Carl's presence is soon known, and a host of individuals "known for their 'contradictory' mores" (166) wind up filling Marc's studio with "their strong perfumes, their little yells, their fussy [tarabiscotée] diction, their short, staccato gestures, their whores' tales [potins de grues]. There is really a freemasonry among those folk. The presence of one of them is signaled, as if by telegraphic waves. Willy-nilly, one is spotted, classified, enrolled in their *confrérie*, necessarily limited, and they are not at all peeved to find a new recruit. Still, it is shocking [agaçant] to have such labels put on one's forehead" (167). The novel ends, as it must, when the full recognition of Renneval's perception of himself and of his permanent separation from Carl becomes evident. Carl writes of the assassination of the archduke (170). Amid the rumblings of war, Carl reaches a decision that Renneval cannot make as he continues to negotiate the various parts of his existence. Carl decides to go AWOL from the army and sends Marc a telegram written in English: "I am leaving Germany to day, going to Switzerland. Shall give you my address from Basel or Lucerne. Charley" (177). In the French army, however, Marc receives letters from Carl with which he cannot deal—he cannot accept the solution Carl has adopted—and he ultimately lets himself be killed in what amounts to a suicide mission. Carl spends the rest of the war in Switzerland, although Marc dies in the early days of the war. After the war a fellow soldier brings the diary to Simon-Pierre, which returns us to the novel's preface.

Published a year later, *Le Naufragé* picks up where *L'Ersatz d'amour* leaves off. It is a much weaker novel for various reasons. In part it follows Carl as he seeks to learn the details of Renneval's death; because Carl is an unconflicted, happily gay character, there is little to learn about any internal differences, thoughts, or reflections. In part because of that, the authors focus on external and episodic moments that serve merely to delay the inevitable final scene in which Carl, having found Renneval's tomb, goes to die on it.

Still, the novel contains a few noteworthy episodes, including a scene with Schatyr-bey, a "Young Turk" who is a eunuch. He says that the Young Turk movement has a lot of eunuchs in its ranks and that in their society eunuchs are "the cream of the intelligentsia" (Willy and Ménalkas, *Naufragé* 69). Still, probably few readers are taken by the argument for castration as a means of dealing with desire, whatever the sort. Elsewhere Carl goes to stay with his friend Léo, who has "straightened out his act" and gotten married. As will become a leitmotif in Callias's other works, including *Erna* and *Metallo*, paternity is dissociated from marriage and compulsory heterosexuality. Léo remarks that despite Carl's commitment to Léo's old way of life and despite Léo's half-hearted commitment to his new way of life, Carl "has the paternal mound [bosse]" more than Léo does (75). These episodes dissociate procreation from heterosexuality, a fact noteworthy in itself, and subtly ask the readers to distinguish biological from psychological functions.

Noteworthy as well are three matters that constitute the first signs of the institutionalization of homosexual culture. There are references to personal ads taken out by "men seeking men," as the current expression goes (Willy and Ménalkas, *Naufragé* 87); the description of a homosocial organization with the name of *Freundschaft* (friendship [82]); and finally, in one of the longer and more boring parts of the novel, an entire scene in which Carl performs as an actor. He is now in Prague, and he is going to act in a fairly declamatory progay play. Because he already speaks Polish, he "will learn to recite easily in Czech without an accent" (107). In all three cases the interesting fact is the normalization of gay relations along the basic cultural lines society defines for its discourses: writing, association, and culture in general. Again, this is not gay culture moving out of the closet but rather the gradual solidification of cultural production that corresponds without total distortion to the desire and dynamics that the gay-male bonds contain.

Published in 1927 with an introduction by Louis Estève, who wrote a book entitled *L'Énigme de l'androgyne, Le Troisième sexe,* signed by Willy alone, reviews the institutions of gay sexuality in its various incarnations *intra muros et extra.* Either written by Willy alone—although this is doubtful—or penned by a ghostwriter entirely in his style, the book dispassionately examines how male homosexuality is manifested in the contemporary world as well as the historical, at least in terms of recent literary history. Never rereleased, as far as I have been able to determine, this book is a fascinating journey through what was reasonably unexplored territory; it is told from a point of view that attempts to be as fair as possible.

The general overview of the field is a means of ensuring that the reader does not bolt too quickly. Guaranteed by Estève's introduction and Willy's renown, the preliminary material begins to normalize male homosexuality. What Willy does is neither repressive nor controlling; rather, he illustrates a view by which talking about homosexuality in the language available to him is a way of normalizing homosexuality until its own language develops. The book as a whole illustrates this very point: gay culture exists, and by making it known, we can hear it speak in its own voices instead of using a language of domination for it.

Willy is ingenious in his choice of discursive models. He wisely avoids the stereotypical discourses of penal codes, abnormal psychology, classical mythology, and republican "acceptance." Willy turns to literature, by and large the popular literature of the sort I have been discussing in this chapter. Look, he says to the reader, male homosexuality is already a part of middle-brow culture; the discursive depiction of male homosexuality already exists within the confines of the world of my own readership. One need not be part of an elite world, peopled by the characters of Proust and Gide, to have access to this material. It is already right here with a long popular history. Readers of *Le Troisième Sexe,* however, do not get to that history for a long time; Willy plants the literary seed but waits several hundred pages before he gets there.

Literature is used as a framing device, but not without irony. Through this irony, which radicalizes a dichotomy of unacceptable positions, Willy creates the ground on which he will rationally and reasonably explore the terrain: "However one takes it, one can distinguish two groups among the authors who have addressed the question: those who are content with protesting their spotless morals without anyone ever having thought of suspecting them, and those who, going beyond the first, profess the most inflexible severity and who would like to line up against a wall, faced with a well-calibrated machine gun, any individual infamous enough to participate in a gymnastics of sex organs different from his own!" (*Troisième Sexe* 30).[21] Willy's dichotomy is interesting because it implies a false opposition, yet it is precisely that false opposition that creates the space in which he can speak.[22] On the one hand, some authors, having chosen to speak about a taboo subject, "protest too much." In so doing they immediately raise a red flag with respect to themselves and their subject, whereas otherwise perhaps no one would have thought them susceptible to participating in the activity or world they describe. Their seeming sympathy for the subject puts them and their writing into question. Willy thus implies that their almost classically Freudian denial is an admission. On the other hand, authors in the second group intensify the position of those in the first; they say nothing about themselves but illustrate inflexible heterosexuality raised to the position of a deontological Kantian absolute. According to this group, homosexuals should be shot for using their body parts in a way other than that described by the owner's manual, for the owner is always straight and has erected himself as the Jansenist god and the jealous guardian and protector of heterosexuality. This position is as suspect as the other, and one may wonder whether the heterosexual marksmen are simply seeking to eradicate evil or are fearful that this evil might be tempting to others. Creating this ambiguity, Willy rejects these two positions.

Willy implicitly carves himself a position in which he spends no time denying his own homosexuality and reconfirming his own heterosexuality; only at the end of the work does he come anywhere close to this rhetorical terrain, and by that point, the afterthought is more amusing than anything else. Nor does he take a stentorian tone or a moralizing position against homosexuals. He writes in a space that shows that him to be sympathetic to the positions, discourses, and cultures of homosexuality, as if it were a subject like any other. The implication is that an author can talk about many subjects that have no personal relation to him. Where sexuality is concerned, however, a reading public seems always to assume that where there is gay smoke, there is gay fire. Willy's position is rather that of the dispassionate observer or the armchair anthropologist looking at other cultures without participating in them or being affected by them.

After a general overview of the situation in a preliminary chapter, the work really starts with a section entitled "Glances across the Borders" (Willy, *Troisième Sexe* 37–85). Not surprisingly, the first stop is in Germany (39–65), with the obligatory reference to Magnus Hirschfeld (46). Willy, however, begins to break away from the typical view that restricts itself to certain layers of society—the intelligentsia, the political, the exhibitionistically tawdry—in his matter-of-fact discussion of places to meet homosexuals, which are also places where homosexuals meet (39–45). Willy strategically removes the protective wall here: seeing homosexuals and seeing homosexuals meet occur in the same space. This strategy first of all rests on a recognition that this space is not abnormal, that there is no real line of separation between the two groups. It rests further on a recognition that this gay subculture makes its own rules for space and that these rules are compossible with those of the straight world, just as the two spaces are the same space. This echoes the statement that Proust makes in deploying the metro as gay cruising ground or that Guy Hocquenghem later makes in his brilliant work *Le Gay Voyage:* although gay life sometimes has its separate spaces, the heterosexual world should realize that its public spaces may be crisscrossed by a visible or invisible gay culture and that therefore public space is always potentially sexualized.

Germany remains the privileged space for gay travel, anthropology, and encounters, but it is not the only one. Italy merits a few pages (Willy, *Troisième Sexe* 66–73), and the Isle of Capri merits the following surrealistic dithyramb: "A sodomic capital in miniature, the Mecca of inversion, a Geneva or Moscow of the future internationalism of homosexuality" (66–67). Even the United States (74–80), one of the great confines of heterosexual Puritanism, is a beacon of hope for the understanding of male homosexuality. Willy mentions gay life among American soldiers, presumably the doughboys whom he had seen in the war and who, when not furnishing sperm so that unhappy hysterics could become unwed mothers, had fun with one another. Moreover, in a wonderfully bizarre moment, he evokes "the cowboys of the Far West," who "pair off in couples [s'arrangent en petits couples]" because of the "rarity of women" (79). Again, the message is strongly worded:

the strange is the familiar, literature already said it, and homosexuality is everywhere, at home and abroad, in realms familiar or even those that are stereotypically exotic and thus always already homosexual, as is the case with Asia (81–85), for "all of Asia is riddled [entachée] with pederasty" (81).

In the next section, entitled "A Little Psychology" (*Troisième Sexe* 87–100), Willy canvasses the usual ground in sexuality, psychology, and biology, both human and animal, with the due and usual references to Hirschfeld, Gide, animal life, and prison life. He thus normalizes the terrain with Hirschfeld and Gide, naturalizes it with the reflections on animal life (much as Gide does with his labored botanical discussions in *Corydon*), and denaturalizes homosexuality at the same time: homosexuality can arise when there are no women, as is the case for cowboys or prisoners. It is the argument made at first by Renneval in *L'Ersatz d'amour.* By giving multiple origins to homosexuality—nature, nurture, and social constraints—Willy makes it more "normal": if we believe Willy, homosexuality is less likely to be perceived as an eradicable illness and more likely to be heard as a minority voice or subculture that is completely heterogeneous in its origins and displays.

The third part, entitled "Some Leaders" (Willy, *Troisième Sexe* 111–48), is essentially a pedigree of homosexuality that lists the accomplishments and works of well-known figures throughout Western history and arts: Alcibiades, Jean-Jacques Rousseau (*Confessions*), Oscar Wilde, Jean Lorrain, Proust, Édouard de Max (whom Willy credits as having written a play entitled *Sardanapale*), Paul Verlaine, and Arthur Rimbaud, among others. Willy does not distinguish between art and artist, between those who are openly gay and those who are openly straight, or between those who are openly gay and those who hide or deny their homosexuality. Again, this strategy normalizes the situation by showing that none of those categories is real: Willy seems to imply that whether one is gay or straight matters only to oneself.

The book's next section adopts a different tone and is sometimes quite amusing, for it is written with the detachment and humor of a slightly ironic moralist. In "The Tour of the 'Curious' [La Tournée des curieux]" (*Troisième Sexe* 149–87) Willy describes gay nightlife at length. As an expert on music halls, soubrettes, and life in the wings, Willy already knows how to describe the demimonde. Because, as Carco demonstrates, the demimonde is a fluid and ambiguous space, our author/tour guide can easily tell the night-blind reader about dances without women, gay bars, coke dens, and gay saunas. He provides a neologism, "pédéros" (163), to describe this erotic and (by definition) therefore exciting, enticing, and orgasmic world of gay nightlife. He tells the uninformed reader about cruising spots in theaters and movies and even meeting places such as "La Petite Cabane," which is "on the side of Montmartre [sur le flanc de la Butte]" (171). Montmartre is semiotically coded for sexuality, and in saying this, Willy is just reinforcing that generalized notion, along with giving some vague directions to the curious.

In addition, this chapter ironically makes light of the opposition. For example, taking a tongue-in-cheek tone, Willy writes: "When those gentlemen and women are treated as dirty, one is wrong; nowadays, they are almost all people with clean bodies. The proof is the great predilection they have for bath houses and steam rooms" (*Troisième Sexe* 178). By collapsing the figurative meaning of *dirty* onto its literal meaning, Willy wipes away the moral soiling and, with a flick of a towel, ridicules the opposition. For this iconoclast, who admires broken class barriers—but always maintains his own position—these gay saunas are wonderful, for Turkish baths foster "the most democratic fraternity among the classes" (180). What more could be desired under the universalism of the Third Republic, the inheritance of the Revolution of 1789, and the liberating progressive light of the twentieth century?

The next, short chapter, "Various Opinions" (Willy, *Troisième Sexe* 189–218), adds little to our understanding, but it does discuss mores, medicine, and women's opinions. The tour de force sixth chapter, "Androgynous Literature" (219–53), introduces one of the most important items for Willy's normalization of male homosexuality: literature, the privileged locus of debate and understanding. "More and more," Willy tells us, "homosexual novels are rife [pullulent]" (225); he cites Proust, Eckhoud, and Binet-Valmer, among others, as examples. This pullulation attests the existence of multiple stories and points of view; it also demonstrates that this supposedly secret homosexuality is really out there all the time, far from hidden and far from secret. Willy mentions a number of contemporary writers, including Francis de Miomandre, whose novel he wrongly entitles *Les Petits Messieurs;* a certain Georges Michel, who wrote *Bohême canaille;* and Carco. He also presents a prehistory to this modern pullulation: a work entitled *La Nouvelle Sodome,* an 1863 work by Edmond Faxy (whom Willy calls *Fazi*), and Jules Méry's book *Monsieur Auguste:* "When it appeared during the Italian War, this precursor novel raised quite a stir, as would *Mademoiselle Giroud, ma femme* a few years later, by Belot, which was a kind of counterweight to it" (233).[23]

The variety of cultures and homosexualities, a veritable congeries of heterogeneous behaviors, ranges from Lang's book *Le Responsable* to the transvestite American trapeze artist Barbette (250–52), of whom Cocteau would write as well. The epilogue to *Le Troisième Sexe* (255–63) continues the understanding implied throughout—until the conclusion. The concluding paragraphs are a less-than-ironic slap and suggest that Willy has decided to assume the persona of Marc Renneval after his first encounters with Carl; indeed, the passage refers to *Ersatz:*

> Relative to unisexuality, I can only repeat the completely personal profession of faith, from my *Souvenirs littéraires,* published by Editions Montaigne.
>
> Born, like the ex-kaiser Wilhelm II, in 1859, I am sure now never to be the prey of the octopus of inversion, whose tentacles I do not fear.
>
> Old impenitent shooter that I am, why would I change where I point my gun? I remain faithful to the game of my young years, all too happy still to be able to catch it. The Woman, I think, is worth more than the Ersatz.
>
> Does that mean she is worth a lot? In this Einsteinian world of relativity, it would seem difficult to me to do better, if, like Jehovah, I had to mold the forms of the Edenic couple with my own hands.[24] (263)

Given the countless proofs of his flaming heterosexuality, probably no one viewed the nearly seventy-year-old author as potential prey for the octopus of inversion. It is thus strange that, after having written a comprehensive and reasonably liberal moral overview of homosexuality, Willy felt compelled to defend his heterosexuality. His credentials are impeccable, and any reader's doubts about his heterosexuality could scarcely matter. Whereas his images of hunting and fishing are laughable in their phallicism, his final image of himself as a pseudo-Creator is pretentious beyond belief. Woman—or the WOMAN—is perfect; the only thing better than Woman is the Creator, who molds the clay to form that ideal that is woman. Since that Creator is definitely masculine, however, why not love the best? Perhaps Willy, after all, enamored of the creation of aesthetic perfection, did lean a bit toward loving the creator.

But perhaps the denial is not so strange. In *Souvenirs* Willy repeats this conclusion but revises it slightly: "As far as I am concerned, I shall never be the prey of the octopus of Homosexuality whose . . . tentacles I disdain. Old impenitent shooter that I am, why would I change where I point my gun? The Woman, I think, is worth more than the Ersatz. I don't imply that she is worth a lot" (141). In this version the octopus is no longer "not feared" but is vaguely disdained, and the woman is far less the Edenic glory than she was before. Has he gotten too old for this? We may never know.

CONCLUSION

The century started with André Gide's revolutionary and daring *L'Immoraliste.* It continued with Gide's *Corydon,* Proust's *Recherche,* and Cocteau's *Enfants terribles.* It was marked by Colette's homoerotic glances and the ways in which she complicates heteronormativity and phallocentrism in the *Claudine* series and *Chéri.* Despite the homophobic rants of André Breton, René Crevel managed to write about homosexuality and "papillae of pleasure." Cocteau silently offered *Le Livre blanc,* films, and hundreds of homoerotic drawings. Gide continued, proposing both the homoeroticism of *Les Caves du Vatican* and the gay characters of *Les Faux-Monnayeurs.* Jouhandeau may have kept his homoerotic writings locked in a drawer, and Gide's "Le Ramier" wouldn't see the light of day until almost a half-century after his death. Nevertheless, a host of lesser writers wrote about gay Albanian kings and bisexual gigolos, about French artists, gay Turkish eunuchs, bathhouses, bars, pickup spots, and an imagined American Far West.

Thus in the first third of the twentieth century French literature began to codify, regularize, describe, and present male homosexuality. What does this mean? A discourse develops outside the popular discourses of everyday life. Literature offers a complicated and privileged code for articulating the subject, so that male homosexuality gets articulated through the time's newly devised forms of plot, character development, and contrast. Literature provides an alternative to popular, psychological, and juridical discourses, but within that alternative it offers a complex, complicated set of mechanisms in which male homosexuality is automatically aestheticized. Male homosexuality as depicted in literature becomes an artistic version of itself.

The artistic depiction of male homosexuality contrasts with the various pathologizing mechanisms offered by the greater world, regardless of the sphere of origin: a psychological discourse founded in a pathology of normality and abnormality, a policing discourse of criminality, a general discourse of misunderstanding in daily life, or even a condemnation to isolation and a solitary life. Literature offers instead a vision of the homosexual integrated into life—into a world in which there are straight and gay people and into a discourse that privileges the aesthetic over the real and the bathetic.

This does not mean that literature replaces the various discourses about abnormality when it comes to describing same-sex desire in men. Far from it. No matter how much some in the academy may retrospectively privilege the writing of Gide and Proust, these writers were and are read by only a small percentage of the public. Moreover, their literary discourse does not really replace the vastly more pervasive discourses of sickness, perversion, and criminality or even the discourses of tolerance and acceptance that began to emerge in the twentieth century. Although it is tempting to attribute those discourses of tolerance and acceptance to the depiction of homosexuality in the normalized discourses of literature, the move toward a more liberal understanding of male homosexuality is probably more related to larger phenomena I have already discussed: the gradual urbanization of modern life and the individual's growing emancipation from the family and religion. Nonetheless, this literature at least shows that normalization can occur.

In addition, this period, in which male homosexuality was often articulated in literature, yielded two far-reaching consequences. First, at least within literature, male homosexuality began to have a history for the future; that is, this period created a literary horizon against which writers to come would have to measure their work, against which they would write, and by which they would be influenced. In the generation of writers immediately after the period in question, Jean Genet is the most well known and important example, but he was only the first in a long line of authors, continuing even today, for whom Proust and Gide have had consequences. I am not suggesting that every contemporary gay writer has studied Proust and Gide. On the contrary, I think this is probably almost as rare among our contemporary writers as it is in the public at large. Rather, Gide and Proust influenced Genet, who influenced those after him, and all these writers have contributed discourses and images that form the landscape of literary homosexuality.

In this regard, Genet's work is striking in its use of literary discourse and form combined with subject matter that is far from the safe bourgeois worlds depicted by Gide and Proust. In Genet's prose, however, every moment of silence is broken by unending narration spinning forth, set somewhere between an oral flow and the printed word. Genet weaves his prose into garlands of literary flowers that are endlessly marked by the oral and all it implies, a written prose that often sounds spoken. Hence the relative strangeness in his work, filled as it is with marks of spoken language yet steadfastly literary, with its use of the imperfect subjunctive, never used ironically, always marking the work as it shifts between the written and the oral. Genet interweaves a textuality and a homosexuality in the playing out of his narratives. His textuality and the depiction of homosexuality are mutual interpretants, and the demarcation between them is never clear. As he writes in *Journal du voleur* (181), "Betrayal, theft, and homosexuality are the essential subjects of this book. A relation exists among them, if not always apparent, at least I seem to recognize a sort of vascular exchange between my taste for betrayal, theft, and my loves."

Thus Genet is the most prominent gay author writing about gay matters after World War II. He takes the tools of literature offered by Proust, Gide, and Cocteau and makes them his own as he becomes in turn a member of the canon. His writing, and especially the far more marginalized subject matter that engages an underworld, will become in turn the material against which later writers will produce their works. Genet's own refiguring of the literary landscape for homosexuality will influence writers as distinct as Renaud Camus, Guy Hocquenghem, Hervé Guibert, and Guillaume Dustan.

The literature of Gide and Proust had a second important consequence: queer theory as it developed in the United States in the 1990s and first decade of the twenty-first century. Elaborated primarily in English departments, queer theory in and for the humanities has privileged the work of Gide, Proust, and Genet (often in translation) and therefore continued to privilege the literary in our understanding of culture in general and queer culture in particular. The literary loci of Proust's *Sodome et Gomorrhe* and, to a lesser extent, those of Gide's *Les Faux-Monnayeurs* and Genet's novels form much of the background for queer studies. Often taken out of context—the contexts of Frenchness, French literature, the absence of puritanism, and the presence of libertinage—the works I have mentioned are a strange substrate for theory.

There is only a century between Proust, Gide, and Willy, on the one hand, and queer theory, Guillaume Dustan, and bareback cybersex in chatrooms, on the other. In inventing modernism, writers such as those in the first group also contributed to the invention of twentieth-century modernity. In questioning modernity, contemporary authors and theorists figure and refigure it into the postmodern. And our contemporary Western world, a world without grand narratives, is perhaps the first one in which the consequences of gender and gender difference, sexual identities and preferences, and sexualities have begun to matter less to some. In part, but only in part, this development is due to writers such as Marcel Proust, André Gide, Jean Cocteau, and Willy, who a century ago bravely wrote male homosexuality back into literature and in so doing helped form what would become a gay aesthetic and a gay sensibility that still mark literature and our world today.

NOTES

Introduction

1. As Marcus notes, the association of Haussmannization with modernity relates only to the public spaces of Paris and not to the redefined private spaces or even the apartment buildings to which I later refer.

2. As I will show later, the question of Proustian vision and nonvision is central to understanding the depiction of male homosexuality in the *Recherche.*

Chapter 1: Proust

1. Gérard Genette characterizes this hint at the novel's future events as "prolepsis." For a discussion of prolepsis, see Genette (105–14); for my discussion of the way it relates to homosexuality, see *The Shock of Men* (72–75).

2. In her excellent study *Proust's Lesbianism,* Elisabeth Ladenson wisely suggests that the nonrepresentation is a way of avoiding censorship: "For one thing, the move from the visual presentation of the seduction of Charlus and Jupien to the auditory presentation of their lovemaking may well have taken its motivation from the author's desire to escape censorship" (73). She goes on to note that the scene in the brothel is in a certain sense "the least genitally oriented." To Ladenson's cogent analysis, I would add the double intratextual reason: the narrator needs (inherently) to know homosexuality, and the path having been prepared, he will eventually be introduced into it. In his cogent analysis of the scene in the male brothel, Mario Lavagetto convincingly shows what has been avoided heretofore: the first-person narrator is "*in* the scene of homosexuality" (119).

3. On learning and apprenticeship—"apprentissage"—in the *Recherche,* see Deleuze's still remarkable pages (36–50).

4. On the contrary, the Duc de Guermantes, although hardly faithful to the duchess, reinforces the correct mores for his class.

5. I now signal Charlus's sense of Marcel's capacity to misread. Marcel will mistake Charlus for a thief or spy. The espionage and voyeurism between Marcel and Charlus goes both ways, as does, eventually, the association of bad looks/looking with some sort of dysfunctionality. As Erman (78) notes, Charlus wonders whether Marcel sees things correctly and, indeed, whether his optic nerve is somehow affected (Proust 2:850).

6. The madness, here indicating that Saint-Loup is madly in love with Rachel, predicts the madness ascribed to Charlus when the latter is trying to pick up the adolescent Marcel.

7. As Deleuze remarks profoundly, "Being sensitive to signs, considering the world as something to be deciphered, is undoubtedly a gift" (37). The narrator has this gift, although as is often the case with a gift, he does not fully recognize it; indeed, learning to accept the gift is the apprenticeship of which Deleuze writes (36–50).

8. From Baden-Powell, who founded the Boy Scouts, and Coubertin, who revived the Olympics, to the free-body/nudist movement mentioned by Suzanne de Callias (see chap. 4), there was an extraordinary association among physical exercise, nudity, and implicit homoeroticism.

9. Interestingly, what others call him differs from what he calls himself. Whereas those in the circle of the Comte de Paris refer to him as "Prince" because of his elegance and pride (109), Charlus deprecates this commonest of titles: "'Today,' he said, 'everyone is a prince; yet you still need something to distinguish you; I shall take the title of prince when I wish to travel incognito'" (114). Should one think that Charlus is traveling incognito when he is in the circle of the Comte de Paris? And what would traveling incognito mean for him?

10. The nucleus of the anecdote is the famous story of Astolphe de Custine. Having made a date with a soldier near Saint-Denis, de Custine received a lesson at the hands of the soldier's friends, who stripped him and threw him out into the forces of nature.

11. "Je passais seul devant le casino en rentrant à l'hôtel, j'eus la sensation d'être regardé par quelqu'un qui n'était pas loin de moi. Je tournai la tête et j'aperçus un homme d'une quarantaine d'années, très grand et assez gros, avec des moustaches très noires, et qui, tout en frappant nerveusement son pantalon avec une badine, fixait sur moi des yeux dilatés par l'attention. Par moments, ils étaient percés en tous sens par des regards d'une extrême activité comme en ont seuls devant une personne qu'ils ne connaissent pas des hommes à qui, pour un motif quelconque, elle inspire des pensées qui ne viendraient pas à tout autre—par exemple des fous ou des espions. Il lança sur moi une suprême œillade à la fois hardie, prudente, rapide et profonde, comme un dernier coup que l'on tire au moment de prendre la fuite, et après avoir regardé tout autour de lui, prenant soudain un air distrait et hautain, par un brusque revirement de toute sa personne il se tourna vers une affiche dans la lecture de laquelle il s'absorba, en fredonnant un air et en arrangeant la rose mousseuse qui pendait à sa boutonnière."

12. As Marivaux (whose name gave French its word for erotic bantering) put it in a title: *On ne badine pas avec l'amour* (One does not banter with love). But love is *precisely* that with which one banters.

13. In his compelling book *La Place de la madeleine,* Serge Doubrovsky considers

the narrator to be asexual (133). I would agree if asexuality were considered to mean nonheterosexuality or hidden homosexuality. The narrator takes great pains to be heterosexual, and asexuality is one narrative feint among others.

14. Erman (110–13) discusses the scene between Marcel and Charlus in *A l'ombre*, and although he remarks that Charlus's plan is to "seduce the hero" (112), he does not draw out the consequences relative to the semiotic and hermeneutic construction of that homosexual construction.

15. The excuse for the narrator is the Proustian aesthetic by which, as Franc Schuerewegen so clearly states: "Homosexuality is a spectacle that he [Proust] seeks to describe rather than explain" (in Schehr and Weiss 122).

16. This detail could clearly be read sympathetically with Eve Kosofsky Sedgwick's notion of the transparency of the closet (67–90).

17. "Sa voix elle-même, pareille à certaines voix de contralto en qui on n'a pas assez cultivé le médium et dont le chant semble le duo alterné d'un jeune homme et d'une femme, se posait au moment où il exprimait ces pensées si délicates, sur des notes hautes, prenait une douceur imprévue et semblait contenir des chœurs de fiancées, de sœurs, qui répandaient leur tendresse. Mais la nichée de jeunes filles que M. de Charlus, avec son horreur de tout efféminement, aurait été si navré d'avoir l'air d'abriter ainsi dans sa voix, ne s'y bornait pas à l'interprétation, à la modulation des morceaux de sentiments. Souvent, tandis que causait M. de Charlus, on entendait leur rire aigu et frais de pensionnaires ou de coquettes ajuster leur prochaine avec des malices de bonnes langues et de fines mouches."

18. After a certain point in the courtyard encounter between Charlus and Jupien at the beginning of *Sodome et Gomorrhe*, even language is of no importance: Charlus's and Jupien's voices quickly turn to grunts and moans in the ensuing scene.

Chapter 2: Un Amour de Charlus

1. In the best analysis of the structures of lesbianism in the novel, Elisabeth Ladenson (*Proust's Lesbianism*) shows the ways in which male and female homosexualities are not always symmetrical.

2. On the performance of a peep show in particular, see Michel Tournier's novel *La Goutte d'or* (188–92), as well as my discussion of it in "Tournier's Theoretical Pretext." On the specificity of the gaze that is generally coded as masculine, the visual figure of phallogocentrism, see Mulvey.

3. Gray (129) puts the deconstruction of the first pages of *Sodome et Gomorrhe* quite succinctly: the "extended figure . . . subtends the encounter in apparent support, but . . . finally breaches its containment as image to invade and overturn the narrative proper." See also my discussion of Proust in *The Shock of Men.*

4. In her article "Rereading Proust" (251–54) Elisabeth Ladenson comments succinctly on Marcel's frequent misprision of class, status, and origin.

5. It is quite astonishing that Marcel has not already figured out that Odette is "the lady in pink," for he has seen her in Tansonville (with Charlus) and then at her house in Paris.

6. Proust makes this character—who eventually is adopted by Charlus, marries Morel, and dies shortly thereafter—sometimes Jupien's niece, sometimes his daugh-

ter. Wondering how Charlus might know Morel, upon the first witnessed meeting of these two, the narrator writes: "I looked for the way in which the Baron might have known Morel. . . . The idea came to me at first that it was through Jupien, whose daughter, one remembers, seemed to be smitten with the violinist" (3:255). Although the confusion is most likely authorial inadvertence, it is an example of the *brouillage*—scrambling—of family relations.

7. Speculating as to whether Charlus is the active or passive sodomite, or even whether sodomy occurs, is no more meaningful than trying to decide how many children Lady Macbeth had. In the relations with Morel, Proust was probably making Charlus a bottom to preserve Morel's sexual integrity (but the reverse argument can be made). What counts is the construction of a potential space for energetics in which Charlus's posterior is potentially the space of passive sodomy: in a classic Lyotardian sense *la bande libidinale* (pun intended).

8. In American gay culture, for example, two old code versions of the musical-gay connection are the question "Is he musical?" meaning, "Is he gay?" and the indication that someone is a "friend of Dorothy," in which reference to Judy Garland's endlessly singing character in *The Wizard of Oz* is meant to indicate that someone is gay. Those specific images do not generally cross U.S. borders, but certainly the idea of "making music together" is an international one.

9. David will come up again as a reference during the whist game played at La Raspelière, where the Verdurin clan is spending the summer. Here David is not the youthful warrior but the old king: "So I shall play that old David" (3:364), which, the editor remarks, is a name for the king of spades.

10. In the scene at the Verdurins' Charlus will illustrate this support tinged with affection as he leans on Morel while the latter is playing whist (3:348). This physical contact is also a sign of familiarity Charlus occasionally takes with the objects of his affection, as when he is "unable to stop himself from pinching the violinist's ear" (3:354). This lack of control, a physical sign of Charlus's obsession with Morel, comes back, for example, during the recounting of a dinner between the two: "M. de Charlus could not refrain from tenderly pinching Morel's ear" (3:396). Charlus's sense of proxemics is often clouded by a homosexualization of the common space in which the body of the other is, at least in part, possessed by him, as was already in evidence in the bathing epilogue at Balbec, when Charlus pinches Marcel's neck (2:125–26).

11. A few lines earlier the narrator, still not in a position to share knowledge with Marcel, has already mentioned prudishness, but "this hypothesis did not even come to mind" (2:580). Given the psychological and social profile of Mme de Villeparisis, it would be hard to attribute a motive to her other than an attempt to avoid the potential compromise of Marcel's virtue.

12. The adjective *lady-like* appears in the text in English.

13. In a broader sociological perspective Splitter (55) calls Morel a "protean trickster," and Jacques Dubois (53) considers him one of the social parasites, wearing a mask in order to arrive.

14. The phrase will come up in *La Prisonnière* as well, in a letter the actress Léa, who is "well-known for the exclusive taste she had for women" (3:720), writes to Morel. She writes exclusively in the feminine and says, "At least you are one of them

[tu en es].” The phrase is made to stand out, for the narrator makes a point of not reproducing the letter except for two brief phrases, because of its “uncouthness.” The narrator continues: “The baron was especially troubled by those words ‘one of them [en était].’ After having ignored it, he had finally, already quite long ago, figured out [appris] that he was ‘one of them [en était].’ But here this notion he had acquired was put into question anew. When he had discovered that he was ‘one of them,’ he had thus believed that his taste, as Saint-Simon says, is not that of women. But here, for Morel this expression ‘one of them [en être]’ took on an extension that M. de Charlus had not known, so much so that Morel proved, according to that letter, that he was ‘one of them,’ by having the same taste as women for women” (3:720). See Ladenson (*Proust’s Lesbianism,* 101–4) for an excellent discussion of this material.

15. The word *tapette* has a number of meanings, one of which indicates a talkative person, which, according to *Le Petit Robert,* “by extension” has come to mean a “passive pederast.” The closest translation in contemporary English would be *fairy,* as opposed to a more generalized *fag* (*pédé*).

16. Along with his notation of misunderstandings, mispronunciations, faulty usages, provincialisms, and the like, one of the techniques Proust uses to create a comic effect and make a more subtle point (whether stylistic, psychological, or textual) is the partial word. Two notable examples are the comment on the name *Cambremer* and Albertine’s correction of Françoise’s grammatical error. In the first case Mme de Saint-Euverte says to Swann: “Well, those Cambremer have rather an astonishing name. It finishes just in time, but it finishes badly!” (1:335). The decomposition of the name into its constituent syllables makes a double scatological joke: it puns on the shortening of *Cambronne* to *Cambre* and *merde* to *mer*—“le mot de Cambronne” being a euphemism for *merde.* But it also implicitly associates the family—perceived as provincial and arriviste—with the referent of the double joke. In the second case Françoise asks Marcel whether she should turn out the lights in his room but makes an error in forming the subjunctive. Albertine, who dislikes Françoise as much as the latter dislikes her, whispers the correction—“éteigne”—but voices only part of it, “teigne,” a half-word that lets her insult Françoise by calling her a “taenia,” or tapeworm (2:656).

17. Although this is not the place to deal with such a question, many of the excesses of cultural studies decried both by historians and literary critics can be blamed on an insufficient contextualization and an inadequate sense of the translatability of modeling systems and discourses.

18. I address these issues because a brothel is necessarily an overly coded sign. Consider, for example, the brothel scene in which Marcel, ready to lose his virginity, meets Rachel, a sort of synecdoche of the brothel; here one could offer an effective reading in which various modeling systems and economies of desire would come into play. I imagine this set against studies of prostitution and extramarital relations in literature, such as those by Charles Bernheimer and Tony Tanner, as well as the historicizing of prostitution, sex, and public health in the work of nineteenth-century writers such as Auguste Morel and Alexandre Parent-Duchâtelet. In *Figures of Alterity* (179–96) I read that scene in a way that considers the locus of exchange and meeting to be one in which a process of literary assimilation takes place, a locus in which

transpires a confusion between the pure and the impure, to borrow a phrase from Colette. This brothel is not so much the economy of women's bodies as it is the locus in which being Jewish is put into question.

19. For the interrelation between cityscapes and the representations of male homosexuality, see Bech 99–115; Chauncey, *Gay New York,* 33–45 and 131–205; and Hocquenghem, *Gay Voyage,* 9–11 and 31–36.

20. The biographical version of literary criticism has done that here in spades, for it has often been noted that Proust himself, in becoming the backer of a male bordello in Paris, helped furnish it with much of the family furniture he received as part of his inheritance. This profanation corresponds to the profanations of the father by Mlle Vinteuil and her friend at Montjouvain and that of the mother discussed so well by Ladenson.

21. This is not the first time that music is associated with the figure of the brothel; in the earlier scene Rachel is associated with an aria from Halévy's *La Juive,* "Rachel, quand du Seigneur." Gray (76–78) sees the algebra scenes not only as an association of the mathematics of the unknown with illicit sexuality but also as evidence of the thickness of reinscribed memory, seen in many other nodal points in the novel.

22. I note in passing the return of vision—"see the tone"—where one would have expected "hear the tone," as if *in* the homosexual scene, the narrator replaces hearing (which had already replaced vision in the hôtel de Guermantes), not as a return, but as the copy of a copy.

23. As he details the various placements of homosexuality in the *Recherche,* Lavagetto (71) shows how the narrator sees and hears things that a more realistic approach would rule out. Lavagetto correctly associates the narrator's interest in homosexuality with a projection into the space in which it occurs. Thus, the "I" remains safely outside homosexuality while safely controlling/mastering the space in which it occurs. Lavagetto shows even that the narrator's lapse may be a Freudian slip. Having discussed the scene of sadomasochism that the narrator observes, Lavagetto turns to the selling of the bed in which the scene ostensibly took place. But Proust places the bed not in the room officially assigned to Charlus but in the one used by Marcel. While some readers may feel that the lapse is more an accident than anything else, it is certainly consonant with what Lavagetto correctly maintains about the representation of homosexuality in the novel.

24. Thus does Charlus mime, in reverse, his own foot imagery. Earlier he says that Marcel is not worthy of kissing his "august toes"; here he offers, "I kiss your feet [Je vous baise les pieds]" (4:394).

Chapter 3: Figures of the Homoerotic

1. Cocteau's relation to Proust is complicated and ambivalent. In *Opium* Cocteau devotes a whole section to reading Proust. Vaguely laudatory but mostly anecdotal, it is not particularly profound, but Cocteau does say one thing to which he will later return: "Marcel Proust did not make characters *à clef,* that goes without saying, but certain friends figured in large doses in his mixtures" (*Romans* 644). Like Gide, although certainly with less vehemence, he finds Proust an easy target. Proust, he writes in a journal entry from 17 March 1942, "sets himself up as a moralist and his night-

life was sleazy [crapuleuse]. To understand the mechanism of his work, one must transport the manias of a vice into a transcendental order—the enigma of the possibilities imagined by a client in certain houses of ill-repute" (*Journal* 45). Ten years later he is rereading Proust and is aghast at the latter's snobbishness (*Passé défini* 1:268). At times Cocteau attacks Proust for aesthetic reasons: he finds the second volume of *Sodome* "unreadable" (1:269) and the first volume of *La Prisonnière* "unbearable" (1:301). Of *Sodome* Cocteau goes on to say that the book "is a mess of badly written sentences, parentheses after which these sentences remain unfinished, vulgar comedy, characters forgotten and rediscovered in a wholly unplanned way." Beyond the aesthetic critique lies a representational one, however, and Cocteau lauds Proust for some of his characters, who he says are drawn with "great physical and psychological [morale] exactness" (1:270). Nevertheless, even though Cocteau praises these characters, he excuses Proust because of his illness, his medicine, and his crises. Cocteau's praise for Proust is faint and his critiques equally banal: he is glad that Proust is true to the original, that the Duchesse de Guermantes and her brother-in-law, the Baron de Charlus, are true to their models of Mme Greffulhe and Robert de Montesquiou. But Cocteau finds fault with Proust's "moral" position, and the question of snobbishness is soon transformed: "Proust is a snob who is wrong to be one. A pederast who is wrong to be one. He will judge snobs and pederasts severely for detouring attention from his person. It is also a delight. To write in the urinals in order to be read" (1:281). Proust fails to rise to the occasion and does not create a mythology out of his intelligence and his observations; Proust's failure is that he is not a poet, that is, not Cocteau: "Proust's magnificent intelligence took its greatest pleasure in painting stupidity. Which is tiring after a while" (1:298). Finally, after a month of struggling with his rereading of Proust, Cocteau concludes wistfully that "nothing is more melancholic, more depressing than no longer loving a work. Alas, I am not like Proust and I shall not forget his [work], as he forgets his grandmother. This work will haunt me like a dead woman" (1:309).

2. In her convincing reading of *L'Immoraliste* and its "homotextuality," Emily Apter (113–24) uses a spatial metaphor different from that of Segal: "Michel's latent homosexuality is *pre*-figured in the 'creux' or hollows of a spoken sentence" (114).

3. I have discussed Gide in various other publications. His writing is one of the discourses I focus on in the introduction to *The Shock of Men* (1–32). Elsewhere I have discussed the question of sexual tourism in Gide and, more recently, the ways in which Gide encrypts homosexuality in *Corydon* and in some of his autobiographical writings (*Alcibiades* 113–30; *Figures* 196–221).

4. Compare the one specific sexual act alluded to in *Le Ramier,* discussed at the end of this section.

5. Leo Bersani (113–29) indicates several clues that he thinks suggest the friends to be gay. I suggest that they may be straight and open-minded. This may seem to be contradictory, but only if we fall into an oppositional pattern. What they are not is a group of latent homosexuals with unconscious homoerotic tendencies. If they are a group of gay men, what Proust would call a "*confrérie,*" then Michel's calling for them seems an odd move, since that would mean he must recognize his own homosexuality and his identification with them. So doing would have produced an entirely different narrative.

6. If, as Bersani suggests, the listeners are gay, is the brother of the transcriber gay as well? Despite the possibility of the occurrence, this is another reason for believing instead that the listeners are sympathetic, straight friends rather than gay men. On an emotional and psychological level, by coming to visit Michel they have shown their faithfulness and their friendship, whereas there is no textual "emoticon" indicating the receptivity, sympathy, or understanding of the scribe's highly placed brother.

7. On Gide and queerness, see Michael Lucey's excellent book. Lucey—and this is not a criticism but rather an observation—refers to *L'Immoraliste* only three times: the first remark indicates that *L'Immoraliste* hints at Gide's homosexuality, the second looks at the question of complicity around the episode of the scissors, and the last occurs in a quotation from Paul de Man. It is precisely because *L'Immoraliste* does not fit with Lucey's queer model of the later Gide that the critic does not address matters in that book.

8. In another shoulder scene, from *Et nunc manet in te,* Gide is in the train returning from Biskra. There are also three young men in the next compartment. Because the heat is "provoking," they are "half undressed." Every time the train stops, Gide can stick his hand out the side window and reach the arm of one of the young men, who seem to enjoy the game, for they laugh. Gide caresses the "dark, downy flesh" and reaches their shoulders (*Souvenirs* 947–48). I thank Naomi Segal for reminding me of this episode.

9. Although Charles is not a figure of rebellion, Segal quite rightly draws a comparison between him and the other "fascinating adolescent," Athalric (179). Segal's excellent reading of *L'Immoraliste* in specific (169–89) and of Gide's work in general is, in the best sense, a queering of discourses about the various false dyads set up as dichotomies: male/female, masculine/feminine, and hetero/homo. Opposed to that binarism, Segal brilliantly proposes fluid dynamics—what she calls hydraulics—as a way of reading and understanding Gide.

10. There is a slightly different spin to masturbation in the opening episode of *Si le grain ne meurt,* where Gide and the concierge's son are "near each other, but not with each other" (*Souvenirs* 81). That is perhaps a childhood innocence before the corruption of civilization. Here, in *L'Immoraliste,* there is a will to return, and that, along with the scene mentioned with Ali in *Si le grain ne meurt,* depends on being with each other.

11. I am not implying that there is a direct causal connection between the love affair and Cocteau's greatest production. On the contrary, in 1920 Cocteau and Radiguet produced a justly neglected horror based on the novel *Paul et Virginie;* they created the libretto for a comic opera whose ineptitude and mediocrity are unequaled by anything else in their work.

12. I recognize that Nijinsky was married and therefore was not technically "gay," but his bisexuality does not affect this reading of the anecdote. Cocteau would go on to have sexual relations with women as well, but that does not affect his basic gay sensibility, at least insofar as the material I am examining is concerned.

13. On the centrality of the limp to Cocteau's work, see Borgal's study.

14. For a discussion of the function of Oedipus in Cocteau's work, see Borgal (77–104).

15. According to Francis Steegmuller (351), Cocteau "says he derived from a cer-

tain Madame Bessont-Fabre the information that in Hebrew 'angel' and 'angle' are synonyms."

16. From his many comments on his own "famous line," I will retain just this one for now. In his diaries from the early 1950s, published as *Le Passé défini,* Cocteau returns to his remark. Referring to a book published six years before, Cocteau writes: "Claude Mauriac is incapable of understanding my sentence: 'I am a lie that always tells the truth.' He quotes it against my person. I meant that every man is a lie since social life and the obligation of being in touch with others weigh him down with masks" (1:51–52).

17. This dynamic can be endlessly modified and pulled in one direction or another, hermeneutic or psychoanalytic, depending on the reader. Cocteau's correspondent, Milorad, sees the *Livre blanc* as something to be deciphered, for a white book is "a collection of documents about a specific problem" (Cocteau, *Lettres à Milorad* 109). The problem, Milorad writes, is the "sexual and sentimental life of the narrator." He goes on to say that the "adjective 'white' also evokes the white page, the absence of the author's signature." Following this line, Milorad elucidates the principal figures of the *Livre blanc:* childhood memories, figures of a centaur, the father, and of course Dargelos. Whereas, writing of *La Corrida du 1er mai* as a kind of reinscription of *Le Sang d'un poète,* Gercke (17) sees the figures of homosexuality as tending toward an inscription of masochism, Milorad views the figure of Dargelos, homoerotic figure par excellence in Cocteau's work, as elaborating a figuration of homosexuality "tinged with sadism and of castration fantasy (Cocteau, *Lettres à Milorad* 123).

18. Although the Dargelos episodes in *Les Enfants terribles* were written after those in *Le Livre blanc,* the more explicit nature of the latter book gives the reader a deeper understanding of the figure than does the relatively cleaned up pages of the former. In addition, as I have indicated, the rhythm of production during these years may make it more appropriate to conceive of this material as part of a linked hypertext rather than a series of works produced in chronological sequence.

19. Cocteau's correspondent, Milorad, puts his finger on the problem when he says that the "narrator of *Le Livre blanc* sees his friends move *normally* toward heterosexuality, while he remains homosexual at heart" (Cocteau, *Lettres à Milorad* 125; emphasis added).

20. This too is a feint, for in giving Marais freedom, Cocteau remains in control. Just as it is he who permits or does not permit familiarity, he gives "permission" for Marais to sleep with others: "I have come to love you so much (more than anything in the world) that I have ordered myself to love you only as a Daddy would. [. . .] It is undoubtedly better to deprive myself of a small part of my happiness and gain your confidence and become brave enough so that you become more free than with a daddy or a mommy" (*Lettres à Jean Marais* 14–15).

21. This sexuality is a fragile thing. In his first film it seems to fragment as its permanence is drawn into question. Gercke reminds us of the importance of the sexualized but impossibly constellated body in the "Hôtel des Folies Dramatiques" sequence of *Le Sang d'un poète.* Gercke says that "Cocteau's hermaphrodite is unable to form a stable body, suspending sexual difference by postponing the completion and specificity of the hermaphrodite's body" (13). But why is this sexual constella-

tion impossible? Cocteau can find no representational system that honestly and straightforwardly represents the sexual self. In Cocteau's world the other is always veering off toward becoming a lie—in other words, toward a loss of erection.

Chapter 4: Willy and Friends

1. In *De Montmartre* Carco assures us of his Zolaesque research: "After the *Lapin* closed, our nights finished at Manière's, in rue Caulaincourt, or in the seedy [mal fréquentés] bars in the rue Lepic, accompanied by people who were scarcely capable of understanding us. It is in those bars that I met Jésus-la-Caille and his boyfriends [petits amis]" (66–67).

2. The French the words for "male" and "female" are more strongly differentiated than are *man* and *woman* in everyday English. The French words insist on the biological aspect.

3. Willy refers to this novel in his assessment of gay literature in *Le Troisième Sexe* (225) but inaccurately calls it *Les Petits Messieurs.* These inaccuracies abound in Willy's book, to which I turn at the end of this chapter.

4. This investment of a larger-than-life orientalism in the figure of a prince is a commonplace of the time. In Marcel Rouff's *Vie et passion de Dodin-Bouffant* the prince occupying the position of the great sybarite is the "Prince d'Eurasie." Rouff was a frequent collaborator with Curnonsky, who was himself Willy's most frequent collaborator, and Willy is at the center of this group of writers, which includes Miomandre and others.

5. The expression *bilateral* for "bisexual" also appears in the 1931 novel *Le Supplice d'une queue,* by François-Paul Alibert (100).

6. Caradec includes Ménalkas in his list of ghostwriters and mentions the author in his discussion of the novel, but he does not say that Ménalkas was a pseudonym for Callias.

7. In French, adjectives agree in gender and number with the common nouns they modify, regardless of the gender of the individual to whom those nouns refer. Only in gender-bending situations, however, such as names given to drag queens, do proper nouns (i.e., names) fail to refer to the individual's gender or biological sex.

8. I am aware that even the limitation of two puts homosexual sex under the limits of normalized heterosexuality. And I realize at the same time that the nonsexual aspects of homosexuality are usually not limited to the dyad but take place in a social setting with a larger number of participants in which dyads and monads can fit.

9. For a reason I have not been able to determine, Tamagne (368–69) considers Erna unhappy and feels that the novel concludes with her marrying a man who has far-right politics and obligates her to stay home.

10. Jean's job as a metalworker in a nearby factory explains the novel's title.

11. I treat the preface as if Willy were the rhetorical author because it seems to speak with his typical voice of authority. The preface is somewhat confused in determining the order of discourse, but the rhetoric is fairly straightforward.

12. Later, in *Le Troisième Sexe,* Willy reduces his own role to that of a grammatically knowledgeable amanuensis. He says that *L'Ersatz d'amour* is the "pathetic autobiography of the painter F.V. that I forced myself to write in correct French (for

the good V. was a native of Antwerp)." That he most likely did little more than correct or improve Callias's text adds a layer of irony to this remark. There is no evidence that the remark is true, nor is there any that it is false. It is, however, vaguely reminiscent of the stories attached to Zola's supposed writing of a homosexual novel and those relating to Marc-André Raffalovich. In all these cases, there is a double leitmotif in which the straight French author, in his liberal and liberated position of authority and iconoclasm, serves merely as the editor for the gay, foreign confessor.

13. Later in the novel, reflecting on his previous prayer, Renneval remarks: "This fling is rather wild [cocasse]. I had asked the Lord to send me a woman, and look at what he sends me. As my old aunt, who led the group of Christian Mothers of her parish, said long ago, 'You can put yourself in the Lord's hands; he knows much better than we do what suits us or not'" (Willy and Ménalkas, *L'Ersatz* 66).

14. Eulenburg returns in a displacement. Just as Marc has gone to Germany, the homosexual paradise, Eulenburg had gone from Germany to Italy, which seems the superparadise for the gay gentry. Carl says: "The Prince von Eulenburg did indeed make love in a boat, in the middle of Lake Como, and with two oarsmen to boot . . . Of course that occurred under the free sky of Italy; what a wonderful country!" (Willy and Ménalkas, *L'Ersatz* 70).

15. Again, one may think of Sartre here and the third case of bad faith, where the homosexual "confesses" to his straight friend.

16. I am obviously playing with stereotypes of sexual conformity here, not examining perfectly real although unconsidered possibilities, such as heterosexual anal penetration or even fellatio. The reader should remember that the position from which this novel starts is the most basic, stereotypical, male-driven, heterosexual one.

17. The image of good food versus bad food as a metaphor for heterosexuality versus homosexuality taken as a make-do option comes up as a gloss on the title: "As for me, I have an 'ersatz' for a mistress. But ersatz may taste good, but it upsets the stomach a bit. One should not make it one's usual meal, but taste of it only in passing . . . I shall go back on a diet of natural foods when I return to France" (Willy and Ménalkas, *L'Ersatz* 66). In another Proustian moment that recalls "the national anthem of our love that is Vinteuil's sonata," which seems to have been based on César Franck's work, Marc and Carl perform the Franck Sonata for Violin and Piano together (75).

18. In *Le Naufragé* the date of his death is given as 14 September 1914, just one month into the war.

19. This reduction of physical space will be repeated in a later scene involving Carl sleeping in Marc's bed in Paris; as I have shown, it is also reprised in *Metallo.*

20. In his *Histoire de la sexualité* Foucault talks at great length about the play of such regulations of the self, from within and without.

21. Technically I should say "his or her own," but because Willy focuses on male homosexuality, I feel comfortable not being inclusive.

22. At the end of *Souvenirs littéraires* Willy does take a position similar to the first one described, but it is somewhat modified, for at least one unnamed critic suggested that he experimented to "document his *Ersatz d'amour*" (Willy, *Souvenirs* 139). Of course, he probably did not write the book, so that it would have been Suzanne de Callias who would have had to experiment, somehow, with male homosexuality. Willy

does not deny homosexuality but presents the matter as an aesthetic and literary one: "Where would we go, if an author could not, without risking suspicion, describe mores other than his own, clean ones?" (139). This is somewhat of a transparent argument, for his first example is André Gide's *Saül,* followed by, among others, Binet-Valmer, Rachilde, Hermant, Whitman (misspelled as "Withmann"), Fazy, Proust, Colette, Miomandre, and Carco, among others (139–40): a savvy mixture of those who are and those who are not of the *confrérie.*

23. On the implications of lesbianism in Belot's novel, see Christopher Rivers's excellent discussion of the novel in his recent reissue and translation of it.

24. Here is the French text without Willy's extravagant indentations: "Relativement à l'unisexualité, je ne puis que répéter la toute personnelle profession de foi, de mes *Souvenirs littéraires,* publiés aux Editions Montaigne. Né, comme l'ex-kaiser Guillaume II, en 1859, je crois être certain, à présent, de ne jamais devenir la proie de la pieuvre Inversion, dont je ne redoute pas les tentacules. Vieux tireur impénitent, pourquoi changerais-je mon fusil de pôle? Je m'en tiens au gibier de mes jeunes années, trop heureux de pouvoir le capturer encore! La Femme, à mon sens, vaut mieux que l'Ersatz. Est-ce dire qu'elle vaille beaucoup? En ce monde einsteinien de la relativité, il me semblerait difficile de faire mieux, si j'avais, comme Jéhovah, à pétrir de mes mains les formes du couple édénique."

BIBLIOGRAPHY

Alibert, François-Paul. *Le Supplice d'une queue.* Paris: Éditions La Musardine, 2002 (1931).

Apter, Emily. *André Gide and the Codes of Homotextuality.* Saratoga, Calif.: Anma Libri, 1987.

Barbedette, Gilles, and Michel Carassou. *Paris Gay 1925.* Paris: Presses de la Renaissance, 1981.

Barthes, Roland. *Roland Barthes par lui-même.* Paris: Seuil, 1975.

———. *Sur Racine.* Paris: Seuil, 1963.

Bech, Henning. *When Men Meet: Homosexuality and Modernity.* Trans. Teresa Mesquit and Tim Davies. Chicago: University of Chicago Press, 1997.

Bell, David F. *Circumstances: Chance in the Literary Text.* Lincoln: University of Nebraska Press, 1993.

Belot, Adolphe. *Mademoiselle Giraud, ma femme.* Introduction by Christopher Rivers. New York: Modern Language Association, 2002.

Benjamin, Walter. *The Arcades Project.* Trans. Howard Eiland and Kevin McLaughlin. Cambridge, Mass.: Harvard University Press, 1999.

Bernheimer, Charles. *Figures of Ill Repute: Representing Prostitution in Nineteenth-Century France.* Cambridge, Mass.: Harvard University Press, 1989.

Bersani, Leo. *Homos.* Cambridge, Mass.: Harvard University Press, 1995.

Bloom, Harold. *The Anxiety of Influence: A Theory of Poetry.* New York: Oxford University Press, 1973; repr., 1978.

Borgal, Clément. *Jean Cocteau ou de la claudication considérée comme l'un des beaux-arts.* Paris: Presses Universitaires de France, 1989.

Callias, Suzanne de. *Jerry: Roman; suivi de Monsieur Fayol et sa fille.* Amiens: Librairie Edgar Malfère, 1924.

Caradec, François. *Feu Willy avec et sans Colette.* Paris: Carrère/Pauvert, 1984.

Carco, Francis. *De Montmartre au Quartier Latin.* Paris: Albin Michel, 1927.

———. *Jésus-la-Caille.* Paris: Ronald Davis et Cie, 1920.

———. *Les Malheurs de Fernande.* Paris: L'Edition, 1918.

Chabanaix, Philippe. "Francis Carco." *Revue des Deux Mondes* 1 (1968): 344–51.

Chauncey, George. *Gay New York: Gender, Urban Culture, and the Making of the Gay Male World, 1890–1940.* New York: Basic Books, 1994.

Christensen, Peter G. "Three Concealments: Jean Cocteau's Adaptation of *The Picture of Dorian Gray.*" *Romance Notes* 27, no. 1 (1986): 27–35.

Cocteau, Jean. *Journal 1942–1945.* Paris: Gallimard, 1989.

———. *Lettres à Jean Marais.* Paris: Albin Michel, 1987.

———. *Lettres à Milorad.* 2d ed. Paris: Le Cherche midi Éditeur (Éditions Saint-Germain-des-Prés), 1975.

———. *Le Passé défini.* 3 vols. Paris: Gallimard, 1983–89.

———. *Mon premier voyage (tour du monde en 80 jours).* Paris: Gallimard, 1936.

———. *Reines de la France.* Paris: Grasset, 1952.

———. *Romans, Poésies, Œuvres diverses.* Paris: Livre de Poche, 1995.

Deleuze, Gilles. *Proust et les signes.* 4th ed. Paris: Presses Universitaires de France, 1976 [1965].

de Man, Paul. *Allegories of Reading: Figural Language in Rousseau, Nietzsche, Rilke, and Proust.* New Haven, Conn.: Yale University Press, 1979.

Desbordes, Jean. *J'adore.* Paris: Grasset, 1928.

Doubrovsky, Serge. *La Place de la madeleine: Ecriture et fantasme chez Proust.* Paris: Mercure de France, 1974.

Dubois, Jacques. *Pour Albertine: Proust et le sens du social.* Paris: Seuil, 1997.

Edelman, Lee. *Homographesis: Essays in Gay Literary and Cultural Theory.* New York: Routledge, 1994.

Erman, Michel. *L'Œil de Proust: Ecriture et voyeurisme dans* A la recherche du temps perdu. Paris: A.-G. Nizet, 1988.

Everdell, William R. *The First Moderns: Profiles in the Origins of Twentieth-Century Thought.* Chicago: University of Chicago Press, 1997.

Genet, Jean. *Journal du voleur.* Paris: Gallimard, 1949.

Genette, Gérard. *Figures III.* Paris: Seuil, 1972.

Gercke, Daniel. "Ruin, Style, and Fetish: The Corpus of Jean Cocteau." *Nottingham French Studies* 32, no. 1 (1993): 10–18.

Gide, André. *Corydon.* Paris: Gallimard, 1924.

———. *Journal 1887–1925.* Paris: Gallimard (Pléiade), 1996.

———. *Le Ramier.* Foreword by Catherine Gide. Preface by Jean-Claude Perrier. Afterword by David H. Walker. Paris: Gallimard, 2002.

———. *Romans; Récits et soties; Œuvres lyriques.* Paris: Gallimard (Pléiade), 1958.

———. *Souvenirs et voyages.* Paris: Gallimard (Pléiade), 2001.

Girard, René. *Des choses cachées depuis la fondation du monde.* Investigations with Jean-Michel Oughourlian and Guy Lefort. Paris: Grasset, 1978.

———. *Mensonge romantique, vérité romanesque.* Paris: Grasset, 1961.

Gray, Margaret E. *Postmodern Proust.* Philadelphia: University of Pennsylvania Press, 1992.

Hermant, Abel. *Le Suborneur.* Paris: Éditions de la Nouvelle Revue Française, 1923.

Hocquenghem, Guy. *Le Gay Voyage: Guide et regard homosexuels sur les grandes métropoles.* Paris: Albin Michel, 1980.

Infantino, Stephen C. *Photographic Vision in Proust.* New York: Peter Lang, 1992.
Jay, Martin. *Downcast Eyes: The Denigration of Vision in Twentieth-Century French Thought.* Berkeley: University of California Press, 1993.
Kristeva, Julia. *Le Texte du roman: Approche sémiologique d'une structure discursive transformationnelle.* The Hague: Mouton, 1970.
Ladenson, Elisabeth. *Proust's Lesbianism.* Ithaca, N.Y.: Cornell University Press, 1999.
———. "Rereading Proust: Perversion and Prolepsis in *A la recherche du temps perdu.*" *Second Thoughts: A Focus on Rereading.* Ed. David Galef. Detroit: Wayne State University Press, 1999. 249–65.
Lavagetto, Mario. *Chambre 43: Un lapsus de Marcel Proust.* Trans. Adrien Pasquali. Paris: Belin, 1996.
Lucey, Michael. *Gide's Bent: Sexuality, Politics, Writing.* New York: Oxford University Press, 1995.
Macris, Pierre. "L'ange et Cocteau." *Revue des Lettres Modernes* 298–303 (1972): 71–90.
Marcus, Sharon. "Haussmannization as Anti-Modernity: The Apartment House in Parisian Urban Discourse, 1850–1880." *Journal of Urban History* 27, no. 6 (2001): 723–45.
Ménalkas [Suzanne de Callias]. *Erna: Jeune fille de Berlin.* Paris: Éditions Cosmopolites, 1932.
Ménalkas [Suzanne de Callias] and Marc de la Roche. *Metallo, mon ami.* Paris: Librarie L. Kra, 1938.
Miomandre, Francis de. *Ces petits messieurs.* Paris: Les Éditions de France, 1934 (1921).
Mulvey, Laura. "Visual Pleasure and Narrative Cinema." *Screen* 16, no. 3 (1975): 6–18.
Proust, Marcel. *A la recherche du temps perdu.* 4 vols. Paris: Gallimard (Pléiade), 1987–89.
Sartre, Jean-Paul. *L'Etre et le néant: Essai d'ontologie phénoménologique.* Paris: Gallimard, 1943.
———. *Saint Genet: Actor and Martyr.* Trans. Bernard Frechtman. New York: New American Library, 1971.
Schehr, Lawrence R. *Alcibiades at the Door: Gay Discourses in French Literature.* Stanford, Calif.: Stanford University Press, 1995.
———. *Figures of Alterity: French Realism and Its Others.* Stanford, Calif.: Stanford University Press, 2003.
———. "Filiations queer?" *Queer: repenser les identités.* Ed. Robert Harvey and Pascal Le Brun-Corder. *Rue Descartes* 40 (2003): 18–26.
———. *Flaubert and Sons: Readings of Flaubert, Zola, and Proust.* New York: Peter Lang, 1986.
———. *The Shock of Men: Homosexual Hermeneutics and French Writing.* Stanford, Calif.: Stanford University Press, 1995.
——— "Tournier's Theoretical Pretext Works Like a Charm." *Studies in Twentieth-Century Literature* 12, no. 2 (1988): 221–38.
Schehr, Lawrence R., and Allen S. Weiss, eds. *French Food: On the Table, on the Page, and in French Culture.* New York: Routledge, 2001.
Schor, Naomi. *Zola's Crowds.* Baltimore, Md.: Johns Hopkins University Press, 1978.

Sedgwick, Eve Kosofsky. *Epistemology of the Closet.* Berkeley: University of California Press, 1990.

Segal, Naomi. *André Gide: Pederasty and Pedagogy.* Oxford: Clarendon, 1998.

Shattuck, Roger. *Proust's Binoculars: A Study of Memory, Time, and Recognition in A la recherche du temps perdu.* New York: Random House, 1963.

Splitter, Randolph. *Proust's Recherche: A Psychoanalytical Interpretation.* New York: Routledge and Kegan Paul, 1981.

Steegmuller, Francis. *Cocteau: A Biography.* Boston: Little, Brown, 1970.

Tamagne, Florene. *Histoire de l'homosexualité en Europe: Berlin, Londres, Paris, 1919–1939.* Paris: Seuil, 2000.

Tanner, Tony. *Adultery in the Novel: Contract and Transgression.* Baltimore, Md.: Johns Hopkins University Press, 1979.

Toepfer, Karl. *Empire of Ecstasy: Nudity and Movement in German Body Culture, 1910–1935.* Berkeley: University of California Press, 1997.

Tournier, Michel. *La Goutte d'or.* Paris: Gallimard, 1985.

Willy [Henri Gauthier-Villars]. *Souvenirs littéraires . . . et autres.* Paris: Éditions Montaigne, 1925.

———. *Le Troisième Sexe.* Introduction by Louis Estève. Paris: Paris-Édition, 1927.

Willy [Henri Gauthier-Villars] and Ménalkas [Suzanne de Callias]. *L'Ersatz d'amour.* Amiens: Librairie Edgar Malfère, 1923.

———. *Le Naufragé.* Amiens: Librairie Edgar Malfère, 1924.

INDEX

LAWRENCE R. SCHEHR is a professor of French at the University of Illinois. He is the author of several volumes, including *The Shock of Men, Alcibiades at the Door, Rendering French Realism, Parts of an Andrology,* and *Figures of Alterity.* He is also the coeditor (with Dominique Fisher) of *Articulations of Difference* and (with Allen S. Weiss) of *French Food.* He is the editor-in-chief of the journal *Contemporary French Civilization.* Prof. Schehr is currently pursuing research on nineteenth- and twentieth-century French literature and culture.

The University of Illinois Press
is a founding member of the
Association of American University Presses.

Composed in 10.5/13 Minion
with Minion display
at the University of Illinois Press
Designed by Paula Newcomb
Manufactured by Maple-Vail Book
Manufacturing Group

University of Illinois Press
1325 South Oak Street
Champaign, IL 61820-6903
www.press.uillinois.edu